1979

The Slave Community

The Slave Community

*Plantation Life
in the Antebellum South*

John W. Blassingame

1

New York
Oxford University Press
1972

For Teasie

Preface

This book describes and analyzes the life of the black slave: his African heritage, culture, family, acculturation, behavior, religion, and personality. In terms of emphasis, it breaks sharply with American historiographical tradition. Even a cursory examination of the literature shows that historians have never systematically explored the life experiences of American slaves. Southern planters, on the other hand, have had an extremely good press in the United States. Historians have analyzed practically every aspect of the planter's behavior, ideology, social and economic position, customs, and politics. Although the 3,954,000 black slaves greatly outnumbered the 385,000 white slaveowners in the South in 1860, the slave has generally been shunted off to the wings on the historical stage.

By concentrating solely on the planter, historians have, in effect, been listening to only one side of a complicated debate. The distorted view of the plantation which emerges from planter records is that of an all-powerful, monolithic institution which strips the slave of any meaningful and distinctive culture, family life, religion, or manhood. The clearest portrait the planter has drawn of the slave is the stereotype of Sambo, a submissive half-man, half-child. Such stereotypes are so intimately related to the planter's projections, desires, and biases that they tell us little about slave behavior and even less about the slave's inner life, his thoughts, actions, self-concepts, or personality.

Any examination of such a new topic as slave life must rest securely on an analysis of new kinds of sources viewed from different angles. The utilization of psychological theory is the first step in this direction. The new insights gained from psychology are useless, however, if they are applied to stereotypes and restricted to traditional sources. Instead, an investigator of the personality development of slaves must depend largely on the personal records left by the slave, especially autobiographies. This is all the more necessary because historians have deliberately ignored these sources. Consequently, a great deal of emphasis has been placed on non-traditional sources in this study in an effort to delineate more clearly the slave's view of bondage and to discover some new insights into the workings of the system.

While relying heavily on those black autobiographies which pass the tests commonly applied to historical sources, I have also systematically examined several hundred white autobiographies, plantation records, agricultural journals, and travel accounts. This approach permits us to view slave life through the eyes of three witnesses. Two of them, the planter and the slave, give an insider's view of the plantation. The third witness, the traveler, views the relation between slave and master from the outside. Although there are no absolute guarantees of truth, this three-dimensional picture of the plantation at least reveals the complexity of the institution and, hopefully, gives us a close approximation of the interaction between masters and slaves.

The inescapable conclusion which emerges from an examination of several different kinds of sources is that there were many different slave personality types. Sambo was one of them. But, because masters varied so much in character, the system was open at certain points, and the slave quarters, religion, and family helped to shape behavior, it was not the dominant slave personality. Rather than identifying with and submitting totally to his master, the slave held onto many remnants of his African culture, gained a sense of worth in the quarters, spent most of his time free from surveillance by whites, controlled important aspects of his life, and did some personally meaningful things on his own volition. This relative freedom of thought and action helped the slave to preserve his personal autonomy and to create a culture which has contributed much to American life and thought.

Like most scholars, I have accumulated many debts in the course of my investigation. I could write much about all of those historians whose published work influenced my thinking, but I hope that the footnote citations and the bibliography truly reflect what I have learned from them. The burdens of research and writing have been lightened by a summer grant from Yale University and the aid of several people. The probing questions raised by Mack Thompson of the University of California at Riverside during an institute at Carnegie Mellon University in 1964 about my first efforts to deal with the topic have continued to influence my thinking. Similarly, Richard Morse's criticisms of an essay I wrote on slave personality during my first year of graduate study at Yale helped me to identify many of the topics I have developed in this book. David B. Davis, Edmund Morgan, and C. Vann Woodward of Yale University, Louis Harlan of the University of Maryland, and John Hope Franklin of the University of Chicago, read several drafts of the manuscript; Joseph Logsdon of Louisiana State University at New Orleans, Thomas Holt, Jerry Thomas, and Lawrence Powell of Yale University, and Nicholas Canady of Louisiana State University at Baton Rouge, commented on the early drafts; Mrs. Dorothy Porter, Curator of the Negro Collection at Howard University, and the staffs of the University of North Carolina and Louisiana State University helped me find many sources. I am deeply indebted to my research assistants Barnett Rubin and Miss Mae Henderson for the hot summer they spent uncovering material on antebellum planters, to Miss Fran Drago of Wesleyan University for helping me to refine my psychological concepts, and to David Robinson of Yale for sharing his knowledge of Africa with me. Mrs. Anne Granger, Mrs. Janet Villastrigo, and Mrs. Rebecca Davis, who had the unenviable task of deciphering my script, cheerfully typed several drafts of the manuscript.

Dedication of this book to my wife is, as only she knows, poor payment for her sacrifices.

J.W.B.

NEW HAVEN, CONNECTICUT
March, 1972

Contents

I   Enslavement, Acculturation, and African Survivals, 1

II   Culture, 41

III   The Slave Family, 77

IV   Rebels and Runaways, 104

V   Plantation Stereotypes and Roles, 132

VI   Plantation Realities, 154

VII Slave Personality Types, 184

Appendix: A Comparative Examination of Total Institutions, 217

Critical Essay on Sources, 227

Select Bibliography, 239

Illustration Sources

Figure 1   *Century Magazine* 31:813
Figure 2   Cornell University Library
Figure 3   Cornell University Library
Figure 4   Library of Congress
Figure 5   W.P.A., *The Negro in Virginia* (Hastings Publishers, N.Y., 1940, copyright, Hampton Institute)
Figure 6   Library of Congress
Figure 7   *Harper's Weekly* 4:344
Figure 8   *Harper's Encyclopedia of United States History,* Vol. 8, New Edition. Revised and Enlarged by Benson John Lossing (Harper & Row, 1915)
Figure 9   Historical Pictures Service of Chicago
Figure 10   Library of Congress
Figure 11
    a.   The Papers of Benjamin Latrobe, Maryland Historical Society
    b.   Curt Sachs, *Les Instruments de musique de Madagascar* (Paris, 1938, copyright, Institut Ethnologie, University of Paris)
    c.   Bernard Ankerman, *Die afrikanischen Musikinstrumente* (Berlin, 1901)
    d.   The Papers of Benjamin Latrobe
    e.   Jean-Sébastien Laurenty, *Les Tambours à fente de l'Afrique Centrale* (Tervuren, Belgium, 1968, copyright, Royal Museum of Central Africa)
    f.   Laurenty, *Les Tambours à fente de l'Afrique Centrale*
Figure 12
    a.   The Papers of Benjamin Latrobe
    b.   Sachs, *Les Instruments de musique de Madagascar*
    c.   Stephen Chauvet, *Musique Nègre* (Paris, 1929, copyright, Société d' éditions geographiques, maritimes et coloniales)

	d.	The Papers of Benjamin Latrobe
	e.	Ankerman, *Die afrikanischen Musikinstrumente*
	f.	Ankerman, *Die afrikanischen Musikinstrumente*

Figure 13   Hamilton W. Pierson, *In the Brush* (New York, 1881)

Figure 14   Muriel and Malcolm Bell, Jr.

Figure 15   Muriel and Malcolm Bell, Jr.

Figure 16   *Century Magazine* 31:808

Figure 17   *Century Magazine* 31:525

Figure 18   *Century Magazine* 31:524

Figure 19   Peter Schnapp. Copyright, Peter Schnapp—*Realités*

Figure 20   The New York Public Library
Astor, Lennox and Tilden Foundations

Figure 21   *Harper's Encyclopedia of United States History*, Vol. 8, New Edition.

Figure 22   *Harper's Encyclopedia of United States History*, Vol. 8, New Edition.

Figure 23   Hampton Institute Library

Figure 24   *Illustrated London News* 38:139

Figure 25   Library of Congress

Figure 26   The Chicago Historical Society

Figure 27   James S. Buckingham, *The Slave States of America* (London, 1842)

Figure 28   Culver Pictures

Figure 29   William Wells Brown, *Narrative of William W. Brown, A Fugitive Slave* (Boston, 1847)

Figure 30   Henry Bibb, *Narrative of the Life and Adventures of Henry Bibb, An American Slave* (New York, 1849)

Figure 31   William Still, *The Underground Railroad* (Philadelphia, 1872)

Figure 32   Culver Pictures

Figure 33   Still, *The Underground Railroad*

Figure 34   Library of Congress

Figure 35   Solomon Northrup, *Twelve Years a Slave* (London, 1853)

Figure 36   Northrup, *Twelve Years*

Figure 37   *Century Magazine* 31:520

Figure 38 *Harper's Monthly Magazine* 15:440
Figure 39 *Harper's Monthly Magazine* 8:456
Figure 40 *Ballou's Pictorial* 14:49
Figure 41 *Harper's Monthly Magazine* 8:457
Figure 42 *Harper's Monthly Magazine* 8:459
Figure 43 *Merry's Museum* 6:111
Figure 44 The New York Public Library
Astor, Lenox and Tilden Foundations
Figure 45 *Harper's Encyclopedia of United States History*, Vol. 8, New Edition.
Figure 46 *Putnam's Monthly* 10:447
Figure 47 *Harper's Encyclopedia of United States History*, Vol. 6, New Edition.
Figure 48 *Harper's Monthly Magazine* 19:729
Figure 49 Frederick Douglass, *My Bondage and My Freedom* (New York, 1855)
Figure 50 Austin Steward, *Twenty-two Years a Slave, and Forty Years a Freeman* (Rochester, N.Y., 1861)
Figure 51 Northrup, *Twelve Years*
Figure 52 Moses Roper, *A Narrative of the Adventures and Escape of Moses Roper from American Slavery* (London, 1840)
Figure 53 Library of Congress
Figure 54 Wilson Armistead, *A Tribute for the Negro* (New York, 1848)
Figure 55 Bibb, *Narrative*
Figure 56 James A. Bear, Jr., editor, *Jefferson at Monticello*, University Press of Virginia (Charlottesville, 1967)

The Slave Community

1 Enslavement Acculturation and African Survivals

Middle Passage:
   voyage through death
      to life upon these shores.

"10 April 1800—
Blacks rebellious. Crew uneasy. Our linguist says their moaning
is a prayer for death,
ours and their own. Some try to starve themselves.
Lost three this morning leaped with crazy laughter
to the waiting sharks, sang as they went under." . . .

  Voyage through death,
          voyage whose chartings are unlove.

A charnel stench, effluvium of living death
spreads outward from the hold,
where the living and the dead, the horribly dying,
life interlocked, lie foul with blood and excrement.

   Deep in the festering hold thy father lies,
   the corpse of mercy rots with him,
   rats eat love's rotten gelid eyes.

   But, oh, the living look at you
   with human eyes whose suffering accuses you,
   whose hatred reaches through the swill of dark
   to strike you like a leper's claw.

                        Robert Hayden

The chains of the American Negro's captivity were forged in
Africa. Prince and peasant, merchant and agriculturalist, warrior
and priest, Africans were swept up into the vortex of the Atlantic
slave trade and funneled into the sugar fields, the swampy rice
lands, or the cotton and tobacco plantations of the New World.

The process of enslavement was almost unbelievably painful and bewildering for the Africans. Completely cut off from their native land, they were frightened by the artifacts of the white man's civilization and terrified by his cruelty until they learned that they were only expected to work for him as they had been accustomed to doing in their native land. Still, some were so morose they committed suicide; others refused to learn the customs of whites and held on to the memory of the African cultural determinants of their own status.

To argue, as some scholars have, that the first slaves suffered greatly from the enslavement process because it contradicted their "heroic" warrior tradition or that it was easy for them because Africans were by nature docile and submissive is to substitute mythology for history. The enslavement of Africans was intimately related to the history of Indian-white relations in the New World and certain historical and anthropological principles. In regard to the latter, historically it has been almost impossible to enslave members of societies who are nomadic food gatherers, herdsmen, hunters, or fishermen. Consequently, Europeans in North America either exterminated the war-like hunting tribes or worked the simple food gatherers to death. Neither group made effective slaves. On the other hand, and in spite of the myths surrounding the "noble red man," when Europeans encountered Indians of a higher culture accustomed to systematic agricultural labor and sedentary habits (as did the Spaniards in Mexico and other parts of South America), the Indians were reduced to slavery or something closely akin to it.

These factors were also operative in Africa. Like many Indians, African hunting, pastoral, and fishing tribesmen were too nomadic or warlike to be captured. As a result, most of the Africans brought to North America were members of agrarian tribes in West Africa, accustomed to hard, continuous labor and a sedentary life. A majority of them belonged to the Ibo, Ewe, Biafada, Bakongo, Wolof, Bambara, Ibibio, Serer, and Arada tribes. Members of the large, well-organized African states and tribes like the Yoruba, Dahomey, Ashantee, Fulani, Kom, Mandingo, and Hausa, with their centralized governments, fast moving cavalries, or disciplined standing armies, rarely fell into the slave trader's hands. It took the British, even with modern weapons, until the first decades of the twentieth century to conquer some of these tribes. On occasion, some of the centralized tribes became so weak that large numbers of them were captured, as happened with the Oyo Yoruba after 1750. For the most part, however, these tribes were almost immune to enslavement. In fact, these were the tribes which made war on their more peaceful (or defenseless) neighbors and sold them and the peoples who fell under their political, economic, military, and cultural hegemony into bondage. Approximately 10 million Africans were brought to the New World between the sixteenth and the mid-nineteenth century.[1]

The tribal origins of the first slaves are important primarily in relation to the extent to which native culture and economic organization prepared the African for one facet of plantation life: systematic labor. While the customary labor of certain tribes made it relatively easy for them to adapt to agricultural labor in the New World, it is not at all clear that there was a close relationship between docility and rebelliousness among slaves and their tribal origin. For example, although South American masters of the sixteenth and seventeenth centuries obtained most of their slaves from what they considered the most "docile" of African tribes, these slaves rose in rebellion after rebellion during the colonial period. In other words, it was not the contrast between the African slave's warrior past and his dependency on the plantation which was primarily responsible for determining his behavior, but rather the interaction between certain universal elements of West African culture, the institutionalized demands of

1. J. F. Ade Ajayi and Dan Espie, *A Thousand Years of West African History* (London, 1965), 157–60, 318–29; M. M. Green, *Ibo Village Affairs* (New York, 1964 [1947]), 32–48, 61–77; J. D. Fage, *A History of West Africa* (London, 1969), 81–95; Daryll Forde and P. M. Kaberry, *West African Kingdoms in the Nineteenth Century* (London, 1967), 37–39, 72–73, 90; Basil Davidson, *The Growth of African Civilization* . . . (London, 1965), 173–233; Philip D. Curtin, *The Atlantic Slave Trade: A Census* (Madison, Wis., 1969), *passim;* Walter Rodney, "Upper Guinea and the Significance of the Origins of Africans Enslaved in the New World," *Journal of Negro History* LIV (Oct. 1969), 327–45.

Figures 2, 3, 4, 5. The Shock of Enslavement

plantation life, the process of enslavement, and his creative response to enslavement.[2]

Although a few chiefs sold their own subjects, household slaves, or criminals, most African slaves were prisoners captured

2. On the economic life of West African tribes, see: Madeline Manoukian, *Tribes of the Northern Territories of the Gold Coast* (London, 1951), 13–23; P. Amaury Talbot, *Tribes of the Niger Delta* (London, 1932), 273–84, 294; Madeline Manoukian, *The Ewe-Speaking People of Togoland and the Gold Coast* (London, 1952), 11–12, 15–20.

Figure 6.   Into the Hold

in tribal wars or kidnapped by slave raiders. After their capture, the Africans were tied together by a rope and then marched hundreds of miles while suffering from thirst, hunger, and exhaustion. Consequently, many either died along the way or were reduced to a very weak and emaciated condition by the time they reached the sea coast. On the coast, the Africans were made to jump up and down, had fingers poked in their mouths and their genital organs handled by a doctor. Those chosen by the Europeans were then branded.[3]

Taken on board ship, the naked Africans were shackled together on bare wooden boards in the hold, and packed so tightly that they could not sit upright. During the dreaded Mid-Passage (a trip of from three weeks to more than three months) the slaves were let out of the hold twice daily for meals and exercise, and women and children were often permitted to spend a great deal of time on deck. The foul and poisonous air of the hold, extreme

3. Elizabeth Donnan, ed., *Documents Illustrative ·of the History of the Slave Trade to America* (4 vols., Washington, 1930–35); Daniel P. Mannix and Malcolm Cowley, *Black Cargoes: A History of the Atlantic Slave Trade, 1518–1865* (New York, 1962), 1–49, 100–130; W. O. Blake, *The History of Slavery and the Atlantic Slave Trade* (Columbus, O., 1860), 93–142; John R. Spears, *The American Slave Trade* (New York, 1900), 1–82.

heat, men lying for hours in their own defecation, with blood and mucus covering the floor, caused a great deal of sickness. Mortality from undernourishment and disease was about 16 per cent. The first few weeks of the trip was the most traumatic experience for the Africans. A number of them went insane and many became so despondent that they gave up the will to live. Slaves in the latter condition were described as having the "fixed melancholy." [4]

Africans were not, however, totally immobilized by shock. Often they committed suicide (especially while still on the African coast) by drowning, or refusing food or medicine, rather than accept enslavement. One captain made it all the way to the West Indies before the Africans began a mass suicide attempt. He asserted that he

> thought all our troubles of this Voyage was over; but on the contrary I might say that the Dangers rest on the Borders of Security. On the 14th of March we found a great deal of Discontent among the Slaves, particularly the Men, which continued till the 16th about Five o'Clock in the Evening, when to our great Amazement about an hundred Men Slaves jump'd over board, and it was with great Difficulty we sav'd so many as we did; out of the whole we lost 33 of as good Men Slaves as we had on board, who would not endeavour to save themselves, but resolv'd to die, and sunk directly down. Many more of them were taken up almost drown'd, some of them died since. . . .[5]

Many of the Africans resisted enslavement at every step in their forced emigration. Conscious of the wrongs they suffered, they began trying to escape on the long march to the coast. Failing this and suicide attempts while still in sight of their native shores, the Africans often mutinied while being transported to the New World and killed their white captors. In spite of their

4. Mannix and Cowley, *Cargoes*, pp. 104–30; *An Abstract of the Evidence Delivered Before a Select Committee of the House of Commons, 1790–91* (London, 1791), 39–44; Spears, *Trade*, 68–81; Blake, *History*, 126–42.

5. Quoted in Donald D. Wax, "Negro Resistance to the Early American Slave Trade," *Journal of Negro History* LI (Jan. 1966), 9–10.

Figure 7.   Middle Passage

chains and lack of arms, they rebelled so frequently that a number of ship owners took out insurance to cover losses from mutinies.[6] In their study of the slave trade, Mannix and Cowley uncovered

6. Wax, "Resistance," 1–15; Lorenzo J. Greene, "Mutiny on the Slave Ships," *Phylon* V (Fourth Quarter, 1944), 346–54; George Francis Dow, *Slave Ships and Slavery* (Salem, 1927), 83, 175, 207; Joshua Coffin, *An Account of Some of the Principal Slave Insurrections* (New York, 1860), 14–15, 33; Donnan, *Documents,* I, 463, II, 232, 266, 397, 460–86, III, 37–42, 51, 119, 318; Harvey Wish, "American Slave Insurrections Before 1861," *Journal of Negro History* XXII (July 1937), 299–320; Spears, *Trade,* 31–35.

fairly detailed accounts of fifty-five mutinies on slavers from 1699 to 1845, not to mention passing references to more than a hundred others. The list of ships "cut off" by the natives—often in revenge for the kidnapping of freemen—is almost as long. On the record it does not seem that Africans submitted tamely to being carried across the Atlantic like chained beasts.[7]

Early records indicate that the Africans continued to resist even after they landed in the New World. Many eighteenth-century travel accounts, memoirs, and slave notices show that a number of the newly imported Africans almost literally ran away as soon as their feet touched American soil.[8] A North Carolina advertisement of 1775 is typical of many:

> ELOPED from the Subscribers on Wednesday the 26th Inst. two newly imported Men Slaves KAUCHEE and BOOHM, about 6 Feet high, and, perhaps 30 Years of Age.—They absconded in Company with three other Slaves about two Months ago, and were taken up at Broad-Creek, about 10 miles off, and brought back by William Gatling of that Place, who has since purchased a Wench who was imported with them; from which it is supposed they are lurking about that Neighborhood.

Even when they did not run away, the Africans were often obstinate, sullen, and uncooperative laborers. An English traveler observed in 1746 that an African born slave, "if he must be broke, either from Obstinacy, or, which I am more apt to suppose, from Greatness of Soul, will require . . . hard Discipline

7. Mannix and Cowley, *Cargoes*, 111.

8. John Brickell, *The Natural History of North Carolina* (Dublin, 1737), 272–74; Alexander Hewatt, *An Historical Account of the Rise and Progress of the Colonies of South Carolina and Georgia* (1779), in B. R. Carrol, ed., *Historical Collection of South Carolina* (2 vols., New York, 1836), I, 331–32, 348; Hugh Jones, *The Present State of Virginia* (Chapel Hill, 1956), 76; Harriet Martineau, *Retrospect of Western Travel* (3 vols., London, 1838), II, 98; Bernard Romans, *A Concise Natural History of East and West Florida* (New York, 1775), 73; Garnett Andrews, *Reminiscences of an Old Georgia Lawyer* (Atlanta, 1870), 10.

. . . you would really be surpriz'd at their Perseverance; . . . they often die before they can be conquer'd." [9]

The psychic impact of what they had undergone was so great that a majority of newly imported Africans, exhausted from the journey which often lasted more than six months from the time of their capture, offered little resistance to their masters. For most slaves in the seventeenth and early part of the eighteenth century, the shock of enslavement was crucial in determining their behavior. Captured and brought to America under the most painful and bewildering conditions, the seventeenth- and eighteenth-century Africans were taken from a society where their status was assured, and thrust into one where customs and languages were totally different and where their prior status was of no import. The African who survived the Mid-Passage, however, had one important advantage, for the experience he was about to face was not entirely unfamiliar to him. Generally, both men and women were accustomed to agricultural labor in Africa and knew of the existence of slavery. In fact, the frequent tribal wars represented a constant reminder of the threat of capture. Even so, enslavement was an unparalleled shock.[10]

Historians have few sources on the initial reactions of Africans to their bondage. From the sketchy accounts which have survived, however, it is possible to obtain a more or less clear idea of their reactions. Fortunately, there were a few African-born slaves who lived to recount stories of their enslavement. One of these, Venture Smith, was born in Guinea in 1729, and brought to the United States when he was eight years old.[11] He remembered that his tribe raised sheep, goats, and cattle. Polygamy was practiced, but apparently a man could not marry an additional wife until he obtained the consent of his other wife or wives. When Venture's father, a wealthy prince, took a third wife

9. Quoted in Wax "Resistance," 11; "Observations on Several Voyages and Travels in America," *William and Mary Quarterly*, Ser. 1, XV (Jan. 1907), 149.

10. Green, *Ibo*, 32–48; Forde and Kaberry, *Kingdoms*, 268–69; Francis Hall, *Travels in Canada and the United States in 1816 and 1817* (London, 1818), 432.

11. Venture Smith, *A Narrative of the Life and Adventures of Venture, A Native of Africa* (New London, Conn., 1798).

Figures 8, 9.
Landing

without his mother's consent, she left him, though she soon re-joined him. Venture remembered his father as "a man of re-markable strength and resolution, affable, kind and gentle, ruling with equity and moderation." He recalled most vividly and pain-fully, however, his father giving cattle and goats to assuage the avarice of African slave raiders, the raiders breaking the bargain, destroying the village, and torturing his father to death: "The shocking scene is to this day fresh in my mind, and I have often been overcome while thinking on it." [12]

The most famous and revealing account we have of the process of enslavement was written by Gustavus Vassa, or Olaudah Equi-ano.[13] The son of an Ibo tribal elder, Olaudah was born in 1745 in a part of the Benin empire (located in what is now Eastern Nigeria). Industrious agriculturalists, his tribe produced corn, tobacco, cotton, plantains, yams, beans, spices, and pineapples and traded for guns, dried fish, and beads. Land was held in common, and everyone worked in the fields. Bullocks, goats, and poultry were also raised. The women wove calico cloth and made earthenware while the men made hoes, shovels, spears, shields, and swords. They had an organized marketing system and used small iron anchor-shaped coins as money.

Often parents promised children in marriage while they were quite young, and the marriage was consummated when the girl came of age. Since the girl became the "property" of her husband's family, her own family was compensated for her loss by gifts from the groom's family. In order to get the new couple started in life, all of their friends and relatives gave them gifts. The girl acquired a new belt to indicate the change in her status, and the marriage ceremony ended with a great feast.

The family was rigidly patriarchal. Olaudah asserted that the marriage bed was so "sacred" and men so jealous of the fidelity of their wives that adultery was punishable by death. The women were bashful and chaste. According to Olaudah, the women were "uncommonly graceful, alert, and modest to a degree of bash-

---

12. Smith, *Narrative,* 11.

13. Gustavus Vassa, *The Interesting Narrative of the Life of Olaudah Equiano, or Gustavus Vassa, The African* (London, 1794), 1–61.

fulness; nor do I remember to have ever heard of an instance of incontinence amongst them before marriage." [14]

Within the patriarchal system, women played important roles. They made the clothes, served as warriors, did the marketing, and worked in the fields alongside their husbands. The care and training of the children was primarily the responsibility of the women. As a result, a deep bond of affection developed between mothers and children. Olaudah was especially favored in this regard because he was the youngest boy: "As I was the youngest of the sons, I became, of course, the greatest favorite with my mother, and was always with her; and she used to take particular pains to form my mind. I was trained up from my earliest years in the arts of agriculture and war: my daily exercise was shooting and throwing javelins; and my mother adorned me with emblems, after the manner of our greatest warriors." [15]

The tribal religion was a complex synthesis of magic, nature worship, and belief in a Supreme Being. The Supreme Being, or Creator, lived in the Sun and governed all events, especially death and captivity. Ancestors, who guarded one against evil spirits, were revered: there were frequent nightly prayers and oblations of the blood of freshly sacrificed animals at their graves. Some members of the tribe believed in transmigration of Souls, and all honored the priest. The priests, succeeded by their sons, foretold events and discovered jealousy, theft, and evidence of poisoning. In addition to their religious duties, the priests were also physicians. Upon the death of a priest, his body, along with his earthly possessions, was buried, after the proper sacrifice of animals, at the end of the day. Some snakes were considered as omens of future events and were not molested.

There were several noteworthy tribal customs. The chief men or elders decided all disputes and meted out punishment for crimes. The people were cheerful and enjoyed music and dancing. According to Equiano, his tribe was "almost a nation of dancers, musicians, and poets. Thus every great event such as a triumphant return from battle or other cause of public re-

14. Vassa, *Narrative,* 14–15.
15. Vassa, *Narrative,* 31.

joicing is celebrated in public dances, which are accompanied with songs and music suited to the occasion." [16] Children were often named after some spectacular event which occurred at the time of their birth. The members of the tribe bathed frequently, practiced circumcision, and had no knowledge of swearing. Fearful of being poisoned, the people always kissed fruit or tasted food to show a friend or stranger that it did not contain poison.

European contact with Africa almost destroyed the society Olaudah knew. After Europeans gained a foothold on the coast, wars, frequently started by avaricious chiefs to obtain slaves, became endemic. Traditionally, prisoners of war had been either returned for ransom or kept as slaves who were treated like, and did the same work as, other members of their master's family; they could even own property. Equiano's father owned many slaves, and his tribe traditionally sold some of their war captives to African slave traders. Europeans changed this by encouraging raids which frequently led to the kidnapping of Ibos in the area by black slave traders.

Olaudah and his sister were kidnapped when he was eleven. At first, they comforted each other. When they were separated, Olaudah cried and refused to eat for several days. Traveling for many days, he was finally sold to a kind African goldsmith. Although his labor was light, he had "an anxious wish for death to relieve me from all my pains." Constantly looking for a way to escape, he was pressed down with grief. He was, he recalled, "quite oppressed and weighed down by grief after my mother and friends, and my love of liberty. . . ." [17]

Olaudah was sold to European slave traders seven months after his capture. Arriving on the coast, he was terrified by the strange ship and the white men with "horrible looks, red faces, and long hair." The boat was a veritable devil's pit. The whites were "so savage" that he was sure they were going to kill and eat him. When he saw a pot of water boiling on the deck, he fainted. The billowing sails and the ability of the whites to make the ship start and stop at will filled him with wonder and convinced him the white men were evil spirits. The groaning men, shriek-

16. Vassa, *Narrative*, 7.
17. Vassa, *Narrative*, 35.

ing women, galling chains, and nauseating, suffocating smell made the hold of the ship "a scene of horror almost inconceivable." On the way to Barbados, two slaves, chained together, jumped overboard and drowned. Although he was anxious about his fate and terrified by the whites, Olaudah was consoled by some members of his own tribe who were on board. Still, the constant flogging of black slaves and white sailors and men dying daily were oppressive. "Every circumstance I met with served only to render my state more painful, and heighten my apprehensions and my opinion of the cruelty of the whites." The voyage was a nightmare; the hold a den of horrors.[18]

When the boat docked in Barbados, a new series of horrors began for Olaudah. Immediately the blacks were painstakingly examined by the eager merchants. Again, the haunting fear of the cannibalistic tendencies of the whites returned, and Olaudah asserted: "there was much dread and trembling among us, and nothing but bitter cries. . . ."[19] This continued until some slaves came on board and explained that the Africans had been brought to the island to work for the whites. Taken off the ship and herded into a stockade, they were amazed by the brick houses of the whites and the horses they rode. The amazement turned to terror a few days later when the Africans were sold by the "shout" or "scramble." Olaudah described the spectacle in the following words:

> We were not many days in the merchant's custody before we were sold after their usual manner, which is this: On a signal given, (as the beat of a drum) the buyers rush at once into the yard where the slaves are confined, and make choice of that parcel they like best. The noise and clamour with which this is attended and the eagerness visible in the countenances of the buyers serve not a little to increase the apprehensions of the terrified Africans. . . . In this manner, without scruple, are relations and friends separated, most of them never to see each other again.[20]

18. Vassa, *Narrative*, 47, 49, 52.
19. Vassa, *Narrative*, 54.
20. Vassa, *Narrative*, 61.

Figure 10.   Selecting Parcels

Most of the Africans were sold in Barbados, but a small group, including Olaudah, were taken to a Virginia plantation. Soon Olaudah was the only newly imported African left on the plantation. He was mortified by his inability to converse with anyone: "I was now exceedingly miserable, and thought myself worse off than any of the rest of my companions; for they could talk to each other, but I had no person to speak to that I could understand. In this state I was constantly grieving and pining, and wishing for death, rather than anything else." [21]

On the Virginia plantation he weeded grass and gathered stones for a few days. Then, called to the mansion to fan his master, Olaudah was terrified by the iron muzzle on the face of the black cook, mystified by the ticking of a clock, and convinced that a portrait on the wall watched his every move and would report any of his transgressions to his master who was asleep.

21. Vassa, *Narrative*, 70–71.

Consequently, he performed his task "with great fear." He spent "some time in this miserable, forlorn, and much dejected state without having anyone to talk to, which made my life a burden," until an English sea captain purchased him.[22]

The narrative of Olaudah Equiano details the process of enslavement and some elements of the cultural baggage Africans brought with them to the New World. The general outline of these elements must be described in order to understand the nature of acculturation. Acculturation in the United States involved the mutual interaction between two cultures, with Europeans and Africans borrowing from each other. When the African stepped on board a European ship he left all of the artifacts or physical objects of his culture behind him. In Africa, as in most societies, these objects were far less important than values, ideas, relationships, and behavioral patterns.

The similarities between many European and African cultural elements enabled the slave to continue to engage in many traditional activities or to create a synthesis of European and African cultures. In the process of acculturation the slaves made European forms serve African functions. An example of this is religion. Most Africans believed in a Creator, or all-powerful God whom one addressed directly through prayers, sacrifices, rituals, songs, and dances. At the same time, they had a panoply of lesser gods each of whom governed one aspect of life. Publicly supported priests, sacred festivals, funeral rites, dirges and wakes, dances and festivals expressing joy and thanksgiving, sacred objects and images, and charms and amulets for protection against evil spirits were the usual elements found in traditional religions. Funerals were especially important to Africans, and often were expensive, drawn-out affairs involving a long period of mourning, and the burial of personal objects with the deceased. All the friends and relatives of the deceased visited his family for a month after his death, delivered their condolences, and periodi-

---

22. Vassa, *Narrative*, 71. At this point, Olaudah Equiano's story merges into English and West Indian history. He led an eventful life. Taken to England in 1757, he worked with Granville Sharp to free English slaves and, in 1788, presented a petition to the Queen calling for the abolition of slavery.

cally arranged great feasts with much singing, dancing, and drinking to prevent the family from brooding over their loss. The merriment was also indicative of the African belief that upon dying one went "home." [23]

Christian forms were so similar to African religious patterns that it was relatively easy for the early slaves to incorporate them with their traditional practices and beliefs. In America Jehovah replaced the Creator, and Jesus, the Holy Ghost, and the Saints replaced the lesser gods. The Africans preserved many of their sacred ceremonies in the conventional Christian ritual and ceremonies: songs, dances, feasts, festivals, funeral dirges, amulets, prayers, images, and priests. After a few generations the slaves forgot the African deities represented by the Judeo-Christian gods, but in many other facets of their religious services they retained many African elements.

The whole question of African survivals in slave culture is so controversial and so limited by inadequate research that one must analyze the primary sources carefully in order to arrive at some tentative conclusions. The debate over this can only be approached by a comparison of African cultural forms with those of the antebellum slaves. Whenever the elements of the slave's culture more closely resemble African than European patterns, we can be relatively certain that we have identified African survivals. Because there are so many universals in culture, however, this procedure almost inevitably leads to an understatement of the African survivals. Then, too, since the slaves had to preserve many of the African elements in their master's language, many Africanisms will be missed because the European equivalents are too obscure for the modern ear to detect. On occasion the Africanisms can be established because of the frequency of such elements in slave culture when compared to European culture.

23. A. B. Ellis, *The Tshi-Speaking Peoples of the Gold Coast of West Africa* (London, 1887), 9–22, 119–48, 222–43; G. T. Basden, *Among the Ibos in Nigeria* (London, 1966 [1921]), 112–34; David P. Gamble, *The Wolof of Senegambia Together with Notes on the Lebu and the Serer* (London, 1957), 71–72, 102–3; Northcote W. Thomas, *Law and Custom of the Timne and Other Tribes* (London, 1916), 29–40; M. J. Field, *Religion and Medicine of the Ga People* (London, 1937), 4–25.

Several aspects of West African culture are so distinctive that it is relatively easy to discover their presence or absence among Southern slaves. Dances, folk tales, music, magic, and language patterns are susceptible to this kind of analysis. Music was central to African culture. Drums, guitars, flutes, piccolos, whistles, and horns were the principal instruments and were played on many occasions. Fast changes in tone, intonation, pitch, timbre, and impromptu variations were characteristic of African songs. Skilled instrumentalists enjoyed a high status, songs accompanied work in the fields and set the pace for rowers. Group participation, improvisation, call and response, rhythmic complexity, and percussions are constant in traditional African music. Often hand clapping or stamping of the feet supply the percussion accompaniment to songs.[24]

Perhaps the most distinctive feature of traditional African music is its rhythmic complexity. In this area the African is far superior to the European. While European music is based characteristically on one rhythm, African tunes often contain three or more patterns. An Englishman who studied traditional African music concluded:

> African rhythm is so complicated that it is exceedingly difficult for a European to analyse it. . . . Broadly speaking, the difference between African and European rhythms is that whereas any piece of European music has at any one moment one rhythm in common, a piece of African music has always two or three, sometimes as many as four. . . . From this point of view European music is childishly simple. . . .[25]

In traditional African dances there was little separation of sacred and secular performances. Usually held in the open air, the dances were elaborate, exhausting affairs. African dances dif-

---

24. J. H. K. Nketia, *African Music in Ghana: A Survey of Traditional Forms* (Accra, 1962); W. E. Ward, "Music in the Gold Coast," *Gold Coast Review* II (July–Dec. 1927), 199–223; Ellis, *Tshi*, 325–28; Basden, *Ibos*, 185–93; Gamble, *Wolof*, 76–77.
25. Ward, "Music," 214.

fered greatly from the traditional, stylized European dance between couples. Instead, women and men danced in separate lines,
moving back and forth toward each other. Traditionally, the
African dance was one of display, involving "seductive" and
rapid movements, and leaping to the furious rhythm of the
drum. Sometimes a large group of people would form a circle
around two dancers while clapping their hands. On other occasions the dance might involve sinuous movements of the upper
torso without moving the feet.[26]

European dances were generally unsuited to the most adul-
terated African rhythm. The uniqueness of the traditional African dances was indicated by an amazed Englishman among the
Ibos:

> The dancers range themselves and begin slow rhythmic
> movements, unconsciously swaying their heads in time with
> the music. As the dance proceeds they appear intoxicated
> with the motion and the music, the speed increases, and the
> movements become more and more intricate and bewilder-
> ing. . . . The twistings, turnings, contortions and springing
> movements, executed in perfect time, are wonderful to be-
> hold. . . . For these set dances . . . the physical strength
> required is tremendous. The body movements are extremely
> difficult and would probably kill a European.[27]

One of the most important cultural forms in West Africa was
the folk tale. Throughout the region story-telling was an art form
including acting, singing, and gestures that served as the favorite
evening entertainment. In many ways traditional African folk
tales were similar to those found in early European societies in
their attempts to explain natural phenomena and various animal
traits, giving animals the power of speech and containing gods
and heroes, creation legends, magic, witches, and morals. Often
accompanied by drums and responses from the audience, West
African tales showed that the people valued family ties, children,

26. Ellis, *Tshi*, 222–43, 325–28; Basden, *Ibos*, 127–34; Gamble,
Wolof, 76–77.
27. Basden, *Ibos*, 131–32.

and knowledge.[28] Animal stories are constant throughout West Africa. The trickster figures—the Nigerian tortoise, the Ghanaian ananse or spider, and the rabbit—are ubiquitous. Congenitally weak, slow moving, or looked down upon by the stronger animals, the tortoise, spider, and rabbit are wise, patient, boastful, mischievous, roguish, guileful, cunning, and they always outwit their stronger foes and triumph over evil.[29]

Regardless of his previous culture, upon landing in the New World the African-born slave had to learn the language of his master. Taught by overseers or native-born slaves, the African acquired a few European words in a relatively casual and haphazard fashion. He began by recognizing his own name and that of his master in his "adopted" language. While they generally had to learn their master's language in order to understand his commands and to communicate with other slaves, many Africans refused to accept a new name.[30] For instance, a Georgia newspaper described two recaptured fugitive slaves in these terms:

> Run aways. . . . TWO NEW NEGROE YOUNG FELLOWS; one of them . . . computed eighteen years of age, of the Fallah country, slim made, and calls himself Golaga, the name given him here Abel; the other a black fellow . . . computed seventeen years of age, of the Suroga country, calls himself Abbrom, the name given him here Bennet.[31]

28. Elphistone Dayrell, *Folk Stories From Southern Nigeria, West Africa* (London, 1910), vii–xvi, 1–6, 20–38, 64–72; Alta Jablow, ed., *An Anthology of West African Folklore* (n.p., 1962), 29–39; Ellis, *Tshi,* 331–43.

29. William Owens, "Folklore of the Southern Negroes," *Lippincott's Magazine* XX (Dec. 1877), 748–55; Basden, *Ibos,* 278–83; Northcote W. Thomas, *The Ibo-Speaking Peoples of Nigeria* (4 vols., London, 1913), I, 139–40; Amaury Talbot, *Tribes of the Niger Delta* (London, 1932), 336–44; G. T. Basden, *Niger Ibos* (London, 1966 [1938]), 424–36.

30. Allen Walker Read, "The Speech of Negroes in Colonial America," *Journal of Negro History* XXIV (July 1939), 247–58; William R. Bascom, "Acculturation Among the Gullah Negroes," *American Anthropologist* XLIII, n.s. (Jan.–March 1941), 43–50; "Eighteenth Century Slaves as Advertised by their Masters," *Journal of Negro History* I (April 1916), 163–216.

31. Read, "Speech," 251.

While some remarkable Africans could converse in English after only eight months in the colonies, it took most of the older ones several years to add a few English words to their vocabulary. Children and younger Africans acquired a knowledge of the new language with relative ease. One Maryland native reported in 1822 that a group of African "boys have been three months only among the English and they now speak it better than most of the blacks in these Southern states." [32] If the African had been "seasoned" in the West Indies, he usually arrived in the South with some knowledge of the English language.

Some Africans consistently refused to abandon their linguistic tie with their homeland. Samuel Hall's mother, captured in Liberia, was typical of many stubborn and proud Africans: "The mother would never work after she was sold into slavery, but pined away, never even learning the language of the people of this country." [33] When newly imported Africans were on large plantations where they had little contact with whites and thus little need to use a European language, they were remarkably successful in retaining elements of their native language.[34]

The acquisition of European languages was an extremely slow process for the Africans, especially during the seventeenth and eighteenth centuries.[35] Eighteenth-century travelers and clergy-

32. P. J. Staudenraus, ed., "Victims of the African Slave Trade, A Document," *Journal of Negro History* XLI (April, 1956), 149.

33. Samuel Hall, *47 Years a Slave* (Washington, Iowa, 1912), n.p.

34. John W. DuBose, "Recollections of the Plantations," *Alabama Historical Quarterly* I (Spring 1930), 66; Marcel (W. F. Allen), "Negro Dialect," *Nation* I (Dec. 14, 1865), 744–45; Marguerite B. Hamer, "A Century Before Manumission: Sidelights on Slavery in Mid-Eighteenth Century South Carolina," *North Carolina Historical Review* XVIII (July 1940), 232–36; Albert H. Stoddard, "Origin, Dialect, Beliefs, and Characteristics of the Negroes of the South Carolina and Georgia Coasts," *Georgia Historical Quarterly* XXVIII (Sept. 1944), 186–95; Sarah H. Torian, ed., "Antebellum and War Memories of Mrs. Telfair Hodgson," *Georgia Historical Quarterly* XXVII (Dec. 1943), 350–56; Samuel H. Chester, *Pioneer Days in Arkansas* (Richmond, 1927), 41–42.

35. William S. Perry, ed., *Historical Collections Relating to the American Colonial Church* (5 vols., Hartford, 1840), I, 264, 280, 344, IV, 197, 222, 224, 305; James B. Lawrence, "Religious Education of the Negro in the Colony of Georgia," *Georgia Historical Quarterly* XIV (March 1930), 41–57; Marcus W. Jernegan, "Slavery and Conversion

men frequently observed that African-born slaves throughout the American colonies did not understand English. The Reverend John Bell of Virginia wrote in 1724 that there were "A great many Black . . . infidels that understand not our language nor me theirs. . . ." The same year the Reverend James Falconer asserted that the adults among the Africans imported into Virginia were "never . . . able either to speak or understand our language perfectly." [36]

As the number of American-born slaves increased, a patois containing English and African words developed in the quarters. For example, the English traveler J. F. D. Smyth in 1773 declared that in conversing with Virginia slaves he could not "understand all of them, as great numbers, being Africans, are incapable of acquiring our language, and at best imperfectly, if at all; many of the others speak a mixed dialect between the Guinea and English." In many areas this pattern continued well into the nineteenth century. Frederick Douglass, who was born on a Maryland plantation around 1817, reported that in his youth the language of the slaves on one isolated plantation was a patois which was

> a mixture of Guinea and everything else you please. . . . there were slaves there who had been brought from the coast of Africa. They never used the "s" in indication of the possessive case. "Capn ant 'ney Tom," "Lloyd Bill," "Aunt Rose Harry." means "Captain Anthony's Tom," "Lloyd's Bill," &c. *"Oo you dem long to?"* means "Whom do you belong to?" *"Oo dem got any peachy,"* means, "Have you got any peaches?" I could scarcely understand them, so broken was their speech. . . .[37]

The center of African linguistic survival was along the Georgia-South Carolina sea coast, where the slaves had little con-

---

in the American Colonies," *American Historical Review* XXI (April 1916), 518–19; Frederick Dalcho, *An Historical Account of the Protestant Episcopal Church, in South Carolina* (Charleston, 1820), 105, 279.

36. Perry, *Church,* I, 282, 293.

37. J. F. D. Smyth, "Travels in Virginia in 1773," *Virginia Historical Register* VI (April 1853), 82; Frederick Douglass, *My Bondage and My Freedom* (New York, 1855), 76–77.

tact with whites. John W. DuBose, a planter in the 1850s, declared that "These low country South Carolina negroes, living through generations of small contact with whites have hardly learned to speak intelligibly. . . . 'Wha um d?' means where is he, she or it to be found? A pronoun or a sex is unknown to them." [38]

During the twentieth century, Lorenzo Turner, a brilliant linguist, found in his fifteen-year investigation of the Gullah dialect used by Negroes on the Georgia-South Carolina sea coast that the language patterns of the blacks were African in nature. African equivalents were substituted for such English words as "tooth," "pregnancy," "alcohol," "partridge," "sweet potato," and countless others. The pronunciation of many English words and the word order of sentences were often African. Like many Africans, the Gullahs frequently employed groups of words to form nouns, verbs, adverbs, and adjectives. Thus, they used *day clean* for "dawn," *a-beat-on-iron* for "mechanic," and *to sweet mouth* for "flatter." As late as the 1940s the Gullah blacks all had African personal names and used more than 4,000 words from the languages of more than 21 African tribes. [39]

In most areas of the South traces of African languages disappeared after two or three generations. As long as fresh Africans were imported during the eighteenth century, however, some African linguistic patterns were retained by blacks even when they spoke English. The end of the African slave trade in the last quarter of the eighteenth and early years of the nineteenth centuries ended the African-English patois in the quarters—after 1830 in most places.

Other African cultural forms were somewhat more resistant to change than language patterns, especially if they did not diverge greatly from English forms. While most of the nineteenth-century slaves were born in the United States, they maintained contact with Africa in various ways. A number had relatives who had been born in Africa and told them stories of their homeland. Samuel Hall, Charles Ball, and Jacob Stroyer learned much of

38. DuBose, "Recollections," 66.

39. Lorenzo D. Turner, *Africanisms in the Gullah Dialect* (Chicago, 1949).

African customs and languages from their African-born relatives. Others sometimes saw freshly imported Africans in the South in the 1840s and 50s.[40]

Clearly one of the general means by which Africans resisted bondage was by retaining their link with their past. Rather than accept the slaveholder's view of his place in society, the African tried to hold onto the African cultural determinants of his status. Charles Ball, who saw many African-born slaves on his plantation, reported many attempts of this nature. Mohammedan slaves continued to pray to Allah and other Africans tried to keep alive memories of their religions and customs. One slave who had been a priest supported by his tribe in Africa did everything the overseer required him to do but according to African custom refused to help his wife in any way. Like other Africans, this slave believed that the spirit of an African who died in the United States returned to Africa. When his son died, the former priest buried a small canoe, bow and arrows, meal, a paddle, and a lock of his hair with the body to aid the child's spirit on its journey to Africa. Maintaining their native concept of beauty, many of the Africans never lost their revulsion for white skin and longed for revenge on the whites for their enslavement. African-born slaves sometimes sang their tribal songs and performed tribal dances for the amusement of their masters and fellow slaves. The result of such practices was the survival of many African cultural forms in the South throughout the antebellum period.[41]

One of the African forms most resistant to European culture was the folk tale. An overwhelming majority of the tales of

40. Jacob Stroyer, *My Life in the South* (Salem, 1890), 9–20; Charles Ball, *Slavery in the United States: A Narrative of the Life and Adventures of Charles Ball* (Lewiston, Pa., 1836), 1–13; John Brown, *Slave Life in Georgia* (London, 1855), 171–200; Austin Steward, *Twenty-Two Years A Slave, and Forty Years a Freeman* (Rochester, New York, 1861), 32–51; Douglass, *Bondage*, 76, 90–91.

41. Stroyer, *My Life*, 44–49; Ball, *Adventures*, 1–13, 112–56, 168–205, 245–58; Robert Sutcliff, *Travels in Some Parts of North America. . . .* (York, England, 1811), 204; Basil Hall, *Travels in North America. . . .* (3 vols., Philadelphia, 1829), II, 184; "Reminiscences of Charles Seton Henry Hardee," *Georgia Historical Quarterly* XII (June 1928), 158–76.

Southern slaves retained the structure and motif of their African prototypes. Anthropologists, Africanists, and folklorists have found so many parallels and identical tales among Africans and Southern slaves that there can be no doubt that many Southern black folk tales were African in origin. In fact, African scholars have traced many of the slave's folk tales directly to Ghana, Senegal, and Mauritius, and the lore of such African tribes as the Ewe, Woloff, Hausa, Temne, Ashanti, and Ibo.[42]

While many of these tales were brought over to the South, the African element appears most clearly in the animal tales. Among Southern slaves such African animals as lions, elephants, and monkeys were retained in folk tales which often included songs and gestures. One Louisiana tale, "Néléphant avec Baleine," is almost identical to a Senegalese story recorded in 1828 describing how the rabbit outwitted the elephant and the whale. The most notable of the African tales imported with few changes are those of the tortoise and the hare and the tar-baby story.[43] The Ewe story of "Why the Hare Runs Away," for instance, contains the basic element of the tar-baby tale. When the hare tricked the other animals and stole their water they set a trap for him by making an "image" and covering it with bird lime:

> The hare came. . . . He approached the image. . . . The hare saluted the image. The image said nothing.
> "Take care," said the hare, "or I will give you a slap."
> He gave a slap, and his right hand remained fixed in the bird-lime. He slapped with his left hand, and that remained fixed also.

42. Daniel J. Crowley, "Negro Folklore: An Africanist's View," *Texas Quarterly* V (Autumn 1962), 65–71; A. B. Ellis, "Evolution in Folklore: Some West African Prototypes of the Uncle Remus Stories," *Popular Science Monthly* XLVIII (Nov. 1895), 93–104; A. J. Gerber, "Uncle Remus Traced to the Old World," *Journal of American Folklore* VI (Oct.–Dec. 1893), 245–57.

43. Alcée Fortier, *Louisiana Folk-Tales* (Boston, 1895); Elizabeth Pringle, *Chronicles of Chicora Wood* (Boston, 1940), 53–55; J. Marion Sims, *The Story of My Life* (New York, 1884), 69–70; Joseph Le Conte, *The Autobiography of Joseph Le Conte* (New York, 1903), 28–30.

"Oh! oh!," cried he, "let us kick with our feet."

He kicked with his feet. The feet remained fixed, and the hare could not get away. . . .[44]

Another good example of the transfer of African forms is the spiritual. Although European words were used in plantation songs, many of them contained African elements. After reviewing a collection of slave songs published in 1867, anthropologist John F. Szwed concluded: "The church songs and spirituals of the Negroes in the Southern United States closely resemble West African song style, particularly in their strong call-and-response patterns."[45] An earlier student not only compared the slave songs with African ones, she compared her notes with recent arrivals from the continent in the 1890s, and talked to former slaves. She wrote:

> During my childhood my observations were centered upon a few very old negroes who came directly from Africa, and upon many others whose parents were African born, and I early came to the conclusion, based upon negro authority, that the greater part of their music, their methods, their scale, their type of thought, their dancing, their patting of feet, their clapping of hands, their grimaces and pantomime, and their gross superstitions came straight from Africa.[46]

According to one old former slave, when she attended antebellum religious services:

> I'd jump up dar and den and holler and shout and sing and pat, and dey would all cotch de words and I'd sing it to some

---

44. A. B. Ellis, *The Ewe-Speaking Peoples of the Slave Coast of West Africa* (Netherlands, 1966 [1890]), 276–77.

45. John F. Szwed, "Musical Adaptation among Afro-Americans," *Journal of American Folklore* LXXII (April–June 1969), 115; see also, Alan Lomax, "The Homogeneity of African-Afro-American Musical Style," in John F. Szwed and Norman Whitten, eds., *Afro-American Anthropology* (New York, 1970), 181–201.

46. Jeanette R. Murphy, "The Survival of African Music in America," *Popular Science Monthly* LV (Sept. 1899), 660–61.

old shout song I'd heard 'em sing from Africa, and dey'd all take it up and keep at it, and keep a-addin' to it, and den it would be a spiritual.[47]

On rare occasions, African words were retained in the slave songs. The writer Lafcadio Hearn transcribed one of these he heard in 1880 from an old African-born slave in New Orleans which contained the Congolese (Fiot) word "Ouendai" or "ouendé," meaning "to go, to continue, to go on."

> *Ouendé ouendé, macaya!*
> Mo pas barrassé, *macaya!*
> *Ouendé, ouendé, macaya!*
> Mo bois bon divin, *macaya!*
> *Ouendé, ouendé, macaya!*
> Mo mangé bon poulet, *macaya!*
> *Ouendé, ouendé, macaya!*
> Mo pas barrassé, *macaya!*
> *Ouendé, ouendé, macaya!*
> *Macaya!* [48]

The significance of the continuing debate over African survivals in black music is not whether African or European patterns predominate or whether the environment of the plantation was the primary determinant of its character. The very existence of the debate is important in any discussion of acculturation for it proves that there is at least a reasonable possibility that there were some survivals of African forms in slave culture. The sophisticated research of ethno-musicologists, anthropologists, and folklorists, coupled with the evidence in a large number of primary sources, suggests that African culture was much more re-

47. Murphy, "Survival," 662.
48. Henry E. Krehbiel, *Afro-American Folksong* (New York, 1914), 39–40. Hearn's translation:

> Go on! go on! *eat enormously!*
> I ain't one bit ashamed—*eat outrageously*
> Go on! go on! eat prodigiously!
> I drink good wine!—*eat ferociously!*
> Go on! go on! eat unceasingly!
> I eat good chicken—gorging myself!
> Go on! go on! etc.

sistant to the bludgeon that was slavery than historians have hitherto suspected.[49]

In many areas, of course, the master tried to prevent the retention of those African cultural forms which he felt were dangerous to his existence. However much scholars may argue about slave music, it is obvious that the slaveholders recognized its revolutionary potential. Clerics rushed forward to teach the psalms to the slaves in an effort to stamp out "heathen" survivals, and masters tried to restrict the slaves' musical activities to prevent the articulation of discontent. Somewhat more sagacious than their Latin American counterparts, Southern planters tried to prevent the slaves from using musical instruments to signal slave uprisings. South Carolinians, recalling that during the Stono rebellion of 1739 the rebels had used a drum to signal other blacks to join them in killing whites, prohibited slaves from beating drums. Similarly, the Georgia slave code provided, since it was "absolutely necessary to the safety of this province, that slaves be prohibited from using and carrying mischievous and dangerous weapons, or using and keeping drums, horns, or other loud instruments, which may call together or give sign or notice to one another of their wicked designs and intentions. . . ."[50]

In spite of all the restrictions, the slaves were able to draw upon their African heritage to build a strong musical tradition. There is overwhelming evidence of the survival of African song and dance forms in the United States in the nineteenth century. The heyday of African cultural influence on Negro slaves, however, was during the eighteenth century. American clergymen and English missionaries were especially horrified at the "idolatrous dances and revels" of the slaves.[51] Alexander Hewatt de-

---

49. For an excellent illustration of the problems involved in the search for African survivals see Melville J. Herskovits, *The Myth of the Negro Past* (Boston, 1958), and E. Franklin Frazier, *The Negro in the United States* (New York, 1949).

50. William A. Hotchkiss, comp., *A Codification of the Statute Law of Georgia, Including the English Statutes in Force . . .* (Savannah, 1845), 813; Howell M. Henry, *The Police Control of the Slave in South Carolina* (Emory, Virginia, 1914), 150.

51. Frank J. Klingberg, *An Appraisal of the Negro in Colonial South Carolina: A Study of Americanization* (Washington, 1941), 12–18.

scribed the general pattern when he wrote in 1779 that in Georgia and South Carolina

> the Negroes of that country, a few only excepted, are to this day as great strangers to Christianity, and as much under the influence of Pagan darkness, idolatry and superstition, as they were at their first arrival from Africa. . . . Holidays there are days of idleness, riot, wantonness and excess: in which the slaves assemble together in alarming crowds, for the purposes of dancing, feasting, and merriment.[52]

There were probably more African survivals in the music and dances in Louisiana than in any other area. Apparently Louisianians encouraged this, for in 1817 the City Council of New Orleans set aside a special place for the slaves to dance. Louisiana slaves certainly took advantage of this opportunity and often performed African dances.[53] While in New Orleans in 1808, Christian Schultz found

> . . . twenty different dancing groups of the wretched Africans, collected together to perform their *worship* after the manner of their country. They have their own national music, consisting for the most part of a long kind of narrow drum of various sizes, from two to eight feet in length, three or four of which make a band. The principal dancers or leaders are dressed in a variety of wild and savage fashions, always ornamented with a number of tails of the smaller wild animals. . . . These amusements continue until sunset, when one or two of the city patrole show themselves with their cutlasses, and the crowds immediately disperse.[54]

The best description of the African dances in New Orleans appears in the diary of Benjamin Latrobe, the famous architect.

52. Hewatt, *Account*, II, 100, 103.

53. Timothy Flint, *Recollections of the Last Ten Years* . . . (New York, 1968 [1826]), 140; Henry C. Knight, *Letters from the South and West* (Boston, 1824), 127; Georges J. Joyaux, "Forest's Voyage aux Etats-Unis de l'Amerique en 1831," *Louisiana Historical Quarterly* XXXIX (Oct. 1956), 457–72.

54. Christian Schultz, *Travels on An Inland Voyage* . . . (2 vols., New York, 1810), II, 197.

On February 21, 1819, Latrobe saw about 500 slaves assembled in a square, dancing in groups around old men beating cylindrical drums, stringed instruments, and calabashes. The men and women danced in separate groups while singing a response to their leaders. In one group

> "A man sung [*sic*] an uncouth song to the dancing which I suppose was in some African language, for it was not French, & the women screamed a detestable burthen on one single note. The allowed amusements of Sunday have, it seems, perpetuated here those of Africa. . . ." [55]

Contrary to the pattern elsewhere, many African customs prevailed in Louisiana right down to the eve of the Civil War. Helene Allain reported that she saw performances almost identical to those described by Schultz and Latrobe in New Orleans in the 1850s.[56] More than thirty years later, Lafcadio Hearn, a new arrival in New Orleans, wrote of the former slaves:

> Yes, I have seen them dance; but they danced the Congo and sang a purely African song to the accompaniment of a drygoods box beaten with sticks or bones and a drum made by stretching a skin over a flour barrel. That sort of accompaniment and that sort of music you know all about; it is precisely similar to what a score of travellers have described. There are no harmonies—only a furious contretemps. As for the dance—in which the women do not take their feet off the ground—it is as lascivious as is possible. The men dance very differently, like savages, leaping in the air. . . .[57]

As persistent as African customs were in New Orleans, they were not restricted to the Crescent City. They were also prevalent on the plantations in Mississippi and Louisiana. For example, Isaac Holmes reported in 1821:

---

55. Benjamin Latrobe, *Impressions Respecting New Orleans: Diary and Sketches, 1818–1820* (New York, 1950), 46–51.

56. Helene Allain, *Souvenirs d' Amérique et de France* (Paris, 1883), 171–72.

57. Quoted in Krehbiel, *Folksong*, 38.

In Louisiana, and the state of Mississippi, the slaves have Sunday for a day of recreation, and upon many plantations they dance for several hours during the afternoon. . . . The general movement is in what they call the Congo dance; but their music often consists of nothing more than an excavated piece of wood . . . one end of which is a piece of parchment which covers the hollow part on which they beat; this, and the singing or vociferation of those who are dancing, and of those who surround the dancers, constitute the whole of their harmony.[58]

In a number of instances, the slaves used musical instruments similar to those used in Africa. Drums, for example, were often made of a hollowed-out piece of wood with an animal skin stretched over it. While the decorative arts degenerated in the South, the slaves continued to carve figures on top of their stringed instruments, as was the traditional practice in Africa. A number of instruments used by the slaves were clearly African in origin. In the latter half of the eighteenth century, Virginia slaves played a three-stringed banjo-like instrument and a "quaqua" or drum which resembled the African "molo" (banjo) and the Yoruba drum, the "gudugudu." Fortunately, Benjamin Latrobe made several sketches of the instruments used by the slaves in New Orleans. Two of them are African drums while the others are very similar to the gourd rattles and mandolins found in many African tribes.[59]

There were several other distinctly African features of the slaves' culture. The strength and longevity of conjurism and voodooism among the blacks illustrate clearly the African element in their culture. In regard to the conjurer, W. E. B. DuBois concluded that in spite of slavery

> some traces were retained of the former group life, and the chief remaining institution was the priest or medicine man.

58. Isaac Holmes, *An Account of the United States of America* . . . (London, 1823), 332; see also, Theodore Pavie, *Souvenirs Atlantiques* . . . (2 vols., Paris, 1833), II, 319–20.

59. Basil Davidson, *The African Genius* (Boston, 1969), 167; Latrobe, *Impressions*, 50; Smyth, "Travels," 85; Thomas Jefferson, *Notes on the State of Virginia* (Boston, 1832), 147.

He early appeared on the plantation and found his function as the healer of the sick, the interpreter of the unknown, the comforter of the sorrowing, the supernatural avenger of wrong and the one who rudely, but picturesquely, expressed the longing, disappointment and resentment of a stolen and oppressed people.[60]

In the United States, many African religious rites were fused into one—voodoo. From the whole panoply of African deities, the slaves chose the snake god of the Whydah, Fom, and Ewe. Symbolic of the umbilical cord and the rainbow, the snake embodied the dynamic, changing quality of life. In Africa it was sometimes the god of fertility and the determiner of good and ill fortune. Only by worshipping the god could one invoke his protective spirit. There were many worshippers of the snake god Damballa among both slaves and whites in nineteenth-century Louisiana. The voodoo priests and priestesses, claiming the ability to make masters kind, to harm enemies, to insure love, and to heal the sick, had many devotees and frequently led the allegedly wild orgies of the snake worshippers in their ceremonies on the shores of New Orleans' Lake Pontchartrain throughout the nineteenth century. Although elements of Catholicism were sometimes grafted onto the ancient rites, the basic ingredients of voodoo worship were traceable directly to the African snake cults.[61]

The funeral rite was an African custom much more widespread than voodoo. Because of labor requirements on the plantation, a deceased slave was often buried at night with the rites being held weeks later. The similarity to African practices is unmistakable. For example, Mrs. Telfair Hodgson reported that on her father's Georgia plantation in the 1850s:

60. W. E. B. DuBois, "The Religion of the American Negro," *New World* IX (Dec. 1900), 618.

61. Lyle Saxon, *Fabulous New Orleans* (New York, 1928), 233–46, 309–22; Werner A. Wegner, "Negro Slavery in New Orleans" (M.A. thesis, Tulane University, 1935), 83–85; Napier Bartlett, *Stories of the Crescent City* (New Orleans, 1869), 100–102; New Orleans *Times*, Oct. 27, 1875; Zora Neale Hurston, "Hoodoo in America," *Journal of American Folk-Lore* XLIV (Oct.–Dec. 1931), 317–417.

Figures 11, 12.
Slave Musical Instruments and African Prototypes

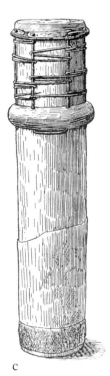

a

b

c

d

e

f

a

b

c

d

e

f

Figure 13. Midnight Slave Funeral

Figure 14.
Graveyard of Slaves
and Their Descendants
at Sunbury, Georgia

> Negro graves were always decorated with the last article used by the departed, and broken pitchers and broken bits of colored glass were considered even more appropriate than the white shells from the beach nearby. Sometimes they carved rude wooden figures like images of idols, and sometimes a patchwork quilt was laid upon the grave.[62]

Not only did Southern slaves decorate graves like their African ancestors, they also retained the practice of celebrating the journey of the deceased to his "home" by dancing, singing, and drinking. According to the traveler Henry Knight, in the Southwest, "When a slave dies, the master gives the rest day, of their [slaves] own choosing, to celebrate the funeral. This, perhaps a month after the corpse is interred, is a jovial day with them; they sing and dance and drink the dead to his new home, which some believe to be in old Guinea." [63]

Even when they were able to maintain some contact with their native culture, Africans could rarely escape the psychic shock of bondage. American slavery was so much more cruel than anything they had known in their native lands that some

62. Torian, "Ante-Bellum and War Memories," 352.
63. Knight, *Letters*, 77, 352.

Figure 15.
Carvings from the Georgia Coastal Area

developed suicidal tendencies. Whether they became suicidal or not, however, most African slaves would have agreed with the poetic lament of Olaudah Equiano:

> Well may I say my life has been
> One scene of sorrow and of pain;
> From early days I griefs have known,
> And as I grew my griefs have grown.
>
> Dangers were always in my path,
> And fear of wrath and sometimes death;
> While pale dejection in me reign'd
> I often wept, my grief constrain'd.
>
> When taken from my native land,
> By an unjust and cruel band,
> How did uncommon dread prevail!
> My sighs no more I could conceal.[64]

In all probability most blacks imported into the American colonies in the seventeenth and early part of the eighteenth cen-

64. Vassa, *Narrative,* 290.

turies received the same shock as Olaudah Equiano. It is possible, however, to place too much emphasis on this in analyzing the development of the slave's personality. Certainly after the end of the trade in America in the latter half of the eighteenth and early part of the nineteenth centuries its importance as an explanation of slave personality declines: only about 400,000 native-born Africans had been brought to the United States before 1807. Since an overwhelming percentage of nineteenth-century Southern slaves were native Americans, they never underwent this kind of shock and were in a position to construct psychological defenses against total dependency on their masters.

All things considered, the few Africans enslaved in seventeenth- and eighteenth-century America appear to have survived their traumatic experiences without becoming abjectly docile, infantile, or submissive. The Africans retained enough manhood to rebel because the Southern plantation was not a rationally organized institution designed to crush every manifestation of individual will or for systematic extermination. The mandatory requirements of the master—labor and obedience—were familiar to the Africans at least in the form of their former occupations and the obeisance they paid to chiefs and elders. Whatever the impact of slavery on their behavior and attitudes, it did not force them to concentrate all of their psychic energy on survival. Once they acquired the language of their master, the Africans learned that their labors, and therefore their lives, were of considerable value. As a result, they were assured of the bare minimum of food, shelter, and clothing. Although provisions were often inadequate and led to many complaints from slaves, they survived.

The most remarkable aspect of the whole process of enslavement is the extent to which the American-born slaves were able to retain their ancestors' culture. While the continuation of the African slave trade in the nineteenth century to Latin America permitted slaves there to maintain, to a certain degree, the purity of African cultural forms, the discontinuation of the trade to United States severely limited the contacts American slaves had with Africans and led to much adulteration of African cultural forms. Even so, and in spite of his disadvantages when compared to his Latin American counterpart, the American slave was able to retain many African cultural elements and an emotional contact with his motherland. This contact, however tenuous, enabled the slave to link European and African forms to create a distinctive culture.

2 Culture

The irony of the situation is that in folk-lore, folk-song, folk-dance, and popular music the things recognized as characteristically and uniquely American are products of the despised slave minority. . . . What accounts for it in the past and promises great momentum to it in the future is the simple fact of the intensification of the emotional side of life by persecution and suffering. . . . This is the Negro's compensation for his hard lot and generation-long sacrifice.

Alain Locke

Antebellum black slaves created several unique cultural forms which lightened their burden of oppression, promoted group solidarity, provided ways for verbalizing aggression, sustaining hope, building self-esteem, and often represented areas of life largely free from the control of whites. However oppressive or dehumanizing the plantation was, the struggle for survival was not severe enough to crush all of the slave's creative instincts. Among the elements of slave culture were: an emotional religion, folk songs and tales, dances, and superstitions. Much of the slave's culture—language, customs, beliefs, and ceremonies —set him apart from his master. His thoughts, values, ideals, and behavior were all greatly influenced by these processes. The more his cultural forms differed from those of his master and the more they were immune from the control of whites, the more the slave gained in personal autonomy and positive self-concepts.

The social organization of the quarters was the slave's primary environment which gave him his ethical rules and fostered cooperation, mutual assistance, and black solidarity. The work experiences which most often brought the slave in contact with whites represented his secondary environment and was far less important in determining his personality than his primary environment. The slave's culture or social heritage and way of life determined the norms of conduct, defined roles and behavioral patterns, and provided a network of individual and group relationships and values which molded personality in the quarters. The socialization process, shared expectations, ideals, and enclosed status system of the slave's culture promoted group identification and a positive self-concept. His culture was reflected in socialization, family patterns, religion, and recreation. Recreational activities led to cooperation, social cohesion, tighter communal bonds, and brought all classes of slaves together in common pursuits.[1]

The few periods of recreation the slave enjoyed and his religious beliefs gave him some hours of joy and a degree of hope amid his sufferings. Since his recreation was less supervised than his labor, these hours were especially important to him. Leisure time and religious activities broke the monotony of daily toil and permitted the slave to play roles other than that of the helpless dependent driven to his tasks. During his leisure hours the slave could take out his anger towards whites in physical contests with other slaves or seek relief in religious devotion by turning to One more powerful than his earthly master. Religious and recreational activities and the differences between the slave's and the master's customs prevented his total identification with the slaveholder's interests and gave him some respite from constant toil.[2]

While some slaves had to use their "leisure" time (usually Saturday afternoons) to perform their personal chores—washing clothes, cleaning cabins, or working on garden plots—Sunday was almost universally a day of rest. The more pious planters also freed the slaves from labor on religious holidays. The largest and most important holidays were the end of labor on the crops before harvesting and Christmas. During these periods, which lasted from four to six days, the restrictions on interplan-

1. Milton M. Gordon, *Assimilation in American Life* (New York, 1964), 19–39; Leslie A. White, *The Science of Culture* (New York, 1949), 121–89.

2. Practically all secondary accounts of slavery discuss what could be generally described as slave "culture," but give little solid information on life in the quarters. See: Charles S. Sydnor, *Slavery in Mississippi* (New York, 1933), 55–66; Joe G. Taylor, *Negro Slavery in Louisiana* (Baton Rouge, 1963), 125–52; J. Winston Coleman, *Slavery Times in Kentucky* (Chapel Hill, 1940), 67–80.

tation visiting were dropped and the planters prepared sumptuous feasts for their slaves. Whole hogs, sheep, or beeves were cooked and the slaves ate peach cobbler and apple dumplings, and frequently got drunk. Often the festival seasons included dances and athletic contests.³

The planters generally had little concern about the recreational activities in the quarters. They did not, however, want their slaves carousing all over the county and wearing themselves out before the day's labor commenced. Consequently, some planters locked the doors of the cabins at night and instituted the patrol system to keep slaves in the quarters after dark. In the face of the resourcefulness of the slaves, their efforts were frequently to no avail. One of the blacks' pastimes was tying vines across trails to trip the horses of the patrollers. The bolder ones fought the patrollers when they were caught at parties without passes. William Webb wrote that when his overseer started locking the cabins at 9 P.M. the slaves crawled out of the chimneys to keep their evening rendezvous.⁴

Many slaves did not have to use these stratagems. Their masters did not try to restrict their recreational activities as long as they did not interfere with the plantation routine. According to Robert Anderson, "The slaves on a plantation could get to-

3. Carl D. Arfwedson, *The United States and Canada in 1832, 1833 and 1834* (2 vols., London, 1834), I, 334; Philip V. Fithian, *Journal and Letters of Philip Vickers Fithian, 1773–1774* (Williamsburg, Va., 1943), 52–83, 121–28, 265; Charles Lanman, *Haw-He-Noo: Or the Records of a Tourist* (Philadelphia, 1850), 139–41; Jacob Stroyer, *My Life in the South* (Salem, 1890), 44–49; Louis Hughes, *Thirty Years A Slave* (Milwaukee, 1897), 13–22, 39–58; Frederick Douglass, *My Bondage and My Freedom* (New York, 1968 [1855]), 251–56; Allen Parker, *Recollections of Slavery Times* (Worcester, Mass., 1895), 40–53.

4. Robert Anderson, *From Slavery to Affluence* (Hemingford, Nebraska, 1927), 29–38; Henry Clay Bruce, *The New Man, Twenty-Nine Years A Slave. Twenty-Nine Years A Free Man* (York, Pa., 1895), 67–72, 96–106; William Grimes, *Life of William Grimes, The Runaway Slave, Brought Down to the Present Time* (New Haven, Conn., 1855), 36–48; William Green, *Narrative of Events in the Life of William Green* (Springfield, 1853), 8–9; Solomon Northrup, *Twelve Years A Slave* (London, 1853), 191–222; Austin Steward, *Twenty-Two Years A Slave, and Forty Years A Freeman* (Rochester, New York, 1861), 32–51; William Webb, *The History of William Webb* (Detroit, 1873), 8–12.

gether almost any time they felt like it, for little social affairs, so long as it did not interfere with the work on the plantation. During the slack times the people from one plantation could visit one another, by getting permission and sometimes they would slip away and make visits anyway." Similarly, Elijah Marrs said his master "allowed us generally to do as we pleased after his own work was done, and we enjoyed the privilege granted to us." [5]

Slaves spent their Sundays fishing, hunting, wrestling, running races, strumming the banjo, singing, dancing, playing marbles, recounting tales, fiddling, drinking whiskey, gambling, or simply visiting and conversing with friends. With or without their master's permission, they often organized dances and parties to which all of the slaves in the neighborhood were invited.

The social leaders at many of these affairs were the house slaves to whom the field slaves looked "as a pattern of politeness and gentility." [6] At one of the balls, Austin Steward recalled that the domestic servants came dressed in their masters' cast-off clothing and brought some of their owners' silverware, table cloths, wine, and food for the guests who were dancing to the tunes played by a slave fiddler. Anderson reported that his overseer once even permitted the slaves to use his master's house for a dance when the master and his family went visiting.

Apparently the European reels, minuets, and schottishes were too sedate and formalized for the slave. In the quarters the dance was more often a test of physical endurance, a means of winning praise and expressing the slave's inner feelings. Often openly lascivious, the dances involved wild gyrations to a furious rhythm. [7] According to a former slave,

5. Anderson, *From Slavery*, 31; Elijah P. Marrs, *Life and History* (Louisville, Ky., 1885), 11.

6. Steward, *Twenty-two Years*, 32.

7. Fithian, *Journal*, 83; Nicholas Cresswell, *The Journal of Nicholas Cresswell, 1774–1777* (New York, 1924), 18–19, 30; James K. Paulding, *Letters From the South . . .* (New York, 1817), 119; Lanman, *Haw-He-Noo*, 144–45; Francis and Theresa Pulzsky, *White, Red and Black* (3 vols., London, 1853), III, 13; John Finch, *Travels in the United States of America and Canada* (London, 1833), 237.

These dances were individual dances, consisting of shuf-
fling of the feet, swinging of the arms and shoulders in a
peculiar rhythm of time developed into what is known today as the Double Shuffle, Heel and Toe, Buck and Wing,
Juba, etc. The slaves became proficient in such dances, and
could play a tune with their feet, dancing largely to an in-
ward music, a music that was felt, but not heard.[8]

The unrestrained exhibitions gave the slave some escape, some
temporary relaxation from toil and refreshed his spirit.

In addition to these activities, several other customs prevented
the slaves from identifying with the ideals of their masters. Because of their superstitions and belief in fortune tellers, witches,
magic, and conjurers, many of the slaves constructed a psychological defense against total dependence on and submission to
their masters. Whatever his power, the master was a puny man
compared to the supernatural. Often the most powerful and
significant individual on the plantation was the conjurer.

The conjurers gained their control over the slaves in various
ways. Shrewd men, they generally were industrious enough to
avoid punishment. They then told the slaves they were not
punished because they had cast a spell on their masters. Claiming the ability to make masters kind, prevent floggings and separations, cause and prevent pain and suffering, insure love and
happiness, the conjurers were often very successful in gaining
adherents. Frequently they were able to do this because they
used their knowledge of the medicinal value of roots and herbs
to cure certain illnesses.

William Webb, who became a conjurer after observing a
skillful practitioner at work, explained how he obtained complete sway over the slaves on one plantation in Kentucky. Observing that the slaves were disgruntled over their master's cruel
treatment, Webb visited the quarters secretly, prayed for better
treatment for the slaves, and then had the slaves collect various
roots, put them in bags, march around the cabins several times,
and point the bags toward the master's house every morning.
When the master started treating his slaves better (because he
had a dream in which they wreaked vengeance on him), the

8. Anderson, *From Slavery*, 30–31.

Figure 16.   The Fiddler

Figures 17, 18. Dance

slaves were completely in Webb's power: they regaled him with sumptuous meals nightly, and the women were especially attentive.[9]

Faith in the conjurer was so strong that slaves often appealed to him to prevent floggings. M. F. Jamison declared that the conjurer on his plantation claimed that he "could prevent the white folks from mistreating you, hence those of us who could believe in such would visit him and have him 'fix' us." In many instances, the conjurer had more control over the slaves than the master had. Henry Clay Bruce felt that conjurers were so successful that the slaves had a mortal fear of them and "believed and feared them almost beyond their masters." [10]

Sometimes the charms the slaves obtained from the conjurers bolstered their courage and caused them to defy their masters. For example, after the powders and roots a conjurer gave to Henry Bibb appeared to prevent him from receiving a flogging, Bibb then had, he wrote,

> great faith in conjuration and witch-craft. I was led to believe that I could do almost as I pleased without being flogged. . . . [after going off the plantation without permission] my master declared that he would punish me for going off; but I did not believe that he could do it, while I had this root and dust; and as he approached me, I commenced talking saucy to him.[11]

The black nurses who cared for the planters' children probably did as much to insure the success of the conjurer as any one else. Because of the tales they heard from their nurses and black childhood playmates, many antebellum whites were con-

9. Henry Bibb, *Narrative of the Life and Adventures of Henry Bibb, An American Slave* (New York, 1849), 24–32; William Wells Brown, *Narrative of William W. Brown, A Fugitive Slave* (Boston, 1847), 90–96; A. M. Bacon, "Conjuring and Conjure Doctors," *Southern Workman* XXIV (Nov. 1895), 193–94, (Dec. 1895), 209–11; Thaddeus Norris, "Negro Superstitions," *Lippincott's Magazine* VI (July 1870), 90–95.

10. Monroe F. Jamison, *Autobiography And Work of Bishop M. F. Jamison, D.D.* (Nashville, 1912), 34; Bruce, *New Man*, 54.

11. Bibb, *Adventures*, 26–27.

vinced of the conjurer's power. William Wells Brown reported that the conjurer on his plantation, one-eyed, ugly Dinkie, terrified everyone in the neighborhood. His usual accouterments certainly must have contributed to this: "He wore a snake's skin around his neck, carried a petrified frog in one pocket, and a dried lizard in the other." [12] Dinkie never worked, never received a flogging, and was never stopped by the patrollers. When the planter sold Dinkie the slave trader brought him back immediately. A new overseer once threatened to whip the conjurer for not going to the fields; Dinkie either frightened or talked him out of it, for he returned to his old carefree ways, and the overseer never bothered him during his tenure on the plantation. Even some of the most refined white ladies visited Dinkie's cabin to have their fortunes told or to obtain love potions. In light of his privileged status and the ritual deference he received from whites, there is little wonder that the slaves stood in "mortal fear" of his power.[13]

While their superstitions sometimes allowed the slaves to exercise power over their masters, they also served as a means of social control in the quarters. The identity of a thief in the quarters, for example, was ascertained by various means. If the accused man could not hold a Bible or a sieve on a string without its turning, he was obviously the culprit. Another method was related to the slaves' superstition about death. They believed that if one stole something from a fellow slave, lied about it, and then drank a bottle of water filled with dust from the grave of a recently departed slave, he would die. Most thieves, not wanting to take the risk, preferred to confess when confronted rather than drink from the bottle.

Among the most important distinctive cultural forms in the quarters were folk songs and tales. It must be acknowledged at the outset that there are innumerable problems involved in using folk tales and songs to delineate the slave's world view. The major problem in attempting to analyze these elements of the culture is that all too many of the eyewitness accounts were recorded long after slavery ended. While undoubtedly many of

12. William Wells Brown, *My Southern Home* (Boston, 1880), 71.
13. Hughes, *Thirty Years*, 13–22; Stroyer, *My Life*, 50–76.

the tales and songs recorded in the nineteenth century reflected the slave experience, they had, in effect, been corrupted by freedom. Even when authentic antebellum sources are used, they are limited because they generally represented only what blacks wanted white folks to hear. When this fact is added to the unfamiliarity of many of the whites with the slaves' language patterns and their general ignorance of music and folklore, the complexities of the problem are manifest. Then, too, many of the profane tales and secular songs were ignored by most witnesses. While some of these problems are insurmountable, others can be eliminated by a strict application of the rules of evidence. This is especially true in regard to slave music. Only evidence from witnesses who actually heard this music before and during the Civil War has been relied upon in this analysis.[14]

The secular songs told of the slave's loves, work, floggings, and expressed his moods and the reality of his oppression. On a number of occasions he sang of the proud defiance of the runaway, the courage of the black rebels, the stupidity of the patrollers, the heartlessness of the slave traders, and the kindness and cruelty of masters.[15] Comments on the latter are especially informative. Nicholas Cresswell declared in 1774 that in the songs of slaves of Maryland, "they generally relate the usage they have received from their Masters and Mistresses in a very satirical stile and manner." William Faux wrote from Charles-

14. Many recent essays on the subject, while often informative, are marred by their heavy reliance on songs written and recorded after the Civil War or those popularized and commercialized by such groups as the Fisk Jubilee Singers and the New Orleans University Singers. See Sterling Stuckey, "The Black Ethos in Slavery," *Massachusetts Review* IX (Summer 1968), 417–37; David McD. Simms, "The Negro Spiritual: Origin and Themes," *Journal of Negro Education* XXXV (Winter, 1966), 35–41; John Lovell, "The Social Implications of the Negro Spiritual," *Journal of Negro Education* XVIII (Oct. 1939), 634–43.

15. George W. Cable, "Creole Slave Songs," *Century Magazine* XXXI (April 1886), 807–28; William C. Bryant, *Letters of a Traveller* (London, 1850), 85–86; Paulding, *Letters*, 126–27; Henry B. Whipple, *Bishop Whipple's Southern Diary* (Minneapolis, 1937), 33–34; Benjamin W. Griffith, "Longer Version of 'Guinea Negro Song' From A Georgia Frontier Songster," *Southern Folklore Quarterly* XXVIII (June 1964), 117.

ton in 1819 of the songs of the slaves: "Some were plaintive love songs. The verse was their own, and abounding either in praise or satire intended for kind and unkind masters." [16]

On a number of occasions the slaves sang sarcastically of the actions of their masters. The Reverend John Long wrote that Maryland slaves sometimes sang:

> William Rino sold Henry Silvers;
> Hilo! Hilo!
> Sold him to de Gorgy trader;
> Hilo! Hilo!
> His wife she cried, and children bawled,
> Hilo! Hilo!
> Sold him to de Gorgy trader;
> Hilo! Hilo! [17]

Frederick Douglass recorded one song indicative of the slave's sense of the planter's oppression:

> We raise de wheat,
> Dey gib us de corn;
> We bake de bread,
> Dey gib us de cruss;
> We sif de meal,
> Dey gib us de huss;
> We peal de meat,
> Dey gib us de skin
> And dat's de way
> Dey takes us in.[18]

Because of their sense of oppression, the blacks occasionally made folk heroes of the rebellious slaves. In the "Dirge of St. Mâlo," Louisiana slaves sang:

> Alas! young men, come make lament
> For poor St. Mâlo in distress!

16. Cresswell, *Journal,* 17–19; William Faux, *Memorable Days in America* (London, 1823), 77–78.

17. John Dixon Long, *Pictures of Slavery in Church and State* (Philadelphia, 1857), 197–98.

18. Douglass, *Bondage,* 253.

> They chased, they hunted him with dogs,
> They fired at him with a gun,
>
>   .   .   .
>
> They dragged him up into the town.
> Before those grand Cabildo men
> They charged that he had made a plot
> To cut the throats of all the whites.
> They asked him who his comrades were;
> Poor St. Mâlo said not a word! [19]

Probably a majority of the secular songs recounted the slave's loves and foibles or served as rhythmic accompaniments to labor.[20] Corn-shucking probably produced more secular songs than any other kind of work. In order to finish the work of removing the husks from his corn, a planter would invite all of the slaves in the neighborhood to gather one night at his barn. The slaves received whiskey and a big meal in payment for their labor.[21] Looking forward to the food and fun (and probably trying to "con" the planter), the slaves marched to the barn singing:

> All dem puty gals will be dar,
>   Shuck dat corn before you eat,
> Dey will fix it fer us rare,
>   Shuck dat corn before you eat,
> I know dat supper will be big,
>   Shuck dat corn before you eat,
> I think I smell a fine roast pig,
>   Shuck dat corn before you eat.
> I hope dey'll have some whisky dar,
>   Shuck dat corn before you eat.

19. Cable, "Creole," 815.
20. Charles Lyell, *Travels in North America, Canada, and Nova Scotia* (2 vols., London, 1855), I, 181; Thomas Low Nichols, *Forty Years of American Life, 1821–1861* (New York, 1937), 357; Timothy Flint, *Recollections of the Last Ten Years* (New York, 1968), 139; Thomas W. Higginson, "Negro Spirituals," *Atlantic Monthly* XIX (June 1867), 692–93; Brown, *Southern Home*, 96.
21. Lanman, *Haw-He-Noo*, 141–44; Garnett Andrews, *Reminiscences of An Old Georgia Lawyer* (Atlanta, 1870), 10–12.

I think I'll fill my pockets full,
Shuck that corn before you eat.[22]

The corn-shucking was a combination of labor and recreation. The slaves enjoyed the evening away from the quarters, meeting friends and sweethearts, drinking the cider or hard liquor, eating cakes and pies, telling tall stories and singing hilarious songs. While shucking the corn they sometimes passed the time by singing this ditty:

Massa an' Missus hab gone far away,
Gone on dey honeymoon a long time to stay,
An' while dey's gone on dat little spree,
I'se gwine down to Charles-Town a purty gal to see.[23]

The most impressive of the work songs that have survived are those created by black steamboat men, deck hands, and rowers. Abounding in rough satire, alluding to sweethearts, masters, and dreams, the boat songs were lusty and sometimes plaintive tunes improvised by the slaves to keep time with their oars.[24] While rowing their master to town, the slaves would set the stroke by singing:

Sing, fellows, for our own true loves.
My lottery prize! Zoè, my belle!
She's like a wild young doe, she knows
The way to jump and dance so well!

Black diamonds are her bright, black eyes.
Her teeth and lilies are alike.
Sing, fellows, for my true love, and
The water with the long oar strike.

22. Brown, *Southern Home*, 92–93.
23. Coleman, *Kentucky*, 75.
24. John Lambert, *Travels Through Canada and the United States of North America in the Years 1806, 1807 and 1808* (2 vols., London, 1814), II, 253–54; Whipple, *Diary*, 13, 33–34; Paulding, *Letters*, 126–27; Catherine Stewart, *New Homes in the West* (Nashville, 1843), 150; Arfwedson, *United States*, I, 378; Sarah H. Torian, ed., "Ante-Bellum and War Memories of Mrs. Telfair Hodgson," *Georgia Historical Quarterly* XXVII (Dec. 1943), 350–56; Bremer, *Homes*, I, 385.

> See! see! the town! Hurrah! hurrah!
> Master returns in pleasant mood.
> He's going to treat his boys all 'round,
> Hurrah! hurrah for master good! [25]

If the master were not aboard, the song might be more melancholy:

> Going away to Georgia, ho, heave, O!
> Massa sell poor negro, ho, heave, O!
> Leave poor wife and children, ho, heave, O! &c. &c.

Boatmen of a more religious bent sang "Michael Row The Boat Ashore":

> Michael boat a music boat,
> Gabriel blow de trumpet horn.
> O you mind your boastin' talk.
> Boastin' talk will sink your soul.
> Brudder, lend a helpin' hand.
> Sister help for trim dat boat.[26]

At their dances the slaves sang merrier tunes often noted more for their rhythmic qualities than for their lyrics. The following was characteristic of many of these tunes:

> Harper's creek and roaring ribber,
> Thar, my dear, we'll live forebber,
> Den we'll go to de Ingin Nation,
> All I want in dis creation,
> Is a pretty little wife and big plantation.[27]

Frequently the songs were composed during the dance:

> I love my darlin', dat I do;
> Don't you love Miss Susy, too?

Once the beat was established, a few lines would be repeated over and over:

25. Cable, "Creole," 822.
26. Paulding, *Letters*, 127; William F. Allen *et al.*, eds. *Slave Songs of the United States* (New York, 1867), 23.
27. Northrup, *Twelve Years*, 167–68.

Sally's in de garden siftin' sand,
And all she want is a honey man.
De reason why I wouldn't marry,
Because she was my cousin
O, row de boat ashore, hey, hey,
Sally's in de garden siftin' sand.[28]

Closely allied with the secular songs was the practice of "patting juba." When slaves had no musical instruments they achieved a high degree of rhythmic complexity by clapping their hands. Solomon Northrup, an accomplished slave musician, observed that in juba the clapping involved "striking the hands on the knees, then striking the hands together, then striking the right shoulder with one hand, the left with the other—all the while keeping time with the feet, and singing. . . ."[29] Often the rhythmic patterns used in juba were little short of amazing. After viewing a performance in Georgia in 1841, a traveler from Rhode Island observed that, while the slaves were patting juba, it was "really astonishing to witness the rapidity of their motions, their accurate time, and the precision of their music and dance. I have never seen it equalled in my life."[30] The South Carolina poet Sidney Lanier declared that in juba the slaves often used "quite complex successions of rhythm, not hesitating to syncopate, to change the rhythmic accent for a moment, or to indulge in other highly-specialized variations of the current rhythmus."[31]

The slaves also used a great variety of musical instruments. Most of these were either made by the slaves themselves or given to them by their masters. The musical instruments they used included fiddles, clarinets, fifes, tambourines, triangles, flutes, castanets, and banjos. The favorites were the banjo, fiddle, and the drum (often made from hollowed-out logs). The effect of castanets was obtained by beating two hollowed-

---

28. Parker, *Recollections,* 66–67.
29. Northrup, *Twelve Years,* 219.
30. Lewis Paine, *Six Years in a Georgia Prison* (New York, 1851), 180.
31. Sidney Lanier, *The Science of English Verse* (New York, 1880), 186–87.

out sticks together or on the floor. Individually or in bands these musicians performed both for the slaves and the master.[32]

Secular music played an especially large role in the life of plantation blacks. The songs expressed their feelings and desires, gave them solace, and lightened their daily burdens. Those slaves who had some special musical skills won the praise of blacks and whites, achieved a degree of self-esteem, and could relieve themselves of sorrow. Solomon Northrup recalled that:

> Alas! had it not been for my beloved violin, I scarcely can conceive how I could have endured the long years of bondage. . . . It was my companion—the friend of my bosom—triumphing loudly when I was joyful, and uttering its soft melodious consolations when I was sad. Often, at midnight, when sleep had fled affrighted from the cabin, and my soul was disturbed and troubled with the contemplation of my fate, it would sing me a song of peace.[33]

The mass of slaves, of course, played no instrument. Their solace came from singing. Robert Anderson asserted that the "steady rhythm of the marching songs carried many a slave across the tobacco and hemp fields ahead of a slave driving overseer, when their tired muscles refused to budge for any other stimulent than that of the rhythm of song, while the weird and mysterious music of the religious ceremonies moved old and young alike in a frenzy of religious fervor." [34]

Folk tales are in many respects easier to analyze than spirituals or secular songs even though the systematic collection of them is more recent. Most folklorists tried in various ways to ascertain the provenience of the tales they recorded. Consequently,

32. Bryant, *Letters*, 86–87; Thomas Ashe, *Travels in America* . . . (New York, 1811), 100; Paulding, *Letters*, 118; Whipple, *Diary*, 50–51; Helen T. Catterall, ed., *Judicial Cases Concerning American Slavery and the Negro* (5 vols., Washington, 1926–1937), I, 365–67; Northrup, *Twelve Years*, 216–17.

33. Northrup, *Twelve Years*, 216–17.

34. Anderson, *From Slavery*, 26.

there is some assurance that slaves actually told these tales around their cabin fires.[35] There was probably less distortion of the folk tales in the transition from slavery to freedom than of the songs. If, as John Mason Brewer has observed, "folk materials offer a true and unbiased picture of the ways in which a given people . . . think and act," they represent valuable materials for the historian.[36] While there are few explicit references to slavery, the patterns and symbolism of the tales often tell us much about the slave's world view.

Primarily a means of entertainment, the tales also represented the distillation of folk wisdom and were used as an instructional device to teach young slaves to survive. A projection of the slave's personal experience, dreams, and hopes, the folk tales allowed him to express hostility to his master, to poke fun at himself, and to delineate the workings of the plantation system. At the same time, by viewing himself as an object, verbalizing his dreams and hostilities, the slave was able to preserve one more area which whites could not control. While holding on to the reality of his existence, the slave gave full play to his wish fulfillment in the tales, especially in those involving animals. Identifying with the frightened and helpless creatures, so similar in their relations to the larger animals to the relationship of the slave to the master, the slave storytellers showed how the weak could survive. Especially in the Brer Rabbit tales, the hero, whether trickster or braggart, always defeated the larger animals through cunning. On occasion the weaker animals (slaves?) injured or killed the stronger ones (masters?). Although it is obviously possible to read too much into these tales, the slave's

35. William Owens, "Folklore of the Southern Negroes," *Lippincott's Magazine* XV (Dec. 1877), 748–55; Walter F. Peterson, ed., "Slavery in the 1850's: The Recollections of an Alabama Unionist," *Alabama Historical Quarterly* XXX (Fall and Winter 1968), 219–27; R. Q. Mallard, *Plantation Life Before Emancipation* (New Orleans, 1892), 62–73; Charles W. Hutson, "My Reminiscences," 25, 52, and George W. Polk, "Some Reflections and Reminiscences," 16, Southern Historical Collection, University of North Carolina.

36. John M. Brewer, *Worser Days and Better Times* (Chicago, 1965), 21.

fascination with weakness overcoming strength cannot be discounted.[37]

Sometimes there are direct references to masters and overseers in these tales. If the slave had suffered at the hands of either, he might thus make them the verbal target of his revenge. A former slaveholder recalled hearing one tale during his childhood in which the slave obviously expressed his hope that some misfortune would befall the overseer:

> Once der was a ole man dat was a conjeror, an' his wife was a witch; an' dey had a son, an' dey larnt him to be a conjeror too; an' every night dey used to get out of deir skins an' go ride deir neighbors. Well, one night de conjeror tetch his son wid his staff an' say, "Horum scarum" (dat mean, "It's pas' de hour o' midnight"). "Come, git up; let's go ride de overseer an' his oldes' son; I had a spite 'gin 'em dis long time." So dey goes to de overseer's house, an' give de sign an' slip t'rough de keyhole. Den dey unbar de door on de inside an' take out de overseer an' his son, widout deir knowin' it; an' de conjeror tetch de overseer wid his switch an' he turns to a bull, an' tetch de overseer's son an' he turns to a bull-yerlin'. Den de conjeror mounts de bull, an' de boy he mounts de bull-yerlin', an' sets off a long way over de creek to blight a man's wheat what de conjeror had a spite again. . . . An' de same minit de overseer was asleep in his bed at home, an' his son was in his bed. An' in de mornin' dey feel very tired, an' know dat de witches been ridin' 'em, but dey never find out what witches it was.[38]

The most explicit and realistic portrayal of slavery appears in the John or Jack series. John frequently makes fools of whites,

37. Langston Hughes and Arna Bontemps, ed., *The Book of Negro Folklore* (New York, 1966); Richard Dorson, *American Negro Folktales* (Greenwich, Conn., 1967); Bruce Jackson, ed., *The Negro and His Folklore* (London, 1967); Joel Chandler Harris, *The Complete Tales of Uncle Remus* (Boston, 1955); Zora Neale Hurston, *Mules and Men* (London, 1935); Alcée Fortier, *Louisiana Folk-Tales* (Boston, 1895), 1–39.

38. Norris, "Negro Superstitions," 95.

pretends to be more ignorant and humble than he is, dissembles, longs for freedom, runs away, is threatened and beaten, and often defies his master and expresses a desire for revenge for his sufferings.[39] In one tale John prays "for God to come git him [master] and take him to Hell right away because Massa is evil." On another occasion Efram prays: "I'm tired staying here and taking these beatings. . . . kill all the white folks and leave all the niggers." [40] Obviously, John was, as Zora Neale Hurston observed, "the wish fulfillment hero of the race." [41] But he also symbolized the discontent of the slaves, the range of actions open to them, a compendium of survival techniques, and a way of bolstering self-esteem.

The existence and content of the folk tales and secular songs can be interpreted in many ways. In the first place, the mere existence of these cultural forms is proof that the rigors of bondage did not crush the slave's creative energies. Through these means the slave could view himself as an object, hold on to fantasies about his status, engender hope and patience, and at least use rebellious language when contemplating his lot in life. The therapeutic value of this should not be dismissed lightly. Not only did these cultural forms give the slave an area of life independent of his master's control, they were important psychological devices for repressing anger and projecting aggressions in ways that contributed to mental health, involved little physical threat, and provided some form of recreation. By objectifying the conditions of his life in the folk tales, the slave was in a better position to cope with them. The depersonalization of these conditions did not, however, distort the slave's sense of the brutal realities of his life.

The slave found some hope of escape from the brutalities of

39. J. Mason Brewer, "Juneteenth," *Publications of the Texas Folklore Society* X (1932), 9–54; Hughes, *Book,* 61–101; Fred O. Weldon, Jr., "Negro Folklore Heroes," *Publications of the Texas Folklore Society* XXIX (1959), 178–82; John Q. Anderson, "Old John and the Master," *Southern Folklore Quarterly* XXV (Sept. 1961), 195–97; Fortier, *Louisiana,* 7–13, 62–69, 89; J. Mason Brewer, "John Tales," *Publications of the Texas Folklore Society* XXI (1946), 81–104.

40. Dorson, *Folktales,* 124–65; Hurston, *Mules,* 96–122, 144.

41. Hurston, *Mules,* 305.

his daily life in conventional religion. His exposure to conventional religious beliefs depended partly, however, on the piety of his master. When planters were non-believers or when they felt that religion spoiled good workers, they tried to prevent their slaves from attending services. One slaveholder, for instance, informed his slaves that "negroes have nothing to do with God" and forbade them to attend church.[42] Fearing insurrectionary plotting, such planters flogged or ran slave preachers off of their estates and broke up religious meetings of the slaves.[43]

The more pious masters often attempted to develop religious principles in their slaves and encouraged them to attend their own churches.[44] Some slaves, however, refused to do this because of their master's actions between Sabbaths. For instance, Moses Roper reported that when his master's slaves learned that he was a Baptist they, "thinking him a very bad sample of what a professing Christian ought to be, would not join the connexion he belonged to, thinking they must be a very bad set of people."[45]

Frequently, while in the first flush of his own conversion, a planter required all of his slaves to attend church. Both master and slave might attend a camp meeting, fervently pray to be saved, be converted, and then moan, shout, cry, faint, and be baptized at the same time. These planters or members of their

42. Henry Box Brown, *Narrative of Henry Box Brown* (Boston, 1851), 28.

43. Bibb, *Adventures*, 20–24, 119–30; Webb, *History*, 5–8; Moses Roper, *A Narrative of the Adventures and Escape of Moses Roper From American Slavery* (London, 1840), 62–63; Grandy, *Narrative*, 52–64; John Thompson, *The Life of John Thompson, A Fugitive Slave* (Worcester, Mass., 1856), 13–19.

44. Clifton H. Johnson, "Abolitionist Missionary Activities in North Carolina," *North Carolina Historical Review* XL (July 1963), 295–320; Trezevant P. Yeatman, "St. John's: A Plantation Church of the Old South," *Tennessee Historical Quarterly* X (Dec. 1951), 334–43; J. S. Bassett, "North Carolina Methodism and Slavery," *Historical Papers Published by the Trinity College Historical Society*, Series IV (Durham, 1900), 1–11; James B. Lawrence, "Religious Education of the Negro in the Colony of Georgia," *Georgia Historical Quarterly* XIV (March 1930), 41–57.

45. Roper, *Escape*, 62.

families taught in the plantation Sabbath schools, held prayer meetings with the blacks at the end of each day, built plantation chapels, hired itinerant white ministers, or preached to the slaves every Sunday themselves.[46] For example, Richard Allen declared that he had a pious master and "while living with him we had family prayer in the kitchen, to which he frequently would come out himself at time of prayer, and my mistress with him." [47]

The slaves acquired many of their religious ideas at the camp meetings they attended with their masters. They, of course, enjoyed the conviviality of these great social gatherings and often sold whiskey and food to both black and white communicants. Many of the slaves, viewing the business opportunities such gatherings provided, cared nothing at all about salvation. William Webb acted the typical businessman at one camp meeting when he made $42 selling ginger cakes and whiskey.

Many of the slaves imitated their master's shouting at both the camp meetings and at their own religious services. Slave preachers often could virtually reproduce the emotional sermons delivered by the white ministers they heard. Frequently attended by all of the blacks in the neighborhood, the slaves' services were similar in many ways to those of their masters: they served as meeting places for friends and sweethearts, furnished avenues for exercising responsibility and leadership, and opportunities for socializing, releasing pent-up emotions, or simply getting drunk.

As long as the slaves communed with whites, their religious instruction was circumscribed. The planters, in spite of their piety, insisted that their slaves not learn any of the potentially subversive tenets of Christianity (the brotherhood of all men, for instance). Consequently, no white minister could give a full exposition of the gospel to the slaves without incurring the wrath of the planters. Most masters saw religion more as a way

46. Thompson, *Fugitive*, 13–19; Peter Randolph, *Sketches of Slave Life* (Boston, 1855), 61–62; W. H. Robinson, *From Log Cabin To The Pulpit* (Eau Claire, Wis., 1913), 74–79; Lucius H. Holsey, *Autobiography, Sermons, Addresses, and Essays* (Atlanta, 1898), 254; Douglass, *Bondage*, 193–95.

47. Richard Allen, *The Life, Experience, and Gospel Labors of the Rt. Rev. Richard Allen* . . . (Philadelphia, 1887), 7.

Figure 19. Invisible Church

of preventing rebellion than as a way of saving the slave's soul. William Wells Brown contended that Missouri planters preferred a religious slave because he was taught "that God made him for a slave; and that, when whipped, he must not find fault, —for the Bible says, 'He that knoweth his master's will, and doeth it not shall be beaten with many stripes!'" [48] Henry Box Brown asserted that in the South "The great end to which religion is there made to minister, is to keep the slaves in docile and submissive frame of mind, by instilling into them the idea that if they do not obey their masters, they will infallibly go to hell. . . ." [49] Indeed, the planters and overseers often preached these virtues to the slaves. Henry Brown also reported that in the tobacco factory in which he worked the overseer taught the slave children in a Sabbath School that in regard to their masters "they must never disobey them or lie, or steal, and if they did they would assuredly 'go to hell. . . .'" [50] White ministers taught the slaves that they did not deserve freedom, that it was

48. W. W. Brown, Narrative, 83–84.
49. H. B. Brown, Narrative, 45.
50. H. B. Brown, Narrative, 45.

God's will that they were enslaved, that the devil was creating those desires for liberty in their breasts, and that runaways would be expelled from the church. Then followed the slave beatitudes: blessed *are* the patient, blessed *are* the faithful, blessed *are* the cheerful, blessed *are* the submissive, blessed *are* the hardworking, and above all, blessed *are* the obedient.[51]

Peter Randolph asserted that the favorite sermon of white ministers was: "servants, obey your masters. Do not *steal* or *lie*, for this is very wrong. Such conduct is sinning against the Holy Ghost, and *in base ingratitude to your kind and loving masters, who feed, clothe, and protect you.*" [52] Lunsford Lane heard similar sermons. He reported that in the Baptist church he

> was often told by the minister how good God was in bringing us over to this country from dark and benighted Africa, and permitting us to listen to the sound of the gospel. . . .
>
> I often heard select portions of the scriptures read. And on Sabbath there was one sermon preached expressly for the colored people, which it was generally my privilege to hear. I became quite familiar with the texts: "Servants be obedient to your masters"—"Not with eye service as men pleasers"—"He that knoweth his master's will and doeth it not, shall be beaten with many stripes," and others of this class: for they formed the basis of most of these public instructions to us. The first commandment impressed upon our minds was to obey our masters, and the second was like unto it, namely, to do as much work when they or the overseers were not watching us as when they were.[53]

Few were deluded by such teachings. In spite of the sermons he heard about obedience, Lunsford Lane felt that "God also granted temporal freedom, which man, without God's consent, had stolen away." [54] When the favorite Episcopal minister of Lane's black congregation told them that God had ordained that they be slaves forever, most of the slaves refused to listen to

51. Robinson, *Pulpit,* 74–79; Lunsford Lane, *The Narrative of Lunsford Lane* (Boston, 1848), 20–21; Webb, *History,* 8–14.

52. Randolph, *Sketches,* 62.

53. Lane, *Narrative,* 20–21.

54. Lane, *Narrative,* 20.

him again. W. H. Robinson asserted that slaves frequently heard white preachers urge them to obey their masters; "But this was not what our people wanted to hear, so they would congregate after the white people retired." [55]

Most slaves, repelled by the brand of religion their masters taught, formulated new ideas and practices in the quarters. The slave's religious principles were colored by his own longings for freedom and based on half-understood sermons in white churches or passages from the Old Testament, struggles of the Jews, beautiful pictures of a future life, enchantment and fear, and condemnation of sin. Frequently the praise meetings started on Saturday or Sunday evenings and lasted far into the night.[56]

A syncretism of African and conventional religious beliefs, the praise meeting in the quarters was unique in the United States. While whites might be carried away by religious frenzy at occasional "Awakenings," slaves had an even more intense emotional involvement with their God every week. In contrast to most white churches, a meeting in the quarters was the scene of perpetual motion and constant singing. Robert Anderson recalled that in meetings on his plantation there was much singing and "While singing these songs, the singers and the entire congregation kept time to the music by the swaying of their bodies, or by the patting of the foot or hand. Practically all of their songs were accompanied by a motion of some kind." [57] A black plantation preacher testified to the uniqueness of the religion in the quarters when he asserted:

> The way in which we worshipped is almost indescribable. The singing was accompanied by a certain ecstasy of motion, clapping of hands, tossing of heads, which would continue without cessation about half an hour; one would lead off in a kind of recitative style, others joining in the chorus. The old house partook of the ecstasy; it rang with their jubilant shouts, and shook in all its joints.[58]

55. Robinson, *Pulpit,* 79.
56. Hughes, *Thirty Years,* 39–58; Webb, *History,* 8–12; Bruce, *New Man,* 72–77; Randolph, *Sketches,* 67–69, 77.
57. Anderson, *From Slavery,* 24–25.
58. James L. Smith, *The Autobiography,* 27.

Besides voodoo ceremonies along the Gulf Coast, the best example of the syncretism of African and conventional religious patterns appears in the "ring shout." H. G. Spaulding gave an excellent description of the "shout" on the Sea Islands in 1863:

> After the praise meeting is over, there usually follows the very singular and impressive performance of the "Shout,"

Figure 20. A Joyful Noise

or religious dance of the negroes. Three or four, standing still, clapping their hands and beating time with their feet, commence singing in unison one of the peculiar shout melodies, while the others walk round in a ring, in single file, joining also in the song. Soon those in the ring leave off their singing, the others keeping it up the while with increased vigor, and strike into the shout step, observing most accurate time with the music. This step is something halfway between a shuffle and a dance, as difficult for an uninitiated person to describe as to imitate. At the end of each stanza of the song the dancers stop short with a slight stamp on the last note, and then, putting the other foot forward, proceed through the next verse. . . . The shout is a simple outburst and manifestation of religious fervor—a "rejoicing in the Lord"—making a "joyful noise unto the God of their salvation." [59]

Shouting, singing, and preaching, the slaves released all of their despair and expressed their desires for freedom. Their expression of the latter was restricted because discreet whites occasionally attended their meetings. Henry Clay Bruce recalled that one old slave preacher once forgot about the white man who was present at the meeting and in his enthusiasm prayed: "Free indeed, free from death, free from hell, free from work, free from white folks, free from everything." [60] Although the preacher was upbraided by the white man later, he had expressed the sentiments of most of his fellows.

The sentiments of the slave often appear in the spirituals. Songs of sorrow and hope rather than of protest, and derivations from Biblical lore, the spirituals rarely contain direct references to slavery. As a consequence of the similarities of themes in the black spirituals and white hymns, a number of scholars contend that the slaves borrowed their songs from whites. While it would be almost as logical to argue the opposite, it must be admitted that the songs the slaves heard in white churches did have a limited influence on the spirituals. For the most part, however,

59. H. G. Spaulding, "Under the Palmetto," *Continental Monthly* IV (Aug. 1863), 196–97.
60. Bruce, *New Man*, 73.

the white hymns were too cold and static to allow for the full expression of the slave's religious sentiments. After listening to the singing of former slaves in South Carolina during the Civil War, Thomas Wentworth Higginson wrote:

> As they learned all their songs by ear, they often strayed into wholly new versions, which sometimes became popular, and entirely banished the others. . . . they sang, reluctantly, even on Sundays, the long and short metres of the hymnbooks, always gladly yielding to the more potent excitement of their own "spirituals." By these they could sing themselves, as had their fathers before them, out of the contemplation of their own low estate, into the sublime scenery of the Apocalypse.[61]

Even when slaves did model their songs on those of whites, they changed them radically. South Carolina slaves, for example, added the following verse to "Blow Your Trumpet Gabriel":

> O, Satan is a liar, and he conjure too,
> And, if you don't mind, he'll conjure you,
> So blow your trumpet Gabriel. . . .[62]

The emphases, words, phrases, structure, and call-and-response pattern of the spirituals differ so strikingly from the songs of whites, that one must look outside the white church to discover their origin.[63] According to a number of antebellum white observers, the spiritual was the unique creation of black slaves.[64]

61. Higginson, "Spirituals," 693–94.
62. Higginson, "Spirituals," 690.
63. Dena J. Epstein, "Slave Music in the United States Before 1860: A Survey of Sources," *Music Library Association Notes* XX (Spring 1963), 195–212, (Summer 1963), 377–90; H. H. Procter, "The Theology of the Songs of the Southern Slave," *Southern Workman* (Dec. 1907), 652–56; Whipple, *Diary*, 36; Francis Hall, *Travels in Canada and the United States in 1816 and 1817* (London, 1818), 358–59; Myrtil Lon Candler, "Reminiscences of Life in Georgia During the 1850's and 1860's," *Georgia Historical Quarterly* XXXIII (June 1949), 110–23.
64. On the origins of the spirituals, see Lucy McKim, "Songs of the Port Royal Contrabands," *Dwight's Journal of Music* XXI (Nov. 8, 1862), 254–55; John Mason Brown, "Songs of the Slave," *Lippincott's*

In 1842, for instance, Charles C. Jones of Georgia noted the slaves' "extravagant and non-sensical chants, and catches and hallelujah songs of their own composing. . . ." [65] An Alabamian, Ella Christian, gave even clearer evidence on this: "When Baptist Negroes attended the church of their masters . . . they used hymn books, but in their own meetings they often made up their own words and tunes. They said their songs had more religion than those in the books." [66]

The spiritual, reflecting the day-to-day experience of the slave, his troubles, and his hopes of release from bondage, was indeed more vibrant and expressive than those songs that came from books. "The songs of the slave," Frederick Douglass wrote, "represent the sorrows of his heart." [67] Whatever their station in life, few white men had shared those sorrows. As a result, the hymns heard in the white churches did not have the same inspiration as the spiritual. One recorder of spirituals, for example, contended that they

> were composed in the fields, in the kitchen, at the loom, in the cabin at night, and were inspired by some sad or awe-inspiring event. The death of a beloved one, even one of the master's family, the hardness of a master or his cruelty, the selling of friends or relatives, and heart-rending separations, a camp-meeting, a great revival, the sadness and loneliness of old age, unusual phenomena such as the bursting of a comet,—any of these might be sources of inspiration. [68]

Frequently, the spirituals dealt with the more prosaic details of slave life. They served, for instance, as a secret means of

---

Magazine II (Dec. 1868); 617–23, "Songs of the Blacks," *Dwight's Journal of Music* IX (Nov. 15, 1856), 51–52; J. M. McKim, "Negro Songs," *Dwight's Journal of Music* XVI (Aug. 9, 1962), 148–49; Bremer, *Homes,* I, 352, 369–71, 393–94.

65. Charles Colcock Jones, *The Religious Instruction of the Negroes in the United States* (Savannah, 1842), 266.

66. James B. Sellers, *Slavery in Alabama* (University, Ala., 1950), 300.

67. Frederick Douglass, *Narrative of the Life of Frederick Douglass* (Cambridge, 1960), 38.

68. A. E. Perkins, "Negro Spirituals From the Far South," *Journal of American Folklore* XXXV (July–Sept. 1922), 223.

communication. Whenever the slaves on one plantation had decided to gather secretly for a dance, prayer meeting, or the clandestine barbecue of a stolen pig, they might let other slaves know of the event by singing:

> I take my text in Matthew, and by Revelation,
> I know you by your garment.
> Dere's a meeting here tonight.
> Dere's a meeting here tonight.[69]

If a slave spotted the master or overseer coming to check on the workers while they were taking an "unauthorized rest," he sang:

> Sister, carry de news on,
> Master's in de field;
> Sister, carry de news on,
> Master's in de field.[70]

The relationship of the spirituals to the slave's actual experiences emerges from a careful study of themes. For example, one of the most striking characteristics of the spirituals was the frequent reference to meeting fathers, mothers, relatives, and friends in Heaven. Although possibly related to ancestor worship in Africa, songs of this nature probably grew out of the slaves' longing to be reunited with loved ones torn away from them by cruel masters. According to Jacob Stroyer, when slaves were sold those remaining on the plantations sang "little hymns that they had been accustomed to for the consolation of those that were going away, such as

> When we all meet in Heaven,
>   There is no parting there;
> When we all meet in Heaven,
>   There is no parting more.[71]

Often the real world of the slave and his reaction to it appeared even more explicitly in the spirituals. In the song "No

69. Allen, *Slave Songs*, 9.
70. Perkins, "Spirituals," 229.
71. Stroyer, *My Life*, 41.

more rain fall for wet you" the slaves described their condition in graphic terms:

> No more rain fall for wet you, Hallelujah,
> No more sun shine for burn you,
> Dere's no hard trials
> Dere's no whips a-crackin'
> No evil-doers in de kingdom
> All is gladness in de kingdom.[72]

The slaves sought some hope, some solace for their suffering in the spirituals. Toiling from day to day, they sang to lighten their burdens:

Breddren, don' get weary, breddren don get weary,
Breddren don't get weary. Fo' de work is mos' done.
Keep yo' lamp trim an' a burnin', Keep yo' lamp trim an' a burnin',
Keep yo' lamp trim an' a burnin', Fo' de work is mos' done.[73]

When there were no whites around, the slaves dropped symbols and expressed their dissatisfaction and longings in unmistakably clear words. In "Hail Mary," for example, the slaves look forward to the coming of a "valiant soldier" to help them bear their cross until they will be

> Done wid driber's dribin', Done wid driber's dribin',
> Done wid driber's dribin', Roll, Jordan roll.
> Done wid massa's hollerin',
> Don wid missus scoldin'.[74]

While William Wells Brown was working for a slave trader, he often heard the slaves singing these words as they were carried to New Orleans:

> See these poor souls from Africa
> Transported to America;
> We are stolen, and sold in Georgia,

72. Allen, *Slave Songs*, 46.
73. Mary Dickson Arrowood and T. F. Hamilton, "Nine Negro Spirituals, 1850–61, from Lower South Carolina," *Journal of American Folklore* XLI (Oct.–Dec. 1928), 582.
74. Allen, *Slave Songs*, 45.

Will you go along with me?
We are stolen, and sold in Georgia,
Come sound the jubilee!

See wives and husbands sold apart,
Their children's screams will break my heart;—
There's a better day a coming,
Will you go along with me?
There's a better day a coming,
Go sound the jubilee! [75]

There were frequent references to freedom and deliverance in the spirituals. Certainly in some cases this must have meant temporal freedom:

O my Lord delivered Daniel
O why not deliver me too?

There is considerable evidence that many of the spirituals refer to the actual longings of the slaves for earthly freedom. Frederick Douglass, for example, recalled that when he and a group of slaves were preparing to escape to the North they sang spirituals:

A keen observer might have detected in our singing of

"O Canaan, sweet Canaan,
I am bound for the land of Canaan,"

Something more than a hope of reaching heaven. We meant to reach the *north*—and the north was our Canaan

"I thought I heard them say,
There were lions in the way,
I don't expect to stay
Much longer here.
Run to Jesus—shun the danger—
I don't expect to stay
Much longer here"

Was a favorite air, and had a double meaning. . . . in the lips of *our* company, it simply meant, a speedy pilgrimage

75. W. W. Brown, *Narrative*, 51.

toward a free state, and deliverance, from all the evils and dangers of slavery.[76]

Generally, the slave's longing for freedom was hidden behind biblical symbols. This was not, however, always the case. On one occasion near Georgetown, South Carolina, a group of slaves forgot to hide their desires and were imprisoned for singing:

> And it won't be long, And it won't be long,
> And it won't be long, Poor sinner suffer here.
> We'll soon be free
> De Lord will call us home.
>
> . . . .
> We'll fight for liberty
> When de Lord will call us home.[77]

Other slaves echoed the desires of their South Carolina brethren. For instance, they often sang the following lines:

> Working all day,
> And part of the night,
> And up before the morning light.
>
> Chorus: When will Jehovah hear our cry,
>   And free the sons of Africa? [78]

Many of the spirituals spoke so directly of the slave's longing for freedom that he could only sing them in secret. Certainly a slave had to be far away from whites when he sang:

> I'se gwine on er journey, tell yo',
> I hyar yo' better go 'long;
> I'se gwine fer de kingdom, tell yo',
> I hyar yo' better go 'long.
> O blow, blow, Ole Massa, blow de cotton horn,
> Ole Jim'll neber wuck no mo' in de cotton an' de corn.[79]

The same was true of the words that Missouri slaves sometimes sang as they contemplated their bondage:

76. Douglass, *Bondage,* 278–79.
77. Allen, *Slave Songs,* 93–94.
78. Long, *Pictures,* 198.
79. *Journal of American Folklore* X (July–Sept. 1897), 216.

O, gracious Lord! When shall it be,
That we poor souls shall all be free;
Lord, break them slavery powers—
Will you go along with me?
Lord break them slavery powers,
Go sound the jubilee!

Dear Lord, dear Lord, when slavery'll cease,
Then we poor souls will have our peace;—
There's a better day a coming,
Will you go along with me?
There's a better day a coming,
Go sound the jubilee! [80]

Whether the slaves stated their desires or intentions explicitly or obliquely, planters often felt they were singing about temporal freedom. One former slave told Lydia Maria Child of white reaction to the song "Better days are coming" around the time of Nat Turner's revolt. The whites, the slave said, "wouldn't let us sing that. They thought we were going to *rise* because we sung 'better days are coming.'" The words of the apparently innocuous song were:

A few more beatings of the wind and rain,
Ere the winter will be over—
Glory, Hallelujah!
Some friends has gone before me,—
I must try to go and meet them—
Glory, Hallelujah!
A few more risings and settings of the sun,
Ere the winter will be over—
Glory, Hallelujah!
There's a better day a coming—
There's a better day a coming—
Oh, Glory, Hallelujah! [81]

In spite of the discontent with their earthly lot revealed in the slaves' sorrow songs, the desire for revenge on whites is

80. W. W. Brown, *Narrative*, 51–52.
81. Maria Chapman, ed., *The Liberty Bell* (Boston, 1839), 42–43.

hidden by symbolism—probably behind the frequent portrayals of a wrathful God, or Moses besieging evil lands (the South?) and smiting sinners (masters?) to force them "to let my people go."

While the spirituals reveal the slave's attitude toward his condition in life, they are, like most sacred songs, primarily reflections of his religious concepts. A content analysis of the spirituals in William F. Allen's *Slave Songs of the United States* (1867) reveals several distinctive features. In an overwhelming majority of the songs the slaves sang of their search for God in the wilderness, rocks, storms, and valleys in order to obtain relief from the pain, weariness, and troubles of the world, or patience to bear them. The strong sense of family and community solidarity is indicated by frequent references to relatives and friends by name. Because the church served as the major social center in the quarters there are numerous references to "going to the meeting." Often the slaves were so filled with the Holy Ghost (the Spirit) that they could forget their oppression in an outburst of shouting and singing. Their joyful noises to the Lord indicated that they valued the ideals of personal honor, godly living, strict morality, integrity, perserverance, faith, freedom, and family life.

For the slave, Satan was a personal Devil, a snake in the grass pulling him toward Hell. Yet he was always optimistic; he was most poetic in depicting the road to Heaven as a way of escaping from his dismal existence on earth. Through the spirituals, the slave sought redemption from sin and communion with God. The God of the spirituals was visible in nature, present in the consciousness of man, omnipotent and omnipresent; He revealed himself directly to men, and was the Father who would help the slaves in their tribulations.

The slave's faith in his God was deep and abiding. He was no abstraction, but a Being who took an interest in the lowly slave and interceded in his behalf. He was the God of freedom to whom slaves prayed for deliverance from bondage. They poured out their troubles to Him and saw visions of Him. He was the great Comforter. Isaac Mason found in times of affliction "that by turning my heart towards God, He would take care of me and provide for my wants." [82] Slavery weighed heavily on William Grimes, he wrote, "yet, under the consolation of religion, my fortitude never left me." God's personal assurance of freedom buoyed up the sagging spirits of many slaves. William Webb prayed for deliverance from a cruel master and asserted that he "found that when I called on God in my trials he sent comfort to my heart, and told me the time would come, when I would be free in this world." [83]

Religious faith often conquered the slave's fear of his master. The more pious slaves persisted in attending religious services contrary to the order of their masters and in spite of floggings. In this test of wills the slave asserted that his master could inflict pain on his body, but he could not harm his Soul. After administering a few floggings, most masters gave up and allowed the slave to go to church when he pleased. Clearly, religion was more powerful than the master, engendering more love and fear in the slave than he could. William Webb's reaction to conversion was similar to that of many slaves: "As soon as I felt in my heart, that God was the Divine Being that I must call on in all my troubles, I heard a voice speak to me, and from that time I lost all fear of men on this earth." [84]

Religious services and recreational activities provided the slave with welcome respites from incessant labor. They not only gave him joy and companionship, they also permitted him to gain some status in the quarters and gave him some hope. By engaging in religious activities, the slave could, for a while, shift his mind from his hopeless *immediate* condition to the bright *future* awaiting him. In his daily tribulations, he could turn either to the conjurer or to God for succor.

Having a distinctive culture helped the slaves to develop a strong sense of group solidarity. They united to protect themselves from the most oppressive features of slavery and to preserve their self-esteem. Despite their weakness as isolated indi-

---

82. Green, *Events*, 3–4; Webb, *History*, 4–8; Isaac Mason, *Life of Isaac Mason as A Slave* (Worcester, Mass., 1893), 24–27.

83. Mason, *Slave*, 27; Grimes, *Life*, 34; Webb, *History*, 7.

84. Webb, *History*, 5.

viduals, they found some protection in the group from their masters. The code of the group, for example, called for support for those slaves who broke plantation rules. The most important aspect of this group identification was that slaves were not solely dependent on the white man's cultural frames of reference for their ideals and values. As long as the plantation black had cultural norms and ideals, ways of verbalizing aggression, and roles in his life largely free from his master's control, he could preserve some personal autonomy, and resist infantilization, total identification with planters, and internalization of unflattering stereotypes calling for abject servility. The slave's culture bolstered his self-esteem, courage, and confidence, and served as his defense against personal degradation.

3 The Slave Family

O, where has mother gone, papa?
What makes you look so sad?
Why sit you here alone, papa?
Has anyone made you mad?
O, tell me, dear papa.
Has master punished you again?
Shall I go bring the salt, papa,
To rub your back and cure the pain?

W. H. Robinson

The Southern plantation was unique in the New World because it permitted the development of a monogamous slave family. In sharp contrast to the South, the general imbalance in the sex ratio among Latin American slaves severely restricted the development of monogamous mating arrangements. For example, in 1860 there were 156 males for every 100 female slaves in Cuba. The German traveler Alexander Humboldt found that there was only 1 female to every 4 male slaves on most Cuban sugar estates and in the San Juan de los Remedios region there was only 1 female to every 19 males. One Cuban plantation that Humboldt visited had 700 males and no female slaves. The imbalance in the sex ratio among Latin American slaves was partly a result of the planter's initial lack of interest in reproducing the slave population and his preference for importing more males than females from Africa. For instance, in the Brazilian coffee-growing county of Vassouras, Stanley Stein found that between 1820 and 1880 70 per cent of the African born slaves were males. Robert Conrad's analysis of ship manifests in the 1830s and 1840s showed that 4 out of every 5 Africans imported into Brazil were males. Whatever the cause, the great disparity in the sex ratio restricted the development of monogamous family patterns among Latin American slaves.[1]

1. Philip D. Curtin, "Epidemiology and the Slave Trade," *Political Science Quarterly* LXXXIII (June 1968), 190–216; Stanley J. Stein,

The physical basis for the monogamous slave family appears clearly in the sex ratio among slaves in the Southern states. The number of females to every 100 male slaves in the United States was 95.1 in 1820, 98.3 in 1830, 99.5 in 1840, 99.9 in 1850, and 99.3 in 1860. When the sex ratio is broken down by ages, there were 99.8 and 99.1 females for every 100 male slaves over 15 years of age in 1850 and 1860 respectively. The excess of males over female slaves was very slight in the South in comparison to the disparity in Latin America. For example, in 1860 only one Southern state, Missouri, had as many as 109 males to every 100 female slaves. In actuality, the sex ratio among slaves was more nearly equal in most Southern states than among whites. In 1860, in the Southern states, there were 106 white males for every 100 white females; in six states there were more than 110 white males for every 100 white females.[2]

Since childhood is the most crucial era in the development of personality, and parents play so large a role in determining behavioral patterns, attitudes, ideals, and values, the slave family must be analyzed in order to understand slave life. The family, while it had no legal existence in slavery, was in actuality one of the most important survival mechanisms for the slave. In his family he found companionship, love, sexual gratification, sympathetic understanding of his sufferings; he learned how to avoid punishment, to cooperate with other blacks, and to maintain his

Vassouras: A Brazilian Coffee County: 1850–1900 (Cambridge, Mass., 1957); Alexander Humboldt, *Personal Narrative of Travels to the Equinoctial Regions of the New Continent, During the Years 1799–1804* (7 vols., London, 1829), VII, 276–79; Alexander Humboldt, *The Island of Cuba* (New York, 1856), 189, 203–16, 249; Carl Degler, *Neither Black nor White* (New York, 1971), 36–39.

2. *Eighth Census of the United States,* I, 594–95; *Compendium of the Seventh Census* (Washington, 1854), 87, 91. For earlier surveys of the slave family, see: Bobby F. Jones, "A Cultural Middle Passage: Slave Marriage and Family in the Ante-Bellum South" (Ph.D., University of North Carolina, 1965); Orville W. Taylor, *Negro Slavery in Arkansas* (Durham, 1958), 189–202; J. Winston Coleman, *Slavery Times in Kentucky* (Chapel Hill, 1940), 57–61; E. Franklin Frazier, *The Negro Family in the United States* (Chicago, 1948); E. Franklin Frazier, "The Negro Slave Family," *Journal of Negro History* XV (April 1930), 198–259.

self-esteem. However frequently the family was broken, it was primarily responsible for the slave's ability to survive on the plantation without becoming totally dependent on and submissive to his master. The important thing was not that the family was not recognized legally or that masters frequently encouraged monogamous mating arrangements in the quarters only when it was convenient to do so, but rather that some form of family life did exist among slaves.

While the form of family life in the quarters differed radically from that among free Negroes and whites, this does not mean that the institution was unable to perform many of the traditional functions of the family. The rearing of children was one of the most important of these functions. Since slave parents were primarily responsible for training their children, they could cushion the shock of bondage for them, help them to understand their situation, teach them values different from those their masters tried to instill in them, and give them a referent for self-esteem other than their master.

Figure 21. Home

If he was lucky, the slave belonged to a master who tried to foster the development of strong family ties in the quarters. Although the slaveholders sometimes encouraged monogamous mating arrangements because of their religious views, they generally did it to make it easier to discipline their slaves. A black man, they reasoned, who loved his wife and his children was less likely to be rebellious or to run away than would a "single" slave. The simple threat of being separated from his family was generally sufficient to subdue the most rebellious "married" slave. Besides, there was less likelihood of fights between slaves when monogamous mating arrangements existed.[3]

A number of planters attempted to promote sexual morality in the quarters, punished slaves for licentiousness and adultery, and recognized the male as the head of the family. On William J. Minor's plantations, slaves had to give a month's notice before their "marriage" or "divorce."[4] One planter asserted in 1836 that he particularly enjoined upon his slaves, "the observance of their marriage contracts. In no instance do I suffer any of them to violate these ties; except where I would consider myself justified in doing so."[5] Hugh Davis of Alabama also sought to promote morality on his plantation. He informed his overseer that "all violations of the right of husband and wife and such other immorality will meet with chastisement[.] From 10 to 50 stripes is

3. William Wells Brown, *Narrative of William W. Brown, A Fugitive Slave* (Boston, 1847), 21–26, 80–90; James Watkins, *Narrative of The Life of James Watkins* (Bolton, England, 1852), 18–21; I. E. Lowery, *Life on the Old Plantation in Ante-Bellum Days: Or A Story Based on Facts* (Columbia, S.C., 1911), 42; William O'Neal, *Life and History of William O'Neal* (St. Louis, 1896), 33–41; James L. Smith, *Autobiography of James L. Smith* (Norwich, Connecticut, 1881), 1–9.

4. J. Carlyle Sitterson, "The William J. Minor Plantations: a Study in Ante-Bellum Absentee Ownership," *Journal of Southern History* IX (Feb. 1943), 59–74; L. Tibbetts to "Sister," Jan. 23, 1853, John C. Tibbetts Correspondence, Jan. 4, 1862. Priscilla Bond Diary, Memoranda Book No. 9, Alexandre DeClouet Papers, Louisiana State University Archives; Philip H. Jones, "Reminiscences of Days Before and After the Civil War," Southern Historical Collection, University of North Carolina; Mathilda Houston, *Hesperos* (2 vols., London, 1850), II, 157–59.

5. *Southern Agriculturalist* IX (Dec. 1836), 626.

the general measure of punishment for stated offenses according to their grade." [6]

White churches (when slaves attended them) sometimes helped to promote morality in the quarters by excommunicating adulterers and preaching homilies on fidelity.[7] For instance, in Liberty County, Georgia, white ministers systematically instructed slaves about their religious duties. R. Q. Mallard, one of the missionaries to the slaves, asserted that slave marriages were

> gladly celebrated by the white pastor or colored minister. . . . We hesitate not to say that the marriages thus contracted were, by the slaves themselves and their masters, generally regarded quite as sacred as marriages solemnized with legal license of the courts; and the obligations as commonly observed as among the same class anywhere. There were as many faithful husbands and wives, we believe, as are to be found among the working white population in any land.[8]

Most planters were far less successful or interested in promoting morality in the quarters than those in Liberty County. The typical experience was related by a Mississippi planter: "As to their habits of amalgamation and intercourse, I know of no means whereby to regulate them, or to restrain them; I attempted it for many years by preaching virtue and decency, encouraging marriages, and by punishing, with some severity, departures from marital obligations; but it was all in vain." [9] It is obvious that most slaveholders did not care about the sexual customs of their slaves as long as there was no bickering and fighting. As a result,

6. Weymouth T. Jordan, "The Management Rules of an Alabama Black Belt Plantation, 1848–1862," *Agricultural History* XVIII (Jan. 1944), 64.

7. Mary W. Highsaw, "A History of Zion Community in Maury County, 1806–1860," *Tennessee Historical Quarterly* V (June 1946), 111–40; William H. Gehrke, "Negro Slavery Among the Germans in North Carolina," *North Carolina Historical Review* XIV (Oct. 1937), 304–24.

8. R. Q. Mallard, *Plantation Life Before Emancipation* (Richmond, 1892), 49.

9. *DeBow's Review* X (June 1851), 623.

planters were generally more interested in encouraging monogamy because it was conducive to discipline than because of any interest in encouraging morality in the quarters. According to one planter, "the general rule of the plantation recognized the relation of man and wife and compelled not virtue perhaps, but monogamy." [10] Many of the plantations were so large that it was impossible for masters to supervise both the labor and the sex life of their slaves. Sexual morality, often imperfectly taught (or violated by whites with impunity), drifted down through a heavy veil of ignorance to the quarters. Consequently, for a majority of slaves, sex was a natural urge frequently fulfilled in casual liaisons. William Wells Brown's mother, for example, had seven children fathered by seven different men, black and white.[11]

The white man's lust for black women was one of the most serious impediments to the development of morality. The white man's pursuit of black women frequently destroyed any possibility that comely black girls could remain chaste for long. Few slave parents could protect their pretty daughters from the sexual advances of white men. This was particularly true when the slaves belonged to a white bachelor or lived near white bachelors. Lucius Holsey's white father, for instance, never married but instead chose successive lovers from among the female slaves on his plantation.[12]

The black autobiographers testified that many white men considered every slave cabin as a house of ill-fame. Often through

10. John W. DuBose, "Recollections of the Plantations," *Alabama Historical Quarterly* I (Spring 1930), 66.

11. Brown, *Narrative*, 1–15; William Grimes, *Life of William Grimes, The Runaway Slave, Brought Down to The Present Time* (New Haven, 1855), 5–14.

12. Grimes, *Life*, 5–14; Annie L. Burton, *Memories of Childhood's Slavery Days* (Boston, 1909), 3–9; Harriet Martineau, *Retrospect of Western Travel* (3 vols., London, 1838), II, 146–48; Thomas Anburey, *Travels Through the Interior Parts of America* (London, 1789), 385; John Davis, *Travels in the United States of America 1798 to 1802* (2 vols., Boston, 1910), I, 70, II, 141; Robert Sutcliff, *Travels in Some Parts of North America in the Years 1804, 1805 and 1806* (York, England, 1811), 53, 101; Victor Tixier, *Travels on the Osage Prairies* (Norman, Oklahoma, 1940), 97.

"gifts," but usually through force, white overseers and planters obtained the sexual favors of black women. Generally speaking, the women were literally forced to offer themselves "willingly" and receive a trinket for their compliance rather than a flogging for their refusal and resistance. Frederick Douglass declared that the "slave woman is at the mercy of the fathers, sons or brothers of her master." [13] Many of the black autobiographers recounted stories of slave women being forced to submit to white men: Henry Bibb's master forced one slave girl to be his son's concubine; M. F. Jamison's overseer raped a pretty slave girl; and Solomon Northrup's owner forced one slave, "Patsey," to be his sexual partner. Slave traders frequently engaged in the same kind of practices. Moses Roper, who once helped a slave trader, declared that the traders often had intercourse with the most beautiful black women they purchased. When Henry Bibb and his wife were sold to a trader in Louisville, Kentucky, the trader forced Bibb's wife to become a prostitute.[14]

A number of white men sought more than fleeting relationships with black women. Frequently they purchased comely black women for their concubines. In many cases the master loved his black concubine and treated her as his wife. Jacob Stroyer declared that the white groom on his master's plantation shared his cabin with his black lover and their two daughters. (One of the girls married a white man after the Civil War.) Two of the black autobiographers, Jermain Loguen and John Mercer Langston, lived in such households. Langston's father was a wealthy Virginia planter, Ralph Quarles, who wanted to abolish slavery. Ostracized by his neighbors because of his abolitionist views, Quarles restricted himself almost solely to the company of his slaves. He took Langston's mother, Lucy, as his concubine, made her mistress of his household, and had four children by her. Eventually he freed her and the children.

13. Frederick Douglass, *My Bondage and My Freedom* (New York, 1968 [1855]), 60.

14. Henry Bibb, *Narrative of the Life and Adventures of Henry Bibb, An American Slave* (New York, 1849), 98–99, 112–16; Moses Roper, *A Narrative of the Adventures And Escape of Moses Roper From American Slavery* (London, 1840), 24, 63–66; Bethany Veney, *The Narrative of Bethany Veney, A Slave Woman* (Worcester, Mass., 1889), 26.

Langston declared that his father treated him "tenderly and affectionately." Early each morning he would rise and tutor his children, and when the boys reached a certain age, he sent them to school in Ohio. Upon the marriage of his daughter to a slave, Quarles purchased and freed her husband and gave them a plantation and some slaves. At his death in 1834, Quarles freed some of his slaves and willed all of his property to his three sons.[15]

Miscegenation often led to complications in the South. Sometimes, white men loved their black concubines more than they did their white wives. Consequently, the white women sued for, and obtained, divorce. Henry Watson asserted that the wife of a Natchez, Mississippi, slave trader divorced him because of his concubine. White women were frequently infuriated by their husbands' infidelities in the quarters and took revenge on the black women involved. When Moses Roper was born, for example, his mistress tried to kill him when she discovered that her husband was Roper's father. To prevent this, the man sold Roper and his mother.

On innumerable occasions white women also had assignations with black slaves. The evidence from Virginia divorce petitions is conclusive on this point: a Norfolk white man asserted in 1835 that his wife had "lived for the last six or seven years and continues to live in open adultery with a negro man. . . ." A Nansemond County white man declared in 1840 that his wife had given birth to a mulatto child and that she had "recently been engaged in illicit intercourse with a negro man at my own house and on my own bed." In many cases the sexual relations between Negro men and white women went undetected because the children resulting from such unions were light enough to pass for white. For example, one Virginian testified that when his white wife gave birth to a mulatto he "did not at first doubt [it] to be his, notwithstanding its darkness of color, and its unusual appearance." One white woman in eighteenth-century Virginia

15. Israel Campbell, *An Autobiography* (Philadelphia, 1861), 228–35; John Mercer Langston, *From the Virginia Plantation To The National Capital* (Hartford, Conn., 1894), 1–36; Jermain Wesley Loguen, *The Rev. J. W. Loguen, As A Slave And As A Freedman* (Syracuse, New York, 1859), 19–37; Jacob Stroyer, *My Life in the South* (Salem, 1890), 30–37.

who had a mulatto child convinced her husband that the child was dark because someone had cast a spell on her. (He believed the story for eighteen years.)[16]

Regardless of the actions of the planters, the courtship pattern in the quarters differed, in many respects, from that of whites. An imperfect understanding of the unnatural puritanical code of their masters freed blacks from the insuperable guilt complexes that enslaved nineteenth-century white Americans in regard to sex. Besides, they argued, they could gain nothing from observing this part of the American creed when whites considered them outside the rest of it. Consequently, freed from social restraints, young slave men pursued their black paramours with a reckless abandon which was often the envy of their white masters.

Sexual conquest became a highly respected avenue to status in the quarters. The slave caroused with black damsels on his own plantation and slipped away, with or without a pass, to other estates until he was smitten by love. He persistently pursued the one of his choice often over a long period of courtship. He flattered her, exaggerated his prowess, and tried to demonstrate his ambition and especially his ability to provide for her. If he won her affections, he often had to obtain the consent of her parents. This was almost always required in the few cases where slave men married free women. In some cases the slaves were engaged for as much as a year before their union was consummated. In the interim, the prospective husband prepared a cabin and furniture for his family, and the prospective wife collected utensils she would need to establish a household.[17]

Love is no small matter for any man; for a slave it represented one of the major crises in his life. Many slaves vowed early in life never to marry and face separation from loved ones. If they had to marry, the slave men were practically unanimous in their desire to marry women from another plantation. They did not want to marry a woman from their own and be forced to watch

16. James H. Johnston, *Race Relations in Virginia and Miscegenation in the South, 1776–1860* (Amherst, Mass., 1970), 253–56.

17. Brown, *Narrative*, 88–90; Solomon Northrup, *Twelve Years A Slave* (London, 1853), 191–222; Stroyer, *My Life*, 15–20.

as she was beaten, insulted, raped, overworked, or starved without being able to protect her. John Anderson declared that when he was contemplating marriage: "I did not want to marry a girl belonging to my own place, because I knew I could not bear to see her ill-treated."[18] Henry Bibb felt the same way. He contended: "If my wife must be exposed to the insults and licentious passions of wicked slavedrivers and overseers; if she must bear the stripes of the lash laid on by an unmerciful tyrant; if this is to be done with impunity, which is frequently done by slaveholders and their abettors, Heaven forbid that I should be compelled to witness the sight."[19] Most of the slaves tried every stratagem to avoid being placed in this position. Moses Grandy summed up the general view when he wrote: "no colored man wishes to live at the house where his wife lives, for he has to endure the continual misery of seeing her flogged and abused, without daring to say a word in her defence."[20]

Unfortunately for most slaves, the master had the final word in regard to their marriage partners. Most slaveholders, feeling that the children their male slaves had by women belonging to other planters was so much seed spewed on the ground, insisted that they marry women on their own estates. Such a practice placed all of the slave's interests under the control of the master and gave the slave fewer excuses to leave the estate. Some masters brought both of the prospective mates together and inquired if they understood the seriousness of their undertaking. If they belonged to different masters it was often more difficult for them to obtain the consent of either one. But, if both the lovers persistently spurned prospective partners on their own plantations, the planters, by mutual agreement, might resolve the controversy. Wealthy masters frequently purchased the female slave and thereby won the loyalty of the male. If the matter could not be resolved by the planters, the love might be consummated in spite of their objections. The marriage ceremony in most cases consisted of the slaves' simply getting the master's permission

18. John Anderson, *The Story of the Life of John Anderson, A Fugitive Slave* (London, 1863), 129.

19. Bibb, *Adventures*, 42.

20. Moses Grandy, *Narrative of the Life of Moses Grandy* (London, 1843), 25.

and moving into a cabin together. The masters of domestic servants either had the local white minister or the black plantation preacher perform the marriage ceremony and then gave a sumptuous feast in their own parlors to the slave guests. Afterwards, the slaves had long dances in the quarters in honor of the couple.[21]

In spite of the loose morality in the quarters, in spite of the fact that some men had two wives simultaneously, there was a great deal of respect for the monogamous family. Whether the result of religious teachings, the requirements of the master, or the deep affection between mates, many slaves had only one partner. Henry Box Brown, for instance, refused his master's order to take another mate after his wife was sold because he felt marriage "was a sacred institution binding upon me." Affection, not morality, was apparently the most important factor which kept partners together. This emerges most clearly in the lamentations and resentments which pervade the autobiographies over the separation of family members. Frequently when their mates were sold, slaves ran away in an effort to find them. The fear of causing disaffection forced planters to recognize the strength of the monogamous family; they frequently sold a slave in the neighborhood of his mate when they moved their slaves farther South. Because they were denied all the protection which the law afforded, slaves had an almost mythological respect for legal marriage. Henry Bibb believed that "there are no class of people in the United States who so highly appreciate the legality of marriage as those persons who have been held and treated as property." [22] In no class of American autobiographies is more stress laid upon the importance of stable family life than in the autobiographies of former slaves.

21. John Brown, *Slave Life in Georgia* (London, 1855), 31–44; Lunsford Lane, *The Narrative of Lunsford Lane* (Boston, 1848), 9–16; Thomas Jones, *The Experiences of Thomas Jones, Who Was A Slave For Forty-Three Years* (Boston, 1850), 29–36; W. H. Robinson, *From Log Cabin To The Pulpit* (Eau Claire, Wis., 1913), 152–63; Charles Sealsfield, *The Americans As They Are* (London, 1828), 133; Tixier, *Travels*, 47; Amelia Murray, *Letters From the United States, Cuba and Canada* (New York, 1856), 224, 351.

22. Henry Box Brown, *Narrative of Henry Box Brown* (Boston, 1851), 57; Bibb, *Adventures*, 152.

After marriage, the slave faced almost insurmountable odds in his efforts to build a strong stable family. First, and most important of all, his authority was restricted by his master. Any decision of his regarding his family could be countermanded by his master. The master determined when both he and his wife would go to work, when or whether his wife cooked his meals, and was often the final arbiter in family disputes. In enforcing discipline, some masters whipped both man and wife when they had loud arguments or fights. Some planters punished males by refusing to let them visit their mates when they lived on other plantations. In any event, these slaves could only visit their mates with their master's permission. When the slave lived on the same plantation with his mate, he could rarely escape frequent demonstrations of his powerlessness. The master, and not the slave, furnished the cabin, clothes, and the minimal food for his wife and children. Under such a regime slave fathers often had little or no authority.[23]

The most serious impediment to the man's acquisition of status in his family was his inability to protect his wife from the sexual advances of whites and the physical abuse of his master. Instead, according to Austin Steward, slave husbands had to "submit without a murmur" when their wives were flogged.[24] Sometimes, in spite of the odds, the men tried to protect their mates. W. H. Robinson's father once told him that he "lay in the woods eleven months for trying to prevent your mother from being whipped." [25] The black male frequently could do little to protect his wife from the sexual advances of whites. Most whites, however, realized that a liaison with a slave's wife could be dangerous. Occasionally, slaves killed white men for such acts. Generally, however, the women had no choice but to submit to the sexual advances of white men.[26] Henry Bibb wrote that "a poor slave's wife can never be . . . true to her husband contrary to the will of her

23. Douglass, *Bondage*, 51.

24. Austin Steward, *Twenty-Two Years A Slave, and Forty Years A Freeman* (Rochester, N.Y., 1861), 18.

25. Robinson, *Pulpit*, 25.

26. Northrup, *Twelve Years*, 176–90, 223–62; Loguen, *Freedman*, 19–25, 38–52; Henry Watson, *Narrative of Henry Watson, A Fugitive Slave* (Boston, 1848), 5–17; Bibb, *Adventures*, 112–18.

Figure 22. The Lonely Hearth

master. She can neither be pure nor virtuous, contrary to the will of her master. She dare not refuse to be reduced to a state of adultery at the will of her master. . . ."[27]

By all odds, the most brutal aspect of slavery was the separation of families. This was a haunting fear which made all of the slave's days miserable. In spite of the fact that probably a majority of the planters tried to prevent family separations in order to maintain plantation discipline, practically all of the black autobiographers were touched by the tragedy. Death occurred too frequently in the master's house, creditors were too relentless in collecting their debts, the planter's reserves ran out too· often, and the master longed too much for expensive items for the slave to escape the clutches of the slave trader. Nothing demonstrated his powerlessness as much as the slave's inability to prevent the forceable sale of his wife and children.[28]

The best objective evidence available concerning the separa-

27. Bibb, *Adventures*, 191–92.

28. Charles Ball, *Slavery in the United States: A Narrative of the Life and Adventures of Charles Ball* (Lewiston, Pa., 1836), 15–22, 258–300; Elkanah Watson, *Men and Times of the Revolution* (New York, 1857), 69; Henry B. Whipple, *Bishop Whipple's Southern Diary* (Minneapolis, 1937), 69, 88–89; John O'Connor, *Wanderings of a Vagabond* (New York, 1873), 110.

tion of mates by planters appears in the marriage certificates of former slaves preserved by the Union army and the Freedmen's Bureau in Tennessee (Dyer, Gibson, Wilson, and Shelby counties), Louisiana (Concordia Parish), and Mississippi (Adams County) from 1864 to 1866. Although these records contain the best material available on the actions of masters in regard to the slave family, they must be used with caution. In the first place, the number of unbroken unions may be exaggerated: those blacks who had retained the strongest sense of family would be most likely to come to the posts to be married. Second, multiple separations by masters were apparently understated (often old slaves simply noted how they were separated from their *last* mate). Third, it was sometimes impossible to determine from the army records whether a childless couple had been united in slavery.

The data concerning the 2,888 slave unions are summarized in Table I.

TABLE I. SLAVE FAMILIES[29]

Unions	Mississippi		Tennessee		Louisiana		Totals	
	No.	Per Cent	No.	Per Cent	No.	Per Cent	No.	Per Cent
Totals	1225	—	1123	—	540	—	2888	—
Unbroken	78	6.3	226	20.1	90	18.1	394	13.6
Broken	1147	93.7	897	79.9	450	81.9	2494	86.3
by: Master	477	39.0	302	26.8	158	29.2	937	32.4
Personal choice	145	11.9	106	9.4	58	10.7	309	10.6
Death	509	41.5	418	37.2	226	41.8	1153	39.9
War	16	1.3	71	6.3	8	0.2	95	3.2

29. Compiled from "Marriage Certificates," Bureau of Refugees, Freedmen and Abandoned Lands, Record Group 105, National Archives; see also: Amelia Murray, *Letters*, 271, 303–4; Carl D. Arfwedson, *The United States and Canada in 1832 and 1834* (2 vols., London, 1834), I, 405–6; Charles Lyell, *A Second Visit to the United States of North America* (2 vols., New York, 1850), I, 209–10.

The most difficult problem involved in analyzing the slave family is defining the term "unbroken." Since the most important characteristic of the slave union which differentiated it from legal marriage was the right the master had to separate mates, this factor must be isolated, and separations caused by death, war-related activities, and personal choice treated as unions "unbroken by masters." Through this technique, we can arrive at an approximation of the role of masters in dissolving slave families. This is not to argue, of course, that casual separations and high mortality rates did not lead to instability in these families. In fact, the dissolution of 50 per cent of the unions was directly attributable to these causes. However intimately related they are to family instability, neither of these factors involved the deliberate intervention of the master for the purpose of separating mates.

It seems logical to treat couples separated by war and death as unbroken unions, since many of them had cohabited together for decades before impersonal forces caused their dissolution. If couples separated by death are dropped from the sample, 66 per cent of the remaining unions were dissolved by masters in Mississippi, 50 per cent in Louisiana, and 43 per cent in Tennessee. This, however, would seem unfair, because it penalizes the planters for events over which they had little control. The issue here is not family stability (which involves an analysis of a number of complex factors) but the extent to which masters deliberately separated their "married" slaves. It is obvious, when all of the factors contributing to dissolution are added together, that the slave family was an extremely precarious institution. Even so, the high mortality rate among slaves was apparently more important in this than any other single factor. In a strict sociological sense, only 13.6 per cent of the unions were unbroken.

The callous attitudes frequently held by planters toward slave unions are revealed clearly in the statistics: 32.4 per cent of the unions were dissolved by masters. An overwhelming majority of the couples were separated before they reached their sixth anniversary. The heartlessness of the planters is revealed more clearly in their separation of slaves who had lived together for decades. Several instances of this appeared in Louisiana: Hosea Bidell was separated from his mate of twenty-five years; Valentine Miner from his after thirty years; and, in the most horrifying case of them all, Lucy Robinson was separated from her mate after living with him for forty-three years. Although such separations made the slave family one of the most unstable institutions imaginable, it should be emphasized that there were numerous unions which lasted for several decades. Those enduring for twenty or thirty years were not uncommon, and a few recorded in Tennessee lasted for more than forty years. If only the actions of masters are considered, 67.6 per cent of the slave unions were unbroken. In other words, in spite of their callous attitudes, masters did not separate a majority of the slave couples.

Many slaves were lucky enough to have masters who refused to intercede in family affairs. In order to relieve themselves of responsibility, many planters gave slave parents complete control of their children. Some masters did not punish slave children but instead asked their parents to do so. On Charles Ball's plantation the overseer did nothing to undermine the authority black males had in their families even when they beat their wives.[30] On large plantations and in cities the slaves were so rarely under the constant surveillance of their masters that there the black male faced no obstacle (other than his mate) in exercising authority in his family. While living in Baltimore, for instance, Noah Davis declared that he had "the entire control" of his family.[31]

There were several avenues open to the slave in his effort to gain status in his family. Whenever possible, men added delicacies to their family's monotonous fare of corn meal, fat pork, and molasses by hunting and fishing. If the planter permitted the family to cultivate a garden plot or to raise hogs, the husband led his wife in this family undertaking. The husband could also demonstrate his importance in the family unit by making furniture for the cabin or building partitions between cabins which contained more than one family. The slave who did such things for his family gained not only the approbation of his wife, but he also gained status in the quarters.[32] According to William

30. J. Brown, *Slave Life*, 62–68; J. Anderson, *Story*, 8–20; Northrup, *Twelve Years*, 176–90.

31. Noah Davis, *A Narrative of the Life of Rev. Noah Davis, A Colored Man* (Baltimore, 1859), n.p.

32. Ball, *Slavery*, 168–205; Grandy, *Narrative*, 52–64.

Figure 23. A Father's Love

Green, in the view of the slaves when one tried to provide for
his family in this manner: "the man who does this is a great
man amongst them." [33] Sometimes, by extra work, slave men
earned enough money to buy sugar and coffee for the family or
to surprise their wives with scarves or dresses. Often, when masters did not provide adequate clothing for their slaves, black men
bought clothes for their children and wives.

Masters, not the black men, determined how much care and
attention slave women received when they were pregnant and
the treatment that infants received. During her pregnancy a

33. William Green, *Narrative of Events In The Life of William
Green* (Springfield, 1853), 9.

93

slave wife usually continued her back-breaking labor until a few weeks before her child was born. Solicitous of the health of the new child, the slave owner generally freed the mother of labor for a few days and often for weeks to nurse the infant. If he were especially interested in rearing slave children (and most masters were), he established a definite routine for nursing the child. The mother either carried the infant to the field with her or returned to the cabin at intervals during the day to nurse it.

The routine of the plantation prevented the lavishing of care upon the infant. In this regard, Frederick Douglas, who did not remember seeing his mother until he was seven years old, asserted: "The domestic hearth, with its holy lessons and precious endearments, is abolished in the case of a slave-mother and her children." [34] On many plantations women did not have enough time to prepare breakfast in the morning and were generally too tired to make much of a meal or to give much attention to their children after a long day's labor. Booker T. Washington's experience was typical: "My mother . . . had little time to give to the training of her children during the day. She snatched a few moments for our care in the early morning before her work began, and at night after the day's work was done." [35] At a very early stage the child was placed in the plantation nursery under the care of old women or placed in the hands of his elder siblings. In either case, he was neglected. Fed irregularly or improperly, young black children suffered from a variety of ills. Treated by densely ignorant mothers or little more enlightened planters, they died in droves.[36]

If he survived infancy, the slave child partook, in bountiful measure for a while, of many of the joys of childhood. One important reason for this was the large size of most slave families. Some of the black autobiographers enjoyed the exquisite pleasure of being the youngest child. Sibling rivalry was apparently minimal. Slave parents, in spite of their own sufferings, lavished love

34. Douglass, *Bondage,* 48.

35. Booker T. Washington, *Up From Slavery* (Cambridge, 1928), 4.

36. John Thompson, *The Life of John Thompson, A Fugitive Slave* (Worcester, Mass., 1856), 13–19; J. Smith, *Autobiography,* 33; Allen Parker, *Recollections of Slavery Times* (Worcester, Mass., 1895), 32–40.

Figure 24. The Auction

on their children. Fathers regaled their children with fascinating stories and songs and won their affections with little gifts. These were all the more important if the father lived on another plantation. The two weekly visits of the father then took on all the aspects of minor celebrations. They were truly this for Elizabeth Keckley, for her father was only allowed to visit his family at Easter and Christmas time. Grandparents, as for all children, loomed large in the life of the slave child. Grandmothers frequently prepared little tidbits for the children, and grandfathers often told them stories about their lives in Africa.

Often assigned as playmates to their young masters, Negro children played in promiscuous equality with white children. Together they roamed the plantation or went hunting, fishing, berry picking, or raiding watermelon and potato patches. Indeed, at first, bondage weighed lightly on the shoulders of the black child.[37] Lunsford Lane, in reflecting on his childhood on a North Carolina plantation, wrote: "I knew no difference between my-

37. R. Anderson, *From Slavery*, 3–8; Stroyer, *My Life*, 15–20; Lucy Ann Delaney, *From the Darkness Cometh The Light Or Struggles For Freedom* (St. Louis, Mo., n.d.), 13; Thomas L. Johnson, *Twenty-Eight Years A Slave: Or The Story of My Life in Three Continents* (London, 1909), 2.

self and the white children, nor did they seem to know any in turn. Sometime my master would come out and give a biscuit to me and another to one of his white boys; but I did not perceive the difference between us." [38]

The pleasures of early childhood and the equality of playmates which transcended color sometimes obscured the young slave's vision of bondage. During this period many of the young blacks had no idea they were slaves. J. Vance Lewis wrote that on a Louisiana plantation during his early childhood: "As a barefoot boy my stay upon the farm had been pleasant. I played among the wild flowers and wandered, in high glee, over hill and hollow, enchanted with the beauty of nature, and knew not that I was a slave, and son of a slave." Sam Aleckson, though in less lyrical terms, declared the same thing. Until he was ten years old, he asserted, "it had never dawned on me that my condition was not as good as that of any boy in the country." Frederick Douglass reported that during his childhood, "it was a long time before I knew myself to be a *slave*." This was true, he said, because "the first seven or eight years of the slave-boy's life are about as full of sweet content as those of the most favored and petted *white* children of the slaveholder . . . freed from all restraint, the slave-boy can be, in his life and conduct, a genuine boy, doing whatever his boyish nature suggests. . . ." [39]

The planters frequently contributed directly to the idyllic existence of the young slaves. Many of the black autobiographers were the favorites of their masters, who, in a number of cases, were their fathers. In such an event, the child would be fondled, taken on horseback rides, or rewarded with numerous gifts and acts of kindness. William Grimes recalled that his master "was very fond of me, and always treated me kindly." Other slaves declared that their masters were indulgent and often gave them sweets and sometimes protected them from parental wrath. Amanda Smith's childhood was typical of this experience. She declared: "I was a good deal spoiled for a little darkey. If I

38. Lane, *Narrative*, 6.

39. J. Vance Lewis, *Out of the Ditch* (Houston, Texas, 1910), 8; Sam Aleckson, *Before the War and After the Union* (Boston, 1929), 113; Douglass, *Bondage*, 38, 40–41.

wanted a piece of bread, and it was not buttered, and sugared on both sides, I wouldn't have it; and when mother would get out of patience with me, and go for a switch, I would run to my old mistress and wrap myself up in her apron, and I was safe. And oh! how I loved her for that." [40]

Most of the slaves, of course, did not have such idyllic childhoods. While J. Vance Lewis recalled that his master's son "was as true a friend as I ever had," the memories of many slaves were clouded with tales of brutal treatment from their little white playmates who were often spurred on by their masters. Others were cuffed about by the planters and flogged for daring to visit the plantation house. Thomas Jones summed up the experience of many slaves when he declared: "I was born a slave. . . . I was made to feel, in my boyhood's first experience, that I was inferior and degraded, and that I must pass through life in a dependent and suffering condition." [41]

Those who were lucky enough to avoid Jones's experience in early childhood knew what he felt by the time they reached their teens. Many began working irregularly at light tasks before they were ten. After that age they usually started working in the fields. Such labor was the first, and irreparable, break in the childhood equality in black-white relations. Lunsford Lane's reaction illustrates the impact of this change:

> When I began to work, I discovered the difference between myself and my master's white children. They began to order me about, and were told to do so by my master and mistress. . . . Indeed all things now made me *feel*, what I had before known only in words, that *I was a slave*. Deep was this feeling, and it preyed upon my heart like a never dying worm. I saw no prospect that my condition would ever be changed.[42]

Most black children learned vicariously what slavery was long before this point. They were often terrified by the violent punish-

40. Grimes, *Life*, 8; Amanda Smith, *An Autobiography* (Chicago, 1893), 22.
41. Lewis, *Ditch*, 9; Jones, *Experience*, 5.
42. Lane, *Narrative*, 7–8.

ment meted out to the black men around them. The beginning of Jermain Loguen's sense of insecurity and brutal awareness of what he was, for example, occurred when he saw a vicious white planter murder a slave and was cautioned to silence by his mother. The shock of seeing their parents flogged was an early reminder to many black children of what slavery was.[43] When young William Wells Brown saw his mother flogged for being late going to the fields he recalled that "the cold chills ran over me, and I wept aloud." [44] The flogging Charles Ball's mother received when he was four years old still retained its "painful vividness" to him forty-seven years later.

In the face of all of the restrictions, slave parents made every effort humanly possible to shield their children from abuse and teach them how to survive in bondage. One of the most important lessons for the child was learning to hold his tongue around white folks. This was especially true on those plantations where the masters tried to get the children to spy on their parents.[45] Sam Aleckson pointed out that as a child he "was taught to say nothing," about the conversations in the quarters. Frequently mothers had to be severe with their children to prevent them from breaking this important rule. Elijah P. Marrs, for example, declared: "Mothers were necessarily compelled to be severe on their children to keep them from talking too much. Many a poor mother has been whipped nearly to death on account of their children telling white children things. . . ." [46]

Many of the slave parents tried to inculcate a sense of morality in their children. The children were taught to be honest and to lead Christian lives.[47] The Reverend Lucius Holsey gave his "intensely religious" mother credit for the moral lessons he had learned as a boy. Henry Box Brown's mother taught him "not to

43. Loguen, *Freedman*, 38–52, 109–22; Watson, *Narrative*, 5–17; Thompson, *Life*, 13–19; Douglass, *Bondage*, 91.

44. W. W. Brown, *Narrative*, 16.

45. Grandy, *Narrative*, 7–18; Ball, *Slavery*, 74–94; Stroyer, *My Life*, 9–14.

46. Aleckson, *Union*, 67; Elijah P. Marrs, *Life and History* (Louisville, Ky., 1855), 11.

47. Aleckson, *Union*, 17–21; Davis, *Colored Man*, 9–17; Stroyer, *My Life*, 24–29; Veney, *Woman*, 7–13.

steal, and not to lie, and to behave myself in other respects."
Strict and pious parents not only taught religious principles to
their children, they also taught them not to rebel against their
masters. William Webb asserted that his mother "taught me
there was a Supreme Being, that would take care of me in all
my trials; she taught me not to rebel against the men that were
treating me like some dumb brute, making me work and refusing
to let me learn." [48] Learning to accept personal abuse and the
punishment of loved ones passively was one of the most difficult
lessons for the slave child. Young Austin Steward indicated this
when he recounted how he felt upon observing a white man
flogging his sister:

> The God of heaven only knows the conflict of feeling I
> then endured; He alone witnessed the tumult of my heart,
> at this outrage of manhood and kindred affection. God
> knows that my will was good enough to have wrung his
> neck; or to have drained from his heartless system its last
> drop of blood! And yet I was obliged to turn a deaf ear to
> her cries for assistance, which to this day ring in my ears.
> Strong and athletic as I was, no hand of mine could be
> raised in her defence, but at the peril of both our lives. [49]

The lessons the slave child learned about conformity were
complex and contradictory. Recognizing the overwhelming power
of the whites, parents taught children obedience as a means of
avoiding pain, suffering, and death. At the same time, they did
not teach unconditional submission. Instead, children were often
taught to fight their masters and overseers to protect their relatives. For instance, W. H. Robinson's father once told him: "I
want you to die in defense of your mother. . . ." [50] On many
occasions the children saw their parents disobey and sometimes
fight their master. Listening to stories of runaways and seeing
slaves interact in the quarters, the slave child had many models
of behavior. In fact, he saw his parents playing two contradictory

48. H. B. Brown, *Narrative*, 16; William Webb, *The History of William Webb* (Detroit, 1873), 3.

49. Steward, *Twenty-Two Years*, 97.

50. Robinson, *Pulpit*, 25.

roles. In the quarters, for example, where he saw his parents most often, his father acted like a man, castigating whites for their mistreatment of him, being a leader, protector, and provider. On the few occasions when the child saw him at work the father was obedient and submissive to his master. Sometimes children internalized both the true personality traits and the contradictory behavioral patterns of their parents. Since, however, their parents' submission was on a shallow level of convenience directed toward avoiding pain, it was less important as a model of behavior than the personality traits they exhibited in the quarters.

When a young slave received his first flogging he was usually so angry that he either wanted to run away or to seek revenge. His parents, upon hearing this, tried to dissuade him, advised him of ways to avoid future punishment, or attempted to raise

Figure 25, 26, 27.　Going South (Figure 26 Courtesy Chicago Historical Society)

his hopes.[51] After receiving his first flogging, for example, Jacob Stroyer vowed to fight the next time he was attacked. His father argued against such action, saying: " 'the best thing for us to do is to pray much over it, for I believe that the time will come when this boy with the rest of the children will be free, though we may not live to see it.' " His father's comments on freedom, according to Stroyer, "were of great comfort to me, and my heart swelled with the hope of the future, which made every moment seem an hour to me." [52]

The degree to which slaves were able to give their children hope in the midst of adversity is reflected in the attitudes the black autobiographers held toward their parents. Fathers were loved and respected because of their physical strength, courage, and compassion. Austin Steward described his father as "a kind, affectionate husband and a fond, indulgent parent." James Watkins admired his father because he was "a clever, Shrewd man." James Mars stood in awe of his father who "was a man of considerable muscular strength, and was not easily frightened into obedience." Although they were not always perfect male models, most slave fathers had the respect of their children. Viewing the little things that they did to make life more pleasant for their children, Charles Ball asserted: "Poor as the slave is, and dependent at all times upon the arbitrary will of his master, or yet more fickle caprice of the overseer, his children look up to him in his little cabin, as their protector and supporter." [53]

Slave mothers, were, of course, held in even greater esteem by their children. Frequently small children fought overseers who were flogging their mothers. Even when they had an opportunity to escape from bondage, many slaves refused to leave their mothers. As a young slave, William Wells Brown did not run away because he "could not bear the idea" of leaving his mother. He felt that he, "after she had undergone and suffered so much

51. J. H. Banks, *A Narrative of Events Of The Life of J. H. Banks* (Liverpool, 1861), 20.

52. Stroyer, *My Life*, 23.

53. Steward, *Twenty-Two Years*, 126; Watkins, *Narrative*, 7; James Mars, *Life of James Mars, A Slave Born and Sold in Connecticut* (Hartford, 1864), 3; Ball, *Slavery*, 211.

for me would be proving recreant to the duty which I owed to her." [54]

The love the slaves had for their parents reveals clearly the importance of the family. Although it was weak, although it was frequently broken, the slave family provided an important buffer, a refuge from the rigors of slavery. While the slave father could rarely protect the members of his family from abuse, he could often gain their love and respect in other ways. In his family, the slave not only learned how to avoid the blows of the master, but also drew on the love and sympathy of its members to raise his spirits. The family was, in short, an important survival mechanism.

54. W. W. Brown, *Narrative*, 31–32.

4 Runaways and Rebels

O, that I were free! . . . O, why was I born a man, of whom to make a brute! I am left in the hottest hell of unending slavery. O, God, save me! God deliver me! Let me be free! Is there any God? Why am I a slave? I will run away. I will not stand it. Get caught, or get clear, I'll try it. . . . I have only one life to lose. I had as well be killed running as die standing.

Frederick Douglass

There is overwhelming evidence, in the primary sources, of the Negro's resistance to his bondage and of his undying love for freedom.[1] The yearning for freedom came with the first realization of the finality, of the fact, of slavery. Lunsford Lane claimed that his first realization that he was a chattel, a thing for the use of others, caused him deep anxiety: "I saw no prospect that my condition would ever be changed. Yet I used to plan in my mind from day to day, and from night to night, how I might be free."[2] Several factors combined to keep the flame of freedom burning: a free Negro kidnapped into slavery explained to his fellows the blessings of liberty; anti-slavery whites, conversing with slaves, dwelt on the blessing denied to them; an old African told speechless young boys about the wonders of his native land; and, above all, each escape of a fellow sufferer produced prayers of success, fed the rumor mill, fired dreams, and raised the level of curiosity about freedom throughout the quarters.

1. William Green, *Narrative of Events In The Life of William Green* (Springfield, Ohio, 1853), 9–14; Lunsford Lane, *The Narrative of Lunsford Lane* (Boston, 1848), 7–8; Elijah P. Marrs, *Life and History* (Louisville, Ky., 1885), 11–16; Austin Steward, *Twenty-Two Years A Slave, and Forty Years A Freeman* (Rochester, New York, 1861), 76–78, 106–15; Jacob Stroyer, *My Life in the South* (Salem, 1890), 24–29; Louis Hughes, *Thirty Years A Slave* (Milwaukee, 1897), 98–114.

2. Lane, *Narrative*, 8.

In spite of all the floggings, there were hopes and dreams.[3] When William Webb talked to the overworked, underfed, and frequently flogged slaves on one plantation he discovered that they still yearned for freedom: "They said they had been thinking they would be free, for a long time, and praying that they would live to see it. . . ."[4] Josiah Henson asserted that "From my earliest recollection freedom had been the object of my ambition, a constant motive to exertion, an ever-present stimulus to gain and to save."[5] Frederick Douglass recalled that as a child, he was "strongly impressed with the idea of being a free man some day."[6]

The slave's constant prayer, his all-consuming hope, was for liberty. Fathers opened family religious observances with prayers for freedom which held out the slender thread of hope to their children. Jacob Stroyer's father, for example, disturbed over the cruel punishment of his son, knelt one night and prayed: "Lord, hasten the time when these children shall be their own free men and women." The prayer raised Jacob's spirits, and he wrote that at that time "my faith in father's prayer made me think that the Lord would answer him at the farthest in two or three weeks." W. H. Robinson recalled that all of the slaves "prayed for the dawn and light of a better day . . . many looked long and eagerly for freedom but died without the sight."[7]

Anything might fan the fires of freedom higher. The overseer's lash, the master's celebration of the Fourth of July, a heated political campaign, the whites' disparagement of abolitionists, a painful reminder of the invidious distinctions between blacks and whites, or a sermon might cause the slave to dream about freedom. According to William Webb, a few literate

3. Moses Roper, *A Narrative of the Adventures And Escapes of Moses Roper From American Slavery* (London, 1840), 10.

4. William Webb, *The History of William Webb* (Detroit, 1873), 26.

5. Josiah Henson, *The Life of Josiah Henson* (Boston, 1849), 25.

6. Frederick Douglass, *My Bondage and My Freedom* (New York, 1968 [1855]), 91.

7. Stroyer, *My Life*, 24; W. H. Robinson, *From Log Cabin To The Pulpit* (Eau Claire, Wis., 1913), 50.

slaves followed the John C. Frémont presidential campaign in 1856 and told others that his election would mean their freedom. When Frémont lost, the slaves were disappointed, but still hopeful. At one meeting they discussed how they could obtain freedom and "some would speak about rebelling and killing, and some would speak, and say 'wait for the next four years.' " Austin Steward declared that a "superbly grand" militia training session made such an impression on him that "it became very hard for me to content myself to labor as I had done. I was completely intoxicated with a military spirit, and sighed for liberty to go out 'on the line' and fight the British . . . besides, I was sick and tired of being a slave, and felt ready to do almost anything to get where I could act and feel like a free man." [8]

The slave understood clearly what freedom was.[9] He only had to feel the scars on his back, recall the anguished cry of his wife and child as they were torn away from him, or to look at the leisure time, delicious and abundant food, and dry house of his master to know, and to know concretely, what liberty meant. Louis Hughes wrote that the slaves often discussed freedom:

> Though freedom was yearned for by some because the treatment was bad, others, who knew it was a curse to be held a slave—they longed to stand out in true manhood— allowed to express their opinions as were white men. Others still desired freedom, thinking they could then reclaim a wife, husband, or children. The mother would again see her child. All these promptings of the heart made them yearn for freedom.[10]

Solomon Northrup contended that even the most ignorant slaves understood the meaning of freedom:

> They understand the privileges and exemptions that belong to it—that it would bestow upon them the enjoyment of domestic happiness. They do not fail to observe the differ-

8. Webb, *History*, 13; Steward, *Twenty-Two Years*, 77–78.
9. Solomon Northrup, *Twelve Years A Slave* (London, 1853), 260; Henson, *Life*, 10–31; Hughes, *Thirty Years*, 75–79; John Brown, *Slave Life in Georgia* (London, 1855), 31–44; Webb, *History*, 13–19.
10. Hughes, *Thirty Years*, 79.

ence between their own condition and the meanest white man's, and to realize the injustice of laws which place it within his power not only to appropriate the profits of their industry, but to subject them to unmerited and unprovoked punishment, without remedy, or the right to resist, or to remonstrate.[11]

The more slaves knew of freedom, the more desirous they were of obtaining it. The continuing conversations about freedom in the quarters shaped Elijah P. Marr's desire for freedom: "I had heard so much about freedom, and of colored people running off and going to Canada, that my mind was busy with this subject even in my young days." The more slaves knew about freedom, Austin Steward averred, "the more we desired it, and the less willing we were to remain in bondage." [12]

It is impossible to measure exactly the extent of the slave's dissatisfaction with his lot. The best objective evidence we have on this appears in Helen T. Catterall's five-volume *Judicial Cases Concerning American Slavery and the Negro*. Restricted to cases which reached colonial or State Supreme Courts between 1640 and 1865, the evidence in Catterall represents only a small part of slave discontent. According to these records, hundreds of slaves sued for their freedom, ran away from their masters, assaulted, robbed, poisoned and murdered whites, burned their master's dwellings, and committed suicide. Hundreds more fought whites in self-defense, and were guilty of insubordination.[13]

The cases reveal that slaves were often unruly, refused to learn trades, killed livestock, and burned plantation buildings in retaliation for mistreatment. Marion J. Russell's survey of the

11. Northrup, *Twelve Years,* 260.

12. Marrs, *History,* 12; Steward, *Twenty-Two Years,* 107.

13. Helen Catterall, ed., *Judicial Cases Concerning American Slavery and the Negro* (5 vols., Washington, D.C. 1926–37); see also William T. Harris, *Remarks Made During a Tour Through the United States of America in the Years 1817, 1818, and 1819* (London, 1821), 57, 67; Harriet Martineau, *Retrospect of Western Travel* (3 vols., London, 1838), II, 97–101, 145–47; Alexander Mackay, *The Western World* (3 vols., Philadelphia, 1849), I, 287.

Supreme Court records revealed several types of discontent and insubordination.

TABLE II. SLAVE DISCONTENT, 1640–1865[14]

State	Suits for Freedom Won	Lost	Unresolved	Total	Runaway	Violence	Discontent and Insubordination
Va.	41	24	6	71	24	4	3
Ky.	41	32	10	83	49	3	5
N.C.	10	6	3	19	56	44	18
S.C.	13	6	4	23	62	33	17
Tenn.	28	4	3	35	27	18	11
Ga.	2	1	2	5	27	11	11
Fla.	1	2	—	3	3	1	—
Ala.	2	5	1	8	33	43	13
Miss.	2	2	1	5	31	28	9
La.	43	38	9	90	160	63	33
Md.	35	45	10	90	24	96	4
D.C.	34	34	20	88	16	16	—
Del.	13	4	1	18	5	—	—
Mo.	11	16	12	39	24	18	8
Ark.	1	5	4	10	11	6	5
Texas	2	—	2	4	9	5	7
Totals	279	224	88	591	561	389	144

14. Marion Russell, "American Slave Discontent in Records of the High Courts," *Journal of Negro History* XXXI (October 1946), 411–34.

As the statistics cited in Table II indicate, the slave's desire for freedom was eventually translated into action. An especially painful flogging or an unusually severe work load frequently led the slave to make a momentous decision: he had had enough, he would run away. Although his immediate purpose might be to escape the overseer's lash or to obtain a temporary respite from incessant labor, the black faced almost insuperable odds. As he plunged into nearby woods or swamps, the overseer, gun in hand, was close on his heels. Almost immediately, or certainly in a few days, he would hear the hounds as they picked up the scent of his tracks. Reaching the woods unscathed, he had to

Figure 28. Escape

fight off the pangs of hunger as well as blood-thirsty wild cats, wolves, and white men. Avid hunters, his master and overseer might know the woods as well, or better, than he did. Besides, any white man might stumble inadvertently onto his hideout. Capture would probably mean cancellation of all passes, inability to travel to the next plantation to see his wife or family, being sold down South, imprisonment in the stocks, being handcuffed to heavy logs at night and to another slave during the day, or having a cow bell hung around his neck or a tall instrument with several prongs covered with little bells attached to his head. At the very least he could look forward to being strung up and flogged severely. And excruciating pain.

The ubiquitous runaway defied all the odds. Sometimes he stayed away until his anger or that of his master subsided. Cold and hungry, he frequently returned after a few days, took his flogging, and went back to work. More often than not, he was caught trying to see his wife or to get the food the sympathetic slaves left for him. On other occasions, however, the runaway eluded his pursuers for weeks, months, or even years, safe in his bailiwick near the plantation. Peter Randolph's brother, for instance, ran away and stayed in the woods seven months while his mother carried him food. Sold South, William Grimes's sister returned to be near her husband, hid in the woods for years, and bore three children there.[15]

The slave who decided to follow the North Star to freedom faced almost insurmountable obstacles. The most formidable one

15. Peter Randolph, *Sketches of Slave Life* (Boston, 1855), 16–19; Hughes, *Thirty Years*, 79–98; Henry Bibb, *Narrative of the Life and Adventures of Henry Bibb, An American Slave* (New York, 1849), 57–93.

Figure 29.   Trailed by Bloodhounds

Figure 30.   Keeping the Wolves at Bay

he had to overcome was the psychological barrier of having to leave a home, friends, and family he loved. Mothers and wives argued passionately against it. Douglass felt that "thousands would escape from slavery . . . but for the strong cords of affection that bind them to their families, relatives and friends." Considering the likelihood of punishment and a harder life in case of failure, ridicule from the other slaves, his ignorance of the world and of geography, his penniless condition, his viewing every white man as his enemy, and his memory of his master's tales of the horrible fate which befell fugitives who succeeded in reaching the North, a slave had to think a long time before he took the first step toward permanent freedom. William Green and his friends often talked about escaping to Canada but he declared that "it requires all the nerve and energy that a poor slave can bring to his support to enable him to make up his mind to leave in this precarious manner." Henry Bibb said that when he left his family enslaved it was "one of the most self-denying acts of my whole life, to take leave of an affectionate wife, who stood before me on my departure, with dear little Frances in her arms, and with tears of sorrow in her eyes as she bid me a long farewell. It required all the moral courage that I was master of to suppress my feelings while taking leave of my little family." On the eve of his escape from bondage, Frederick Douglass expressed what most slaves probably felt upon contemplating escape: "I was making a leap in the dark. . . . I was like one

111

going to war without weapons—ten chances of defeat to one of victory." [16]

The slaves who escaped were extremely resourceful men. Seven of the fugitive autobiographers escaped from cities and eleven of them from plantations. Since so many of the fugitives had served in so many capacities as slaves, it is difficult to classify them according to occupation. Four had been house slaves all of their lives; seven had been craftsmen all of their lives; six were house servants when they escaped, six were craftsmen; and six were field slaves. Weekends, Christmas holidays, and the months when corn was still standing in the fields were their favorite times for running away. They mailed themselves in boxes, hid, often with the aid of black sailors or sympathetic white captains, in the holds of North-bound ships, disguised their sex, paid poor whites to write passes for them, or when literate, wrote their own passes; they stowed away on steamboats, pretended to be so loyal and so submissive that their masters took them to the North where they disappeared; or they passed for white. A limited amount of material was needed to begin the journey, but it was often crucial. A warm jacket, some pepper, a gun or knife, and a small cache of food (a couple of ears of corn would suffice) were essential. All the material could be stolen from the master. The bolder slaves took their master's fastest horse and any money they could find.

Slipping away on the weekend or during the Christmas revelries, the fugitive could be far away from his immediate neighborhood by the time he was missed. But just in case his trail had not gotten cold by then, he used a liberal supply of pepper to throw the dogs off his trail. Remaining in the woods at night, he avoided all inhabited areas. His two greatest enemies were the white man and hunger. The latter problem he solved by appropriating ears of corn from the fields or barns, chickens from chicken houses, or, if desperate, he begged for food in the slave quarters or ate garbage. But the white man was, by far, the runaway's most deadly enemy. If the slave was surprised by an ignorant white man, he flashed any piece of paper with writing

16. Douglass, *Bondage*, 333; Green, *Events*, 15; Bibb, *Adventures*, 46; Douglass, *Bondage*, 422.

Figure 31.　Fighting off Pursuers

on it in front of his face and usually succeeded in deceiving his adversary. When accosted by a white man he could not deceive, he ran. If cornered, he sometimes fought and killed his pursuers.[17]

One of the most objective and revealing sources of information on the character of the fugitive appears in the runaway slave notices in antebellum Southern newspapers. Unbiased attempts of owners to recover property worth hundreds of dollars, the notices were carefully composed, dispassionate descriptions of the fugitives, indicating their character, clothing, motives, and identifying marks. Even so, the notices are somewhat misleading in regard to slaves with exceptional talents. Since such slaves were more valuable, planters were more likely to try to recover them than the common slave. Even so, it is possible to draw some generalizations from the notices about the character of the fugitives. Most of them were young, robust men. In Louisiana most of them were between the ages of sixteen and twenty-five. In a collection of 134 runaway slave notices from eighteenth-century

17. William Craft, *Running A Thousand Miles For Freedom: Or the Escape of William and Ellen Craft From Slavery* (London, 1860), 12–80; John Anderson, *The Story of the Life of John Anderson, A Fugitive Slave* (London, 1863), 8–126; Henson, *Life*, 40–58.

newspapers, 76 per cent of the fugitives were under 35, and 89 per cent of them were men.[18]

Most studies of the notices indicate that there was no uniformity of personality types among the fugitives. For instance, Orville W. Taylor systematically examined notices in Arkansas newspapers and found they showed "among other things, that slaves were as individualistic as white people, despite the regimentation of slavery."[19] The major thing to remember about these notices is that they contained information which would help to distinguish the fugitive from the mass of slaves. Most of the fugitives had no readily identifiable behavioral patterns which set them apart from their fellows.

Those who were different in character from most slaves fell into two relatively broad categories. One group was composed of what Southerners called Sambo, the slave who allegedly viewed his master as his father and identified with his interest. The fugitive Sambo often stuttered, whined, laughed, grinned, trembled, was "easily frightened or scared," "rather stupid," "addicted to lying," or had a "sly," "down guilty" look, or "shuffled" and had a "low voice," or "a small impediment in speech when frightened" in the presence of whites.[20] He was a very complex fellow. Frequently, in the same sentence in which the terms cited above appeared, the planters observed that the slave was artful, could read and write, and had probably forged a pass, and stolen money, horses, and clothes. A Virginia planter wrote in 1784 that Dick had "a very roguish down look . . . is artful and plausible . . ." Another Virginia planter in 1793 described Will as "of a black complexion, round shouldered and down look, when spoken to is apt to grin, is an artful sensible fellow,

18. "Eighteenth Century Slaves as Advertised by their Masters," *Journal of Negro History* I (April 1916), 163–216; Lorenzo J. Greene, "The New England Negro As Seen In Advertisements for Runaway Slaves," *Journal of Negro History* XXIX (April 1944), 125–46; John W. Coleman, *Slavery Times In Kentucky* (Chapel Hill, 1940), 218–44; James B. Sellers, *Slavery in Alabama* (University, Alabama, 1950), 277–81; Joe Gray Taylor, *Negro Slavery in Louisiana* (Baton Rouge, 1963), 174–79.

19. Orville W. Taylor, *Negro Slavery in Arkansas* (Durham, 1958), 225.

20. See footnote 18.

much accustomed to driving a wagon, is good at any kind of plantation business, tolerably ingenious, and I am informed, has a pass. . . ." In the same year, a Maryland planter wrote that his Jem "has a great hesitation in his speech, and when he laughs shows his gums very much, takes snuff, one of his legs is sore; he is very artful and can turn his hand to any thing. . . ." [21]

The fugitive Sambo was a bundle of contradictions. On the one hand, he was the epitome of loyalty and docility, and completely trusted by his master. On the other, in spite of his "loyalty," he ran away. A South Carolina master in 1786 indicated how much of an enigma Sambo was when he observed that one of his fugitive slaves was

> sensible and artful, speaks quick, and sometimes stutters a little; HE MAY POSSIBLY HAVE A TICKET THAT I GAVE HIM TWO DAYS BEFORE HE WENT AWAY, DATED THE 6TH OF APRIL, MENTIONING HE WAS IN QUEST OF A RUNAWAY, AS I DID NOT MENTION WHEN HE WAS TO RETURN, HE MAY ENDEAVOUR TO PASS BY THAT. . . .[22]

How could a slave so completely gain the confidence of his master that he would be sent out to look for a runaway slave and then become a fugitive himself?

Did Sambo grin and look down all the while that he was "artfully" and "ingeniously" planning to escape? Was he only playacting when he grinned? Did he reveal his true character when he stepped out of the Sambo role or did the master misperceive his character, read too much into his "down look," while being selectively inattentive to his artfulness and roguish behavior? Many of these questions plagued the planters. For example, a Maryland slaveholder wrote in 1755 lamenting the escape of James: "That this Slave should run away and attempt getting his liberty, is very alarming, as he has always been too kindly used, if any Thing, by his Master, and one in whom his Master has put great Confidence, and depended on him to overlook the rest of the Slaves, and he had no Kind of provocation to go off."

---

21. *Maryland Gazette*, Aug. 26, 1784; "Eighteenth Century Slaves Advertised," 189, 203.

22. *South Carolina Gazette*, May 1, 1786.

Other planters were apparently less mystified by the contradiction inherent in an overly simplified perception of Sambo. An Alabama planter obviously suspected that the Sambo role involved a great deal of play-acting. He warned other whites to be wary of a fugitive who was "a smooth tongued fellow and when spoken to used the word 'master' very frequently, particularly when accused of any misdemeanor." [23]

The other character type which appears in the notices is the rebellious slave. The rebellious fugitive was very artful, cunning, a "well set, hardy villain," "of good sense, and much ingenuity," "saucy," "very surly," "very great rogue," "sober and intelligent," "bold," "fights like the Devil when arrested," and often stole large sums of money and took along a "nice short shot gun." Many of these fugitives were habitual runaways and quick to try to get revenge when punished.[24] The archtype of the rebellious fugitive was "Sarah" whom a Kentucky planter described in 1822 as

> the biggest devil that ever lived, having poisoned a stud horse and set a stable on fire, also burnt Gen. R. Williams stable and stock yard with seven horses and other property to value of $1500. She was handcuffed and got away at Ruddles Mills on her way down the river, which is the fifth time she escaped when about to be sent out of the country.[25]

Throughout the antebellum period groups of slaves occasionally banded together in attempting to escape. Often this occurred when they were being taken to the deep South to be sold. A group of blacks being transported through Southampton County, Virginia, killed two whites in 1799 in an attempt to escape. Seventy-seven slaves mutinied on a Mississippi River steamer in 1826, killed five white men on board and escaped to Indiana. When slaves lived near swamps, impenetrable forests, or near

---

23. "Eighteenth Century Slaves Advertised," 202; Sellers, *Alabama*, 279–80.
24. See footnote 18.
25. Coleman, *Kentucky*, 233.

Figure 32. Conspirators

frontier areas, they often banded together in such mass efforts.[26] After a Spanish decree welcomed English slaves to Florida in 1733, often as many as twenty South Carolina slaves marched in a body to the colony, occasionally killing whites along the way. The most impressive of the South Carolina incidents began at Stono in September 1739, when a group of slaves sacked and burned the armory. Then they began marching toward a Spanish fort in Florida which contained a colony of runaway slaves and was manned by a black militia company. Beating a drum as they marched, the slaves attacked all of the plantations along the way, and killed twenty or thirty whites before a militia com-

26. Herbert Aptheker, *American Negro Slave Revolts* (New York, 1943), 218–19, 276–79; Herbert Aptheker, "Maroons within the Present Limits of the United States," *Journal of Negro History* XXIV (April 1939), 167–84; Herbert Aptheker, "Additional Data On American Maroons," *Journal of Negro History* XXXIII (Oct. 1947), 452–60.

Figure 33. Resistance

pany killed or captured most of them. A contemporary wrote of the Stono uprising: "Several Negroes joined them, they called out liberty, marched on with colours displayed, and two drums beating." [27]

Few states were immune to organized mass escape attempts. In July 1845, seventy-five slaves from three Maryland counties armed themselves and began marching toward the Pennsylvania state line. Caught and surrounded by whites near Rockville, Maryland, several of the blacks were killed and thirty-one recaptured. A similar dash for freedom occurred in August 1848 in Kentucky when a white college student led a group of seventy-five slaves toward the Ohio River. Pursued by the slaveholders, the fugitives fought two battles with them, but all were eventually killed or recaptured. Thirty slaves in Missouri emulated the Kentucky fugitives in 1850 when they armed themselves and began marching toward freedom. Later, surrounded by heavily armed whites, the slaves held out for a while and then surrendered.[28]

27. Edward McCrady, "Slavery in the Province of South Carolina," *Annual Report of the American Historical Association for the Year 1895* (Washington, 1896), 631–73.

28. Aptheker, *Revolts*, pp. 337–43; John Finch, *Travels in the United States of America and Canada* (London, 1833), 241–42; Henry C. Knight, *Letters from the South and West* (Boston, 1824), 29.

For the most part, the possibility of a large body of slaves marching undetected to a free state was remote. Realizing this, many runaways built "free" or "maroon" communities in the swamps and mountains in the South.[29] The character of the maroon settlements and their inhabitants appears in a report from Alabama in 1827. In that year a group of whites reported that:

> A nest of runaway negroes was discovered last week in the fork of the Alabama & Tombecke [Tombigbee] Rivers, by a party from the upper end of Mobile County. . . . The negroes were attacked and after a very severe action they were conquered. Three negroes were shot . . . several were taken prisoner and others escaped. They had two cabins, and were about to build a Fort. . . . Some of these negroes have been runaways several years, and have committed many depredations on the neighbouring plantations. They fought desperately.[30]

The maroon communities represented one of the gravest threats to the planters. In the first place, these communities undermined the master's authority and emboldened other slaves to join them. For example, a group of North Carolina planters complained in December 1830 that their "slaves are become almost uncontrollable. They go and come when and where they please, and if an attempt is made to stop them they immediately fly to the woods and there continue for months and years Committing depredations on our Cattle hogs and Sheep. . . . patrols are of no use on account of the danger they subject themselves to. . . ."[31] Second, and perhaps more important, the maroons often engaged in guerrilla-like activities, plundering and burning plantations, stealing stock, and attacking, robbing, and murdering whites. If they obtained enough arms or allied themselves with poor whites and Indians they could terrorize almost any isolated white community. Sometimes their activities were rationally planned, systematic attacks on the plantations.

29. Aptheker, *Revolts,* 336.
30. Aptheker, *Revolts,* 280.
31. Aptheker, *Revolts,* 289.

This was certainly the case in Accomack County, Virginia, in 1781. A resident of the county declared, "We have had most alarming times this Summer all along shore, from a sett of Barges manned mostly by our own negroes who have run off—These fellows are dangerous to an individual singled out for their vengeance whose property lay exposed—They burnt several houses." [32] On other occasions maroons formed outlaw bands and raided plantations in order to obtain supplies. The Norfolk *Herald* described one of these bands when it announced in 1823 that whites in the county

> have for some time been kept in a state of mind peculiarly harassing and painful, from the too apparent fact that their lives are at the mercy of a band of lurking assassins, against whose fell designs neither the power of the law, nor vigilance, or personal strength and intrepidity, can avail. These desperadoes are runaway negroes (commonly called outlyers) . . . Their first object is to obtain a gun and ammunition, as well to procure game for subsistence as to defend themselves from attack, or accomplish objects of vengeance. [33]

The maroon was a resourceful black man who, having obtained his freedom, challenged any white man to take it away from him. If his hideout was discovered, he was willing to die defending it. For instance, when a group of North Carolina whites attacked a maroon camp in August 1856, the slaves fought back and killed one of them. Then, the "negroes ran off cursing and swearing and telling them to come on, they were ready for them again." [34] On a number of occasions the maroons fought pitched battles with militia in the seventeenth and eighteenth centuries. Later, improvements in roads and communications facilities enabled whites to concentrate large bodies of armed men in the vicinity of the camps and to destroy them. Smaller maroon camps, however, continued to develop in inaccessible swamps in the South, and as long as the slaves did not attack

32. Aptheker, *Revolts*, 207.
33. Aptheker, *Revolts*, 276.
34. Aptheker, *Revolts*, 346.

surrounding plantations they might go undetected for years.[35] The largest semi-permanent maroon communities grew up in areas where there was international rivalry over borders, or which were near sympathetic Indian tribes. Although some of the tribes like the Choctaw and Chickasaw held blacks in bondage similar to that on Southern white plantations, most of the other tribes either welcomed the blacks as freemen or subjected them to a relatively mild form of slavery. Under the latter group of Indians, blacks performed light labor, owned property, and intermarried with their masters. The closest relations between red and black men developed in Florida when a branch of the Creek tribe, the Seminoles, moved into the Spanish territory. Some of the Seminoles owned black slaves who were almost indistinguishable from free men. These blacks were joined by groups of runaways from South Carolina and Georgia who accepted the Spanish invitation to desert their Protestant masters. By 1836 there were probably about 1,200 maroons living in the Seminole towns. Better acquainted with whites than the Indians were, the maroons and slaves often acted as interpreters for their red masters. By the mid-nineteenth century so many of the Indians and blacks had intermarried that they were almost indistinguishable.[36]

Aided by Indian wars and Spanish and British intrigues on the Georgia-Alabama border of Florida, large numbers of slaves escaped and joined the maroons. A special inducement was held out to runaways when during the War of 1812 the British built a fort on the eastern side of the Appalachicola River for themselves and their black and red allies. Abandoning the fort in

35. Aptheker, *Revolts,* 171–83, 196–217, 277–89, 342–51; Ulrich B. Phillips, *American Negro Slavery* (Baton Rouge, 1966), 509–10; James McKaye, *The Mastership and its Fruits* (New York, 1864), 7–12.

36. J. Lutch Wright, "A Note on the First Seminole War as Seen by the Indians, Negroes, and Their British Advisers," *Journal of Southern History* XXXIV (Nov. 1968), 565–75; Kenneth W. Porter, "Negroes and the Seminole War, 1817–1818," *Journal of Negro History* XXXVI (July 1951), 49–80; Wilton M. Krogman, "The Racial Composition of the Seminole Indians of Florida and Oklahoma," *Journal of Negro History* XIX (Oct. 1934), 412–30; Joshua R. Giddings, *The Exiles of Florida* (Columbus, Ohio, 1858).

1816 but leaving behind guns and cannon for their allies, the British inadvertently incited the First Seminole War. Three hundred runaway slaves immediately took over the fort and cultivated land located within fifty miles of it. Led by the maroon Garçon, the runaways attacked a group of sailors from a U.S. gunboat in July and scalped most of them. After a short artillery duel the gunboat was successful in blowing up the fort's magazine, killing most of the blacks. The survivors were recaptured and returned to their owners.

Seeking revenge for their fallen comrades, the Negroes and Indians began drilling in separate units under their officers. In 1817 and 1818 between 400 and 600 runaways joined with the Seminoles in raiding plantations in Georgia, killing the whites and carrying off slaves. On April 16, 1818, Andrew Jackson captured one of the Seminole towns in which the blacks, after their initial retreat, fought valiantly.[37] According to one observer: "They fought desperately, and did not give way until eighty out of three hundred and forty were killed." Unable to follow the survivors into the trackless swamps, Andrew Jackson unilaterally ended what he called "this savage and negro war." [38]

The presence of hundreds of runaway slaves plagued every effort to make a permanent peace with the Seminoles before 1865. The Seminoles were so steadfast in their refusal to agree to the return of the fugitives to their owners that when the U.S. acquired Florida in 1819 plans began almost immediately to remove the Indians to the West. The role of the blacks in the controversy was summarized by an Indian agent in 1821:

> It will be difficult to form a prudent determination, with respect to the maroon negroes, who live among the Indians, on the other side of the little mountains of Latchiova. Their number is said to be upwards of three hundred. They fear being again made slaves, under the American government; and will omit nothing to increase or keep alive mistrust among the Indians, whom they in fact govern. If it should

37. Kenneth W. Porter, "Relations Between Negroes and Indians Within the Present Limits of the United States," *Journal of Negro History* XVII (July 1932), 287–367.
38. Porter, "Relations," 333–34.

become necessary to use force with them, it is to be feared the Indians would take their part.[39]

Fearing that they would be returned to slavery if they ever gathered at a central point to be transported to the West under military supervision, the maroons took a leading part in stirring up resistance to removal among the Seminoles. The immediate cause of the Second Seminole War was intimately related to the problem of the maroons. The war can be traced to the kidnapping and enslavement of the wife of the Seminole chief, Osceola. She was the daughter of a Negro fugitive. As a result of this, in December 1835 the Indians, after being informed by a Negro guide of the route of a company of American soldiers, massacred about 100 of the troops. Negro warriors fought in most of the battles during the next seven years and were so numerous in some of them that on one occasion General Thomas Jesup declared: "This, you may be assured, is a negro, not an Indian war. . . ."[40]

Among the several black warriors, Abraham was the most impressive. After escaping from his Florida master, Abraham became a Seminole slave and interpreter for his master. Later, he won his freedom and married the widow of a chief. Considered one of the most dangerous of the maroon leaders, Abraham was described by one white officer as "the most noted, and for a time an influential man in the [Seminole] nation. He dictated to those of his own color, who to a great degree controlled their masters. They were a most cruel and malignant enemy. For them to surrender would be servitude to the whites; but to retain an open warfare, secured to them plunder, liberty, and importance."[41]

Peace efforts were hindered because planters always rushed in to claim those Negroes who were captured or who surrendered. Between 1835 and 1843 about 500 blacks were returned to their owners in Florida and Georgia. Since the maroons always renewed hostilities when any of their number were returned to slavery, army officers began pleading with the War Department to treat the blacks as prisoners of war to be removed

39. Porter, "Relations," 334.
40. Porter, "Relations," 341.
41. Porter, "Relations," 341.

to the Southwest. General Jesup, for instance, wrote in 1837 that "The negroes rule the Indians and it is important that they should feel themselves secure: if they should become alarmed and hold out, the war will be renewed." Failing in their efforts to prevent the re-enslavement of the maroons, the military officers tried to convince the rapacious planters that it would be better to remove the rebellious blacks to the Southwest rather than add them to their plantation force and possibly incite revolts. One officer tried to demonstrate this by describing the character of the maroons: "The Negroes, from the commencement of the Florida war, have, for their numbers, been the most formidable foe, more blood-thirsty, active, and revengeful than the Indian. . . . Ten resolute negroes, with a knowledge of the country, are sufficient to desolate the frontier, from one extent to the other." The war ended in 1842 only after Zachary Taylor guaranteed the blacks that they would be taken to the Southwest.[42]

In spite of widespread maroon activity and individual resistance among slaves in the South, there have been considerably fewer large-scale slave rebellions in the United States than in Latin America. The explanation for this lies in the differences between conditions in Latin America and in the South. A chronic shortage of military forces and high slave to white population ratio (7 to 1 in the British West Indies, 11 to 1 in Haiti, 20 to 1 in Surinam) severely limited the ability of South American and Caribbean masters to control plantation blacks. Faced with an underdeveloped communication and transportation network, along with the propinquity of plantations to jungles, swamps, and mountains, Latin American masters found it difficult to prevent slaves from rebelling or escaping to the "trackless wilderness." When the slaves did escape to the almost impenetrable forests, they were able to form free communities in relative security. The military forces were so weak in Latin America that it once took a Cuban army two months to dislodge 700 slaves from a mountain stronghold, while a colonial Mexican army took months to reach the site of a slave revolt in the mining region and then could not defeat the rebels. Al-

42. Porter, "Relations," 342, 347.

though an ignorant slave may not have known in advance that the army was weak, the existence of the slave communities was public knowledge. These communities stood, moreover, as an open invitation for escape and a monument to the weakness of the master class. Besides, blacks had before them the knowledge and tradition of successful slave resistance. Of overriding importance in the apparent greater inclination of Latin American slaves to rebel was the constant importation of Africans and a slave population composed of from 60 per cent to 70 per cent males.[43]

Having the advantage over their Latin American counterparts in practically every respect, Southern planters were able to crush every slave rebellion with relative ease, and more importantly, to prevent the development of a tradition of successful revolt in the quarters. Unless he were totally blind, a slave could not fail to perceive how hopeless revolt was, given the size and undeniably superior firepower of the whites. In this regard, the few revolts which did occur in the United States are convincing evidence of the indomitability of the Southern slave. After all, he had far less chance of success than his Latin American brother.

There has been so much controversy surrounding the whole question of slave rebellions that one has to apply a very strict definition to the word "revolt." Consigning conspiracies to the general category of "resistance," a revolt is defined in this study as any concerted action by a group of slaves with the settled purpose of and the actual destruction of the lives and property of local whites. In addition, the activities must have been recognized as an insurrection by public officials who called out the armed forces of the locale to destroy the rebels. Applying this rigid definition, there were at least nine slave revolts in America between 1691 and 1865. Although most of the large-scale conspiracies occurred in cities, most of the actual rebellions took place in plantation counties.[44]

43. Hubert H. S. Aimes, *A History of Slavery in Cuba, 1511 to 1868* (New York, 1967), 89, 160, 264; Stanley Stein, *Vassouras: A Brazilian Coffee County, 1850–1900* (Cambridge, Mass., 1957), 30–130; David M. Davidson, "Negro Slave Control in Colonial Mexico, 1519–1650," *Hispanic American Historical Review* XLVI (Aug. 1966), 235–53.

44. Thomas W. Higginson, *Black Rebellion* (New York, 1969); Harvey Wish, "American Slave Insurrections Before 1861," *Journal of*

A few of these revolts must be analyzed in order to under-stand the full range of the black man's reaction to slavery. In 1712 several Africans formed a plot in New York City to burn the town, to destroy all whites "for some hard usage they appre-hended to have received from their masters," and to obtain their freedom. Sealing an oath of secrecy by sucking each other's blood and rubbing powder prepared by a black conjurer on their bodies to make them invincible, the conspirators armed them-selves with guns, pistols, swords, daggers, knives, and hatchets. On the night of April 6th, they set fire to several buildings and then murdered or wounded at least sixteen whites who came to put out the blaze. When the alarm was sounded and troops called out, the rebels retreated and were later captured by the militia. At least six of the rebels committed suicide rather than surrender. The twenty-five rebels who were captured and con-victed were either burnt alive, hanged, or broken on the wheel.[45]

A larger uprising occurred in Louisiana's St. Charles and St. John the Baptist parishes in 1811. Led by a free Negro, Charles Deslondes, 400 slaves killed two whites and burned several plan-tations in St. John early in January. Gaining adherents along the Mississippi River, the insurgents formed into units of as many as 500 slaves and began marching the 31 miles to New Orleans. Before they reached the city, U.S. troops attacked and killed 66 slaves in open battle. Later, 16 leaders were executed in New Orleans, and their heads were placed on poles on roads leading from the city.[46]

The most destructive of all the slave revolts occurred near Jerusalem, Southampton County, Virginia, in 1831.[47] Fortu-

---

Negro History XXII (July 1937), 299–320; William S. Drewry, *Slave Insurrections in Virginia* (1830–1865) (Washington, 1900); Marion D. deB. Kilson, "Towards Freedom: An Analysis of Slave Revolts in the United States," *Phylon* XXV (Summer 1964), 175–87.

45. Kenneth Scott, "The Slave Insurrection in New York in 1712," *New York Historical Society Quarterly* XLV (Jan. 1961), 43–74; "Journal of Rev. John Sharpe," *Pennsylvania Magazine of History and Biography* XL (1916), 421.

46. Aptheker, *Revolts*, 249–51.

47. F. Roy Johnson, *The Nat Turner Slave Insurrection* (Murfrees-boro, N.C., 1966).

nately, a white lawyer, Thomas R. Gray, recorded the confession of "the leader of this ferocious band" and "the origin and progress of this dreadful conspiracy." According to Gray, the rebellion "was not instigated by motives of revenge or sudden anger, but the results of long deliberation and a settled purpose of mind." Nat Turner, the arch rebel, was born in October 1800, on the plantation of Benjamin Turner. Nat was a precocious child and so impressed his fellow slaves by his knowledge of things that had happened before his birth that they predicted he would be a prophet. Like many other slaves, Nat was strongly influenced by his father, mother, and his religious grandmother. His parents taught him to read and stressed his uniqueness and great destiny. Of them he wrote, "my father and mother

Figure 34. Capture

strengthened me . . . saying in my presence, I was intended for some great purpose. . . ." [48]

Restless, inquisitive, and observant, Nat learned to read quickly and was admitted to religious services in his master's household. Because of his ability to read, the slaves looked up to him and chose young Nat as their leader "when they were going on any roguery, to plan for them." As he grew to manhood, Nat consolidated his leadership over the slaves "by the austerity of my life and manners, which became the subject of remark by white and black—Having soon discovered to be great, I must appear so, and therefore studiously avoided mixing in society, and wrapped myself in mystery, devoting my time to fasting and prayer." [49]

From his prayers, fasts, and revelations from the Lord, Nat was convinced, he declared, "that I was ordained for some great purpose in the hands of the Almighty." Several things confirmed this for him. Upon reaching manhood he recalled vividly that both whites and blacks during his childhood had often said "that I had too much sense to be raised, and if I was, I would never be of any use to any one as a slave." Apparently Nat's discontent with slavery was inspired by his father, who had managed to escape. When Nat was placed under a new overseer he too ran away but returned to the plantation after remaining in the woods for thirty days. His fellow slaves were dismayed at his voluntary return, "saying if they had my sense they would not serve any master in the world." [50]

Shortly after this Nat had a vision where he saw "white spirits and black spirits engaged in battle, and the sun was darkened—the thunder rolled in the Heavens, and blood flowed in streams—and I heard a voice saying, 'Such is your luck, such you are called to see, and let it come rough or smooth, you must surely bare it.'" [51] Meditating on this and other revelations, seeking religious perfection, Nat had decided in 1828 that he was destined to wreak the vengeance of the Lord on the plant-

48. Johnson, *Turner*, 228–30.
49. Johnson, *Turner*, 231.
50. Johnson, *Turner*, 232–33.
51. Johnson, *Turner*, 234.

ers. Choosing four trusted lieutenants, Nat communicated his
desire for rebellion to them. After discussing many plans the
conspirators decided to strike on July 4, 1831. Because of Nat's
illness as a result of anxiety the revolt was postponed.

On August 20th the original conspirators, joined by Will and
Jack, barbecued a pig and drank a bottle of brandy. To make
sure of the new recruits, Nat queried Will, who declared that
"his life was worth no more than others, and his liberty as dear
to him. I asked him if he thought to obtain it? He said he would,
or lose his life." Now confident of his men, Nat decided to strike
first at the home of his master, Joseph Travis, who, he asserted,
"was to me a kind master, and placed the greatest confidence in
me; in fact, I had no cause to complain of his treatment of me."
Nat entered the house of his sleeping master and then opened
the door for the other rebels. Armed with a dull light sword,
Nat failed in his first attempt to kill his master who was dis-
patched by Will. Hoping to gather a large black army from the
surrounding plantations before an alarm could be raised, the
conspirators decided that until they had taken sufficient arms
from the whites, "neither age nor sex was to be spared (which
was invariably adhered to)." [52]

Parading silently through the night and led in military ma-
neuvers by Nat, the rebels left a trail of ransacked plantations,
decapitated bodies and battered heads across Southampton. At
the Whitehead plantation, Nat caught Margaret Whitehead
"and after repeated blows with a sword, I killed her by a blow
on the head, with a fence rail." By mid-morning of August 21st
the little band had grown to forty men, some of them mounted.
Determined "to carry terror and devastation" throughout the
county, Nat used his cavalry to lead attacks on plantations and
to prevent the escape of whites.[53] After several white families
had been massacred and the rebels had increased to sixty men,
Nat turned toward the little town of Jerusalem. By this time,
however, the alarm had been spread, and the insurgents were
confronted by eighteen armed white men.

Nat and his men immediately charged the small band of

52. Johnson, *Turner*, 235–36.
53. Johnson, *Turner*, 239.

white men and chased them over a hill where they were joined by a large number of additional whites. At this point Nat's men panicked and beat a hasty retreat. Still, he did not give up the struggle: "After trying in vain to collect a sufficient force to proceed to Jerusalem, I determined to return, as I was sure they would make back to their old neighborhood, where they would join me, make new recruits, and come down again." [54] His men scattered, Nat at first attempted to recruit more, but the militia prevented this, and he "gave up all hope for the present." He had been in hiding for two weeks, hoping to escape, when an armed white man captured him. Nat was lodged in jail and executed. More than forty blacks were either executed or murdered as an aftermath of the revolt.

A short, coal-black man, Turner was fearless, honest, temperate, religious, and extremely intelligent. Gray asserted that Turner "for natural intelligence and quickness of apprehension, is surpassed by few men I have ever seen." He knew a great deal about military tactics, and had a "mind capable of attaining anything. . . ." [55] Feeling no remorse for the fifty-five whites killed during the rebellion, Turner calmly contemplated his execution. Gray gave the best characterization of him when he wrote:

> He is a complete fanatic, or plays his part most admirably.
> . . . The calm, deliberate composure with which he spoke
> of his late deeds and intentions, the expression of his fiend-
> like face when excited by enthusiasm, still bearing the
> stains of blood of helpless innocence about him; clothed
> with rags and covered with chains; yet daring to raise his
> manacled hands to heaven, with a spirit soaring above the
> attributes of man; I looked on him and my blood cur-
> dled in my veins. [56]

The black rebels and runaways "curdled" the blood of many Southern whites. The ubiquitous runaway was the "bogey man"

54. Johnson, *Turner*, 240–41.
55. Johnson, *Turner*, 244.
56. Johnson, *Turner*, 244–45.

for young whites, "worrisome property" for his master, and a hero in the quarters. Symbolic of black resistance to slavery, the rebel and the runaway indicate quite clearly that the black slave was often ungovernable.

5 Plantation Stereotypes and Institutional Roles

Because my mouth
Is wide with laughter
And my throat
Is deep with song,
You do not think
I suffer after
I have held my pain
So long.

Because my mouth
Is wide with laughter,
You do not hear
My inner cry,
Because my feet
Are gay with dancing,
You do not know
I die.

Langston Hughes

Personal relations on the plantation were, as in most institutions, determined by spatial arrangements, the frequency of interaction between high- and low-powered individuals, and how the high-powered individual defined the behavioral norms. In practice, of course, many of the institutionally defined roles were imperfectly played. Before one can examine the *actual* behavior on the plantation, however, the societal images and the planter's expectations of the slave must be compared. In the final analysis, the planter's expectations were more closely related to the slave's actual behavior than publicly held stereotypes. Even so, neither the planter's expectations nor the stereotypes were proscriptive. In other words, the slave did not necessarily act the way white people expected him to behave or the way they perceived him as behaving.

Antebellum Southern novelists, dramatists, and journalists were so influential in the creation and reflection of public attitudes toward slaves that their works must be examined. An investigation of this literature is also mandatory because its impact has been so pervasive that twentieth-century historians have often uncritically accepted the most popular literary stereotype as an accurate description of slave personality. In many instances, historians have been misled by analyzing only one literary stereotype. The accuracy of the literary treatment of the plantation can only be determined, however, when several of the stereotypes of the slave are examined. This is all the more necessary because the legitimacy of each stereotype is tied irrevocably to the legitimacy of all the others.

The portrait of the slave which emerges from antebellum Southern literature is complex and contradictory.[1] The major slave characters were Sambo, Jack, and Nat. The one rarely seen in literature, Jack, worked faithfully as long as he was well treated. Sometimes sullen and uncooperative, he generally refused to be driven beyond the pace he had set for himself. Conscious of his identity with other slaves, he cooperated with them to resist the white man's oppression. Rationally analyzing the white man's overwhelming physical power, Jack either avoided contact with him or was deferential in his presence. Since he did not identify with his master and could not always keep up the façade of deference, he was occasionally flogged for insubordina-

---

1. Francis P. Gaines, *The Southern Plantation: A Study in the Development and Accuracy of a Tradition* (New York, 1925); Tremaine McDowell, "The Negro in the Southern Novel Prior to 1850," *Journal of English and Germanic Philology* XXV (Oct. 1926), 455–73; Charles E. Burch, "Negro Characters in the Novels of William Gilmore Simms," *Southern Workman* LII (April 1923), 192–95; Jack B. Moore, "Images of the Negro in Early American Short Fiction," *Mississippi Quarterly* XXXII (Winter 1968–69), 47–57; Sterling A. Brown, *The Negro in American Fiction* (Washington, D.C., 1937), 1–47; John H. Nelson, *The Negro Character in American Literature* (Lawrence, Kansas, 1926), 23–48, 86–92; Catherine J. Starke, *Black Portraiture in American Fiction* (New York, 1971), 30–45.

tion. Although often proud, stubborn, and conscious of the wrongs he suffered, Jack tried to repress his anger. His patience was, however, not unlimited. He raided his master's larder when he was hungry, ran away when he was tired of working or had been punished, and was sometimes ungovernable. Shrewd and calculating, he used his wits to escape from work or to manipulate his overseer and master.

Nat was the rebel who rivaled Sambo in the universality and continuity of his literary image. Revengeful, bloodthirsty, cunning, treacherous, and savage, Nat was the incorrigible runaway, the poisoner of white men, the ravager of white women who defied all the rules of plantation society. Subdued and punished only when overcome by superior numbers or firepower, Nat retaliated when attacked by whites, led guerrilla activities of maroons against isolated plantations, killed overseers and planters, or burned plantation buildings when he was abused. Like Jack, Nat's customary obedience often hid his true feelings, self-concept, unquenchable thirst for freedom, hatred of whites, discontent, and manhood, until he violently demonstrated these traits.[2]

Sambo, combining in his person Uncle Remus, Jim Crow, and Uncle Tom, was the most pervasive and long lasting of the three literary stereotypes. Indolent, faithful, humorous, loyal, dishonest, superstitious, improvident, and musical, Sambo was inevitably a clown and congenitally docile. Characteristically a house servant, Sambo had so much love and affection for his master that he was almost filio-pietistic; his loyalty was all-consuming and self-immolating. The epitome of devotion, Sambo often fought and died heroically while trying to save his master's life. Yet, Sambo had no thought of freedom; that was an empty boon compared to serving his master.[3]

The Sambo stereotype was so pervasive in antebellum Southern literature that many historians, without further research,

2. Howard Braverman, "An Unusual Characterization by a Southern Ante-Bellum Writer," *Phylon* XIX (Summer 1958), 171–79; Calvin H. Wiley, *Life in the South: A Companion to Uncle Tom's Cabin* (1852); Bayard R. Hall, *Frank Freeman's Barbershop* (1852).

3. For portraits of Sambo risking his life to save his master see: Hector, Cato, Scipio, Braugh, and Tom in William Gilmore Simms, *The Yemassee* (1832), *The Foragers* (1855), *Mellichampe* (1836); *Southward Ho!* (1854), and *The Partisan* (1835).

argue that it was an accurate description of the dominant slave personality. According to historians of this stripe, the near unanimity of so many white observers of the slave cannot be discounted.[4] While this is obviously true, it does not follow that the Sambo stereotype must be treated uncritically. Instead, it must be viewed in the context of the other slave stereotypes, and from the perspective of psychology and comparative studies of literature.

Any attempt to generalize about individual and group personality traits based on stereotypes must assess the degree to which "outsiders" are able to perceive someone else's behavior correctly. Since so much of one's personality is socially non-perceivable, hidden, or invisible, the way other people describe an individual is not totally reliable as an index of his attitudes and behavior. Consequently, students must be cautious in equating societal images with personality traits. There is too much distortion in people's perception, observation, and interpretation of the behavior of other individuals for historians to rely solely upon their reports. Prior experiences, situational factors, cultural frames of reference, and selective inattention all influence perception of individual behavior.[5] So many of these factors may be operative in society that *sham* characteristics are attributed to a group or individual. According to psychologist Gustav Ichheiser:

> The sham characteristics are those which are attributed to an individual from the point of view of other people. They might, or might not, reflect themselves in his own conception about himself. They can originate entirely through misinterpretations by others without his participation, or he can directly or indirectly share the responsibility for their development through pretending to have the characteristics. The given individual does not possess these sham characteristics but only seems to possess them.[6]

One of the best examples of how external forces and cultural frames of reference lead to the ascription of sham characteristics

4. Stanley Elkins, *Slavery: A Problem in American Institutional and Intellectual Life* (New York, 1963), 86–89.
5. Gustav Ichheiser, *Appearances and Realities* (San Francisco, 1970).
6. Ichheiser, *Appearances*, 95.

to a group appears in the changing stereotypes of the Chinese. When California needed laborers in the mid-nineteenth century, the newspapers characterized the Chinese as a thrifty, sober, tractable, inoffensive, and law-abiding group. Twenty years later, Californians were competing with Chinese laborers. They began to describe the Chinese as clannish, criminal, debased, servile, deceitful, vicious, filthy, and loathsome.[7]

In light of these observations, scholars cannot accept the Sambo stereotype uncritically. Instead, they must try to examine the roots of this conception of the black slave: First, and most important, was the American attitude toward Negroes or Africans as a race. Most antebellum whites firmly believed that Africans were ignoble savages who were innately barbaric, imitative, passive, cheerful, childish, lazy, cowardly, superstitious, polygamous, submissive, immoral, and stupid.[8] For instance, Dr. Samuel A. Cartwright, a Louisiana physician, wrote that Africans were "endowed with a will so weak, passions so easily subdued, and dispositions so gentle and affectionate" that they had "an instinctive feeling of obedience to the stronger will of the white man." In 1850, "L.S.M." argued that Negroes were naturally "good-tempered, unambitious, unintellectual, incapable of civilization, and unfit for amalgamation . . ." An anonymous contributor to the *Christian Examiner* contrasted "the submissive, obsequious, imitative negro" to other races.[9]

7. Earl Raab, ed., *American Race Relations Today* (Garden City, N.Y., 1962), 29–57; Otto Klineberg, *The Human Dimension in International Relations* (New York, 1964), 33–48; Sigmund Freud, *Psychopathology of Everyday Life* (New York, 1951), 66–67, 73–76.

8. Milton Cantor, "The Image of the Negro in Colonial Literature," *New England Quarterly* XXXVI (Dec. 1963), 452–77; Matthew Estes, *A Defense of Negro Slavery, as it Exists in the United States* (Montgomery, Ala., 1846), 50–70; Henrietta Tolbert, "A Study of the Inferiority of the Negro in American History" (M.A., Howard University, 1939), 1–98; L.A., "The Diversity of Origin of the Human Race," *Christian Examiner* XLIX (July 1850), 110–45; "Uncle Tom at Home," *Putnam's Monthly* VIII (July 1856), 1–10; Dr. Cartwright, "On the Caucasians and the African," *DeBow's Review* XXV (July 1858), 45–56.

9. Cartwright, "Caucasians," 47–48; L.S.M., "The Diversity of the Races; Its Bearing upon Negro Slavery," *Southern Quarterly Review* XIX (April 1851), 412; L.A., "Diversity," 144.

Most whites felt that the "natural" traits of Negro character were so deeply ingrained that they were immutable. Regardless of climate, condition, or circumstance, the Negro retained his native African characteristics. Julien Virey, a Frenchman whose works were widely read in America, supported this view when he asserted: "All the facts which have been collected, concur to prove how constant and indelible are the natural and moral characteristics of negroes in every climate, notwithstanding a diversity of circumstances, which condemn him to indolence and degradation." [10]

Sambo became a universal figure in antebellum Southern literature partly because he belonged to a subordinate caste. Traditionally writers in caste and slave societies, representing and identifying with the ruling class and supporting the status quo, have drawn unflattering stereotypes of the lowest caste. David B. Davis, for example, concluded from his study of several slave societies that, almost universally, slaves were described as loyal, faithful, lazy, irresponsible, and untrustworthy. According to Davis, "The white slaves of antiquity and the middle ages were often described in terms that fit the later stereotype of the Negro." Similarly, nineteenth-century Russian writers portrayed the white serfs as callous, shiftless, dishonest, lazy, hypocritical, and stupid.[11]

The greatest confusion in the comparative study of literary stereotypes of slaves has been caused by cursory examinations of Brazilian and Southern literature. From such examinations it appears at first glance that there was not only a great diversity of types, but no Sambo character in Brazilian literature. In order to place this in true perspective, one must understand that we are comparing the literature of a slaveholding region (the South) produced largely by white pro-slavery advocates with the literature of a nation produced by slaveholders, abolitionists, and black writers. Since Brazilian writers varied so much in character, there

10. Julien J. Virey, *Natural History of the Negro Race* (Charleston, 1837), 19.

11. David B. Davis, *The Problem of Slavery in Western Culture* (Ithaca, N.Y., 1966), 59; Hannah S. Goldman, "The Tragic Gift: The Serf and Slave Intellectual in Russian and American Fiction," *Phylon* XXIV (Spring, 1963), 51–61.

was naturally greater diversity in the portrayal of slaves than in the South. When, however, Northern, abolitionist, and black writers are added to Southern writers, the same range of slave characters appear in American as in Brazilian literature. Like their American counterparts and contrary to the allegations of some historians, Brazilian writers often portrayed the slaves as Sambos. Brazilian novelists, poets, and dramatists frequently characterized slaves as indolent, faithful, immoral, submissive, ignorant, happy, patient, docile, irresponsible, promiscuous, loyal, and lazy.[12]

The commitment of Southern writers to drawing unflattering stereotypes of subordinate groups was so great that they even characterized some whites in terms remarkably similar to their picture of Sambo. For example, they portrayed non-slaveholding white Southerners as "poor whites" who were densely ignorant, irresponsible, lawless, lazy, shiftless, dirty, careless, stupid, listless, unambitious, dishonest, and morally degraded.[13] Frances Kemble typified this attitude when she described the poor whites as "filthy, lazy, ignorant, brutal, proud, penniless savages, without one of the nobler attributes which have been found occasionally allied to the vice of savage nature." [14]

Another factor which compelled Southern writers to portray the slave as Sambo was their need to disprove the allegations of anti-slavery novelists. Facing the withering attack of the abolitionists, they had to prove that slavery was not an unmitigated evil.

12. Raymond S. Sayers, *The Negro in Brazilian Literature* (New York, 1956), 73–83, 121–26, 138–39, 145–64, 186–97; Lorenzo D. Turner, *Anti-Slavery Sentiment in American Literature Prior to 1865* (Port Washington, N.Y., 1966); Carl Degler, *Neither Black nor White* (New York, 1971), 12–13.

13. Gaines, *Plantation,* 1–17; William R. Taylor, *Cavalier and Yankee* (Garden City N.Y., 1963), 156–67, 279–94; A. N. J. Den Hollander, "The Tradition of 'Poor Whites'" in William T. Couch, ed., *Culture in the South* (Chapel Hill, N.C., 1934), 403–31; Frank Lawrence Owsley, *Plain Folk of the Old South* (Baton Rouge, La., 1949), 1–22; Clement Eaton, *The Growth of Southern Civilization* (New York, 1963), 150–76; J. E. Cairnes, *The Slave Power* . . . (New York, 1862), 54–79; Paul H. Buck, "The Poor Whites of the Ante-Bellum South," *American Historical Review* XXXI (October 1925), 41–54.

14. Frances Anne Kemble, *Journal of a Residence on a Georgian Plantation in 1838–1839* (New York, 1961), 182.

The loyal contented slave was a *sine qua non* in Southern literary propaganda. Whether he existed in fact was irrelevant to the writer. Without Sambo, it was impossible to prove the essential goodness of Southern society.[15]

Another of the important reasons for the pervasiveness of the Sambo stereotype was the desire of whites to relieve themselves of the anxiety of thinking about slaves as men. In this regard, Nat, the actual and potential rebel, stands at the core of white perceptions of the slave. With Nat perennially in the wings, the creation of Sambo was almost mandatory for the Southerner's emotional security. Like a man whistling in the dark to bolster his courage, the white man *had* to portray the slave as Sambo. This public stereotype only partially hid a multitude of private fears, which reached the proportion of mass hysteria at the mere mention of the word "rebellion." Generally, historians have been so intent upon proving that these fears were groundless that they have ignored the relationship between the countless rumors of rebellions and the white man's stereotype of the slave and the slave's actual behavior. If whites really believed that a majority of slaves were Sambos, how could they also believe that these pathetically loyal and docile blacks would rise up and cut their throats?

Judging from the ease with which whites conjured up Nat, they apparently felt that the relationship between the planter and the slave was one of continual war requiring eternal vigilance in order for the master to maintain the upper hand. In a sense, this is indicated by the constant changes in the slave codes. If the slave had accepted the Sambo role, there would have been little need to continue changing the codes after the first generation of American-born slaves had grown to adulthood. Slaveholders apparently never believed in Sambos, for they were constantly searching for new ways to guarantee the subordination of slaves. Was this search simply a result of the formulation of new management techniques, or did it reflect slave behavior which contradicted the Sambo stereotype?

15. Jeanette Tandy, "Pro-Slavery Propaganda in American Fiction of the Fifties," *South Atlantic Quarterly* XXI (Jan. 1922), 41–50, (April 1922), 170–78; Jay B. Hubbell, *Southern Life in Fiction* (Athens, Ga., 1960).

From an analysis of the constantly recurring rumors of insurrections, it is obvious that many whites considered black slaves dangerous, insubordinate, bold, evil, restless, turbulent, vengeful, barbarous, and malicious. The white man's fear and his anxiety about the slave was so deep and pervasive that it was sometimes pathological. An epidemic of runaways, a group of whispering slaves, mysterious fires, or almost any suspicious event caused alarm, apprehension, and a deepening state of paranoia among whites.[16]

Considering the overwhelming power of the whites, the censorship of news about insurrections, and the general reluctance of men to parade their fears, the constant discussion of Nat among antebellum Southern whites appears at first glance to be remarkable. After all, no white man could possibly be anxious about his safety if a majority of the slaves were thought to be Sambos. Perhaps the Governor of the colony of Virginia gave a clearer insight into the white man's characterization of slaves when in 1723 he urged the legislators to pass more oppressive laws because he was "persuaded you are . . . well acquainted with the cruel dispositions of these creatures. . . ." Similarly, a South Carolina white wrote that "We regard our negroes as the 'Jacobins' of the country, against whom we should always be on guard. . . ."[17] It is obvious that many whites did not believe the slaves were innately docile. Too many governors received requests for arms and troops from thousands of whites, the U.S. Army marched and countermarched too often, too many panic-stricken whites spent their nights guarding their neighborhoods to believe that most Southern whites equated the Sambo stereotype with the dominant slave personality.

Thinking about Nat kept whites "in a state of mind peculiarly harassing and painful," and "a state of perpetual anxiety and ap-

16. Herbert Aptheker, *American Negro Slave Revolts* (New York, 1943); Thomas W. Higginson, "Nat Turner's Insurrection," *Atlantic Monthly* VIII (Aug. 1861), 173–87; Robert N. Elliott, "The Nat Turner Insurrection As Reported in the North Carolina Press," *North Carolina Historical Review* XXXVIII (Jan. 1961), 1–18; Donald B. Kelley, "Harper's Ferry: Prelude to Crisis in Mississippi," *Journal of Mississippi History* XXVII (Nov. 1965), 351–72.

17. Aptheker, *Revolts*, 14, 15.

prehension, than which nothing could be more painful." The stereotype of Nat forced some whites to conclude that to live among black slaves was "really a dreadful situation to be in." [18] The character of the slave was felt to be such that it led to a deep and abiding fear among large numbers of whites. Many of them slept behind barricaded doors with pistols under their pillows. One Louisiana planter recalled that "I have known times here, when there was not a single planter who had a calm night's rest; they then never lay down to sleep without a brace of loaded pistols at their sides." [19]

It is almost impossible to square the white's fear of Nat with the predominance of the Sambo stereotype in plantation literature. Apparently both slave characters were real. The more fear whites had of Nat, the more firmly they tried to believe in Sambo in order to escape paranoia. This psychological repression was augmented by public acts to relieve anxiety. Every effort was made to keep the slaves in awe of the power of whiteness and ignorant of their own potential power. The congregation of crowds of slaves, their independent movement, possession of arms, and degree of literacy, were all strictly regulated. The rebellious slave was punished swiftly and cruelly to discourage others. The oppressive acts consisted of cropping ears, castrating, hanging, burning, and mutilating. The army, the militia, and the entire white community stood ready to aid any embattled region. In all of these actions, the whites demonstrated that, even if slaves did not revolt, they were considered rebellious. Consequently, Southern whites restricted their own freedom of speech, censored their newspapers, interfered with the U.S. mails, and lynched abolitionists to make sure that no one incited the rebellious slaves.[20]

18. Aptheker, *Revolts*, passim.

19. Fredrika Bremer, *The Homes of the New World* (2 vols., New York, 1853), II, 190. For similar expressions see: James H. Johnston, *Race Relations in Virginia* (Amherst, Mass., 1970), 27, 116–21; Kemble, *Journal*, 379; Emily P. Burke, *Reminiscences of Georgia* (Oberlin, 1850), 156–58; James Stirling, *Letters from the Slave States* (London, 1857), 59.

20. Clement Eaton, *Freedom of Thought in the Old South* (New York, 1951), 89–117; Herbert Aptheker, *One Continual Cry: David Walker's Appeal to the Colored Citizens of the World* (New York, 1965), 45–53.

The slaveholder apparently sought peace of mind by claiming that unrest among slaves was the result of the hellish designs of outside incendiaries. This was so much a part of writings about insurrections that John Brown's raid on Harpers Ferry in 1859 has all the appearance of a self-fulfilling prophecy. Many Southerners were able to convince themselves that their slaves would remain perfectly content and docile as long as they imbibed none of the ideals of fanatics.

Like most men, the Southern white men learned to live with their fears. After all, they were more numerous, better organized, armed, educated, and more mobile than slaves. Any actual rebellion could be crushed relatively easily. Through cruelty or kindness a planter might discourage his own slaves from bloodthirsty acts, even if there were an insurrection. In addition to this rational view of the situation, the planter tried to reduce the anxiety produced by the incongruity between the Sambo and Nat stereotypes by pushing Nat deep into his subconscious. Firmly trying to believe in Sambo, the planter knew that in the final analysis his superior firepower would enable him to survive.

When these stereotypes held by antebellum whites are compared, some interesting questions about planter psychology and slave behavior emerge. Did the contradictory portraits of Sambo and Nat indicate that Southerners were not entirely sure that the slave's actual personality was indeed the same as the Sambo stereotype? This question lies at the heart of white reaction to Nat Turner's bloody revolt. Admittedly a favored slave, with a kind master, Nat gave no prior indications of his desire for revenge. Did this mean that the wide grins and servile bows represented the impenetrable masks of the black slaves' character? Were they all "Jacobins"? Did they view their masters as good fathers to be loved or as cruel tyrants to be exterminated? If the latter, could more and more oppressive legislation insure their subordination? Regardless of what was done, would a white man's family ever be secure from the vengeance of the black slave? These questions haunted the Southern white man, and their very existence raises doubts about the predominance of the Sambo personality on the antebellum plantation. How much stock can be placed in the Sambo stereotype when antebellum Southern whites questioned it as a representation of the typical slave?

Their uncertainty was indicated clearly in debates in the Virginia legislature after Nat Turner's revolt. One legislator observed that the widespread fear of revolt was caused by

> the suspicion eternally attached to the slave himself, the suspicion that a Nat Turner might be in every family, that the same bloody deed could be acted over at any time and in any place, that the materials for it were spread through the land and always ready for a like explosion. Nothing but the force of this withering apprehension, nothing but the paralyzing and deadening weight with which it falls upon and prostrates the heart of every man who has helpless dependents to protect, nothing but this could have thrown a brave people into consternation, or could have made any portion of this powerful Commonwealth, for a single instant, to have quailed and trembled.[21]

Any attempt to reconcile the white man's "suspicion that a Nat Turner might be in every family" with the widespread existence of the Sambo stereotype places the historian on the horns of a dilemma. On the one hand, the persistent fear of the slave in the absence of revolts may indicate that there was overwhelming circumstantial evidence and hundreds of individual acts which convinced whites that slaves were ungovernable. On the other, the white man may have been grossly in error when he perceived the slave as rebellious; and if the latter was true, then the antebellum white man is not a good witness, for it follows that he may also have been grossly in error in stereotyping the slave as Sambo. It is possible, however, to deal with these contradictory portraits. For various reasons, often having more to do with whites than blacks, antebellum whites apparently focused on two extreme forms of slave behavior—childlike docility and rebellion—in formulating the Nat and Sambo stereotypes. Both stereotypes were probably blown out of proportion to their relationship to the actual behavior of most slaves. In effect, each of the stereotypes is so contrary to the other that the legitimacy of each as a representation of typical slave behavior is limited. Perhaps the only thing that the white man's stereotypes of the

21. Eric Foner, ed., *Nat Turner* (Englewood Cliffs, N.J., 1971), 113.

slave as Sambo, Jack, and Nat does is to indicate the range of personality types in the quarters. Without supporting evidence, none of these literary stereotypes can be accepted as indicative of the dominant slave personality. At any rate, few, if any planters depended on literary stereotypes in managing their plantations. Although many of them may have held the Sambo stereotype, they had a different set of expectations for their own slaves. Obviously, if Sambo represented the sum of the master's expectations, the slaveholder could not have survived. Lazy, inefficient, irresponsible, dishonest, childish, stupid Sambo was a guarantee of economic ruin. Whatever the literary stereotypes, the institutionally defined roles and behavior expected of planters, overseers, and slaves were quite clear. The best definition of these roles appears in contracts and numerous essays on plantation management in antebellum journals.[22]

In these rules, the planter explained the ideal which guided his relationship with slaves and his perception of their personalities gained from years of experience. According to most advisers on slave management, the plantation was somewhat like an army camp: authority descended downward from the master, to the overseer, to the slave driver. The planter was comparable to a general, a ship captain, or an unlimited monarch directing the lives of a large group of people toward one objective: large profits. The first requirement in achieving this objective was to maintain regularity and order in everything. It was the planter's duty to calculate how many supplies were required, how large a crop to plant, and how much labor could be performed.

In order to obtain the maximum labor at the cheapest cost, the planter had to construct healthy cabins, provide adequate, wholesome food and proper clothing, permit recreation, and provide medical attention for his slaves. If the slaves adhered to

22. *Southern Agriculturalist* VII (April 1834), 117–83; IX (Feb. 1836), 70–75; (Nov. 1836), 580–84; *Southern Cabinet* I (May 1840), 279–80; *Southern Cultivator* X (Aug. 1852), 227–28; *American Farmer* II (March 16, 1821), 402; X (Oct. 17, 1828), 244; *Farmer's Register* II (Sept. 1834), 248–49; (Feb. 1835), 579–80; V (May 1837), 32–33; *DeBow's Review* XV (June 1851), 621–25; XXI (Sept. 1856), 277–79.

certain moral precepts, rested during the hottest part of the day, spent all of their time on the plantation, marched to the fields, ate, and went to bed at the sound of bugles or bells, and were kept under proper subjection, they would be healthy and industrious. In his relations with slaves, the planter had to maintain strict discipline and require unconditional obedience. He also had to maintain a great degree of social distance between himself and his slaves. In this regard, a Virginia planter asserted: "All conversation with a negro is forbid, except about his work. This is important; he should be kept as far from his master as possible, but with no accompanying *harshness;* he ought to be made to feel that you are his superior, but that you respect his feelings and wants." [23]

Advisers on plantation management insisted that, while being aloof from slaves, planters had to enforce all rules rigidly. Proper discipline, they contended, was maintained by the certainty rather than the severity of punishment for infractions. Closely allied with the certainty of punishment as an inducement to labor was the use of flattery, praise, and rewards. Most planters felt that little could be gained from deriding or threatening slaves.

Since the master had the most power and authority on the plantation, he defined the institutional roles. A representative definition of plantation roles appeared in an article in *DeBow's Review* in 1855:

> The master should never establish any regulation among his slaves until he is fully convinced of its propriety and equity. Being thus convinced, and having issued his orders, implicit obedience should be required and rigidly enforced. Firmness of manner, and promptness to enforce obedience, will save much trouble, and be the means of avoiding the necessity for much whipping. The negro should feel that his master is his lawgiver and judge; and yet is his protector and friend, but so far above him, as never to be approached save in the most respectful manner. That where he has just

23. *American Farmer* VII (May 1852), 397.

Figure 35. The Stake-Out

cause, he may, with due deference, approach his master and
lay before him his troubles and complaints; but not on false
pretexts or trivial occasions. . . .[24]

Placed in the position of a general planning strategy, the
planter had to depend on the overseer to carry out the tactics and
see to the day-to-day operation of the plantation. Most advisers

24. *DeBow's Review* XIX (Sept. 1855), 361–62.

contended that the overseer was an "indispensable agent" on the plantation. He had to wake the slaves at daylight and drive them to the fields, attend the sick and prevent malingering, supervise the planting, tillage, and harvesting of the crops; and show the slaves how to perform their work, keep a daily record of plantation events, see that the slave's food was properly prepared, and maintain fences and tools in good repair. In managing slaves in such a fashion as to insure a large quantity and high quality of the money crop, the overseer was required to "push the hands fast," preserve the health and morals of slaves by prohibiting the use of alcohol, interplantation visiting, theft of plantation stock and produce, and trading with whites. He had to supervise and examine the work of each slave, regularly inspect each cabin and person to insure cleanliness, order, and sobriety, and ring the bell or blow the bugle to signal "lights out" in the quarters and then make sure that each laborer received enough rest to complete his task the next day. Overseers, one planter argued, should

> be accustomed to early rising, and to steady, settled customs and ways. Let them learn regularity in arranging plantation business *in advance,* in order to avoid delay, confusion and loss of work; regularity in settling every one to their work betimes; in closely watching the driver or drivers, urging them on to their duty, and by a vigilant eye over every individual labourer's progress, as the day advances, ascertaining that none of these, and of course, that none of the business of the place is getting behind hand.[25]

The overseer had to be especially adept at keeping slaves under proper subjection. Speaking to them only in regard to their work, he was required to keep them under almost constant surveillance. Consequently, he had to remain on the plantation at all times. Most planters enjoined the overseer from maiming, scarring, or disabling their property. Instead, he was to treat slaves with "care & humanity," and punish them in a "humane" fashion free from passion. In addition, the overseer was not to "use abusive language to nor to threaten the negroes, as it makes them unhappy

25. *American Farmer* XI (Oct. 16, 1829), 42.

and sometimes induces them to run away." The overseer had to be careful not to become so familiar with slaves that they learned all of his secrets and shortcomings. An Alabama planter wrote: "The overseer must hide all his faults if possible from the negroes —but if not possible then never in any event what ever request or require the Negroes to conceal his faults from the employer— In such case the overseer is unmanned—better to retire at once from a place he can but disgrace, when afraid his hands will tell on him—" [26]

Planters and overseers defined the role of the slave in very explicit terms. The institutionally defined role of the slave required him to identify with his master's interest, to be healthy, clean, humble, honest, sober, cheerful, industrious, even-tempered, patient, respectful, trustworthy, and hard-working. This was the kind of slave the master *wanted*: a laborer who identified so closely with his master's interest that he would repair a broken fence rail without being ordered to do so. Systematic labor, implicit obedience, and unconditional submission (as child to parent or soldier to general) was expected of slaves.

The extent to which slaves acted the way their masters expected them to behave can be explained partially by examining "role theory." According to the proponents of this theory, a person's behavior is generally determined by the socially defined roles or the behavioral patterns expected of him in certain situations. A policeman, for instance, behaves differently in his law enforcer, father, husband, and Sunday School teacher roles. Man learns these roles by becoming an object, or learning how several other people define how a husband, father, or policeman should act. This process begins when the child discovers how his parents expect him to behave. A person internalizes the roles (accepts them as a part of himself, as a legitimate, desirable way of behaving) expected of him to the degree that the sanctions and rewards attached to them are great enough.[27] The relationship of this

26. J. Carlyle Sitterson, "The William J. Minor Plantations: A Study in Ante-Bellum Absentee Ownership," *Journal of Southern History* IX (Feb. 1943), 63; Weymouth T. Jordan, "The Management Rules of an Alabama Black Belt Plantation, 1848–1862," *Agricultural History* XVIII (Jan. 1944), 57.

27. William F. Knoff, "Role: A Concept Linking Society and Person-

behavior to personality, however, is not a deterministic one. Indeed, several psychologists have pointed out that there is no demonstrable one-to-one relationship between the roles we play and our personality. In fact, Jones, Davis, and Gergen assert that a person only reveals his true self when he fails to play roles. They declared: "The performance of social roles tends to mask information about individual characteristics because the person reveals only that he is responsive to normative requirements." [28]

The plantation, like most large institutions, permitted deviations from the roles it defined. Sociologist Florian Znaniecki noted this characteristic of institutions when he observed that role proscriptions do not mean "that every individual who performs a specific role always has to conform strictly with all the norms which regulate his conduct. For, as a matter of fact, the cultural patterns of most roles allow for variations, changes, and even some failures and transgressions." [29] An individual is frequently able to deviate from role expectations because he does not have to play the role continuously; part of his behavior is immune from surveillance. Because there is no continuous social interaction, Robert K. Merton concluded that the lack of observability "allows for role-behavior which is at odds with the expectations of some in the role-set to proceed without undue stress." [30]

Many individuals do not internalize the behavioral patterns of a specific role because in their daily lives they play so many roles and their behavior and attitudes are different for each of them.

ality," *American Journal of Psychiatry* CXVII (May 1961), 1010–15; Ralph H. Turner, "Role-Taking, Role Standpoint, and Reference Group Behavior," in Edward E. Sampson, ed., *Approaches, Contexts, and Problems of Social Psychology* (Englewood Cliffs, N.J., 1964), 219–31; Reinhard Bendix, "Compliant Behavior and Individual Personality," *American Journal of Sociology* LVIII (Nov. 1952), 290–303; Bruce J. Biddle and Edwin J. Thomas, eds., *Role Theory: Concepts and Research* (New York, 1966), 144–48, 195–200, 282–87, 313–17.

28. Edward E. Jones, Keith E. Davis, and Kenneth Gergen, "Role Playing Variations and Their Informational Value for Person Perception," in Biddle and Thomas, *Role,* 172.

29. Florian Znaniecki, *Social Relations and Social Roles* (San Francisco, 1965), 274.

30. Robert K. Merton, "Instability and Articulation in the Role-Set," in Biddle and Thomas, *Role,* 284.

The behavior of a worker, for example, who is promoted to fore-
man may become more pro-management. When he is demoted
to a worker, he may become more anti-management. The more
roles a person plays the less likely is he to internalize the attitudes
and behavior of any one of them. Generally this is facilitated because many roles are peripheral and involve little emotional involvement. Even when there is strong pressure to conform to role
expectations, a person has several options other than internalization. He may have a counternorm, or adhere to the values of his
subgroup at the same time that he behaves in the accepted
pattern.[31]

It is obvious from the writings of the planters that the slaves
did not internalize the roles and automatically submit uncondi-
tionally to their masters. Consequently, the primary guarantee of
obedience was the lash. While accepting the central role of
coercive force in maintaining plantation discipline, however,
slaveholders recognized its limitations. As a result, they argued
that several techniques had to be combined in order to control
the slaves. One slaveholder declared that in managing slaves:
"Love and fear, a regard for public opinion, gratitude, shame,
the conjugal, parental, and filial feelings, these all must be appealed to and cultivated." [32] Reason and persuasion, slaveholders
argued, had to be among the primary instruments of slave management.[33]

Many of the planters asserted that the frequent punishment

31. Seymour Lieberman, "The Effects of Changes in Roles On the
Attitudes of Role Occupants," in Henry Clay Lindgren, ed., *Contem-
porary Research in Social Psychology* (New York, 1969), 317–31;
Daniel Katz and Robert L. Kahn, *The Social Psychology of Organizations*
(New York, 1966), 171–206.

32. "Plantation Life—Duties and Responsibilities," *DeBow's Review*
XXXIX (Sept. 1860), 362.

33. John Perkins, "Relation of Master and Slave in Louisiana and
the South," *DeBow's Review* XV (Sept. 1853), 275–77; F. A. Shoup,
"Has the Southern Pulpit Failed?" *North American Review,* CXXX
(June 1880), 585–603; A Mississippi Planter, "Management of Negroes Upon Southern Estates," *DeBow's Review* X (June 1851), 621–
27; "Instruction of Slaves," *Littell's Living Age* (Jan. 24, 1846), 179–
81; "Management of Cotton Estates," *DeBow's Review* XXVI (May
1859), 579–80.

of slaves was an indication of bad management. According to one slaveholder, "The best evidence of the good management of slaves, is the keeping up of good discipline with little or no punishment." [34] The use of coercion was an indication that the slave did not identify with the master's interest and refused to play the submissive role. One planter noted this when he observed: "The master should make it his business to show his slaves, that the advancement of his individual interest, is at the same time an advancement of theirs. Once they feel this, it will require but little compulsion to make them act as becomes them." [35] The extent of the planters' failure is revealed in their frequent resort to compulsion.

Inasmuch as the planters defined the roles and applied the sanctions to insure conformity, practically all advisers on plantation management insisted that the behavior of the slaves was a reflection of the way planters treated them. A Maryland slaveholder observed in 1837:

> The character of the negro is much underrated. It is like the plastic clay, which may be moulded into agreeable or disagreeable figures, according to the skill of the moulder. The man who storms at, and curses his negroes, and tells them they are a parcel of infernal rascals, not to be trusted, will surely make them just what he calls them; and so far from loving such a master, they will hate him. Now, if you be not suspicious, and induce them to think, by slight trusts, that they are not unworthy of some confidence, you will make them honest, useful, and affectionate creatures.[36]

How, exactly, did the planters characterize slaves? For the most part, they felt that there was great variability among them. Most advisers admonished overseers and planters to try to determine the range of personality types in the quarters. One Virginia planter, for example, noted:

> In the management of slaves, the temper and disposition of each negro should be particularly consulted. Some require

34. *Southern Agriculturalist* VII (July 1834), 368.
35. *Southern Agriculturalist* IX (Dec. 1836), 626.
36. *Farmer's Register* V (Sept. 1837), 302.

Figure 36.   The Flogging

spurring up, some coaxing, some flattering, and others nothing but good words. When an overseer first goes upon a plantation to live, He should study their dispositions well, before he exerts too much rigor. Many a noble spirit has been broken down by injudicious management, and many a lazy cunning fellow has escaped, and put his work on the shoulders of the industrious. Give me a high spirited and even a high tempered negro, full of pride, for easy and comfortable management. Your slow sulky negro although he may have an even temper, is *the devil* to manage.

The negro women are all harder to manage than the men. The only way to get along with them is by kind words and flattery. If you want to cure a sloven, give her something nice occasionally to wear, and praise her up to skies whenever she has on any thing tolerably decent.[37]

If there is any validity at all in the essays on plantation management and publicly held stereotypes, there was a great variety of personality types in the quarters. The first premise of the planter was that there were so many different kinds of slaves that he had to combine several techniques in order to manage them. When the slaveholder considered the best way to get the maximum labor from his slaves he did not assume that a majority of them were Sambos; there was little room for romanticizing when there was cotton to be picked. Even in the publicly held stereotypes, slave behavior ran the whole gamut from abject docility to open rebellion. The predominance of the Sambo and Nat stereotypes explain a great deal more about the white man's character than about the behavior of most slaves.

37. *Southern Agriculturalist* VIII (July 1834), 368.

6 Plantation Realities

And in this society in which the infant son of the planter was commonly suckled by a black mammy, in which gray old black men were his most loved story-tellers, in which black stalwarts were among the chiefest heroes and mentors of his boyhood, and in which his usual, often practically his only, companions until he was past the age of puberty were the black boys (and girls) of the plantation—in this society in which by far the greater number of white boys of whatever degree were more or less shaped by such companionship and in which nearly the whole body of whites, young and old, had constantly before their eyes the example, had constantly in their ears the accent, of the Negro, the relationship between the two groups was, by the second generation at least, nothing less than organic. Negro entered into white man as profoundly as white man entered into Negro—subtly influencing every gesture, every word, every emotion and idea, every attitude.

Wilbur J. Cash

The behavior of the black slave was intimately bound up with the nature of the antebellum plantation, the behavior of masters, the white man's perceptions and misperceptions, and a multitude of factors which influenced personal relations. In the final analysis, the character of the antebellum plantation was one of the major determinants of the attitudes, perceptions, and behavior of the slave. There was so much variation in plantations, overseers, and masters, however, that the slave had much more freedom from restraint and more independence and autonomy than his institutionally defined role allowed. Consequently, the slave did not have to be infantile or abjectly docile in order to remain alive. It was primarily because of the variegated pattern of plantation life that Sambo did not emerge as the dominant slave personality in the quarters.[1]

1. John Q. Anderson, "Dr. James Green Carson, Ante-Bellum Planter of Mississippi and Louisiana," *Journal of Mississippi History* XVIII (Oct. 1956), 243–67; Winthrop M. Daniels, "The Slave Plantation in Retro-

The plantation did, however, give a certain uniform pattern to the slave's life, especially in terms of labor requirements. According to the black autobiographers, most field hands rose before dawn, prepared their meals, fed the livestock, and then rushed to the fields before sunrise. Failure to reach the field on time often brought the overseer's lash into play. Depending upon the season or the crop, the laborer would grub and hoe the field, pick worms off the plants, build fences, cut down trees, construct dikes, pull fodder, clear new land, plant rice, sugar, tobacco, cotton, and corn, and then harvest the crop.

Frequently, after working from dawn to sunset, the weary slaves then had to care for the livestock, put away tools, and cook their meals before the horn sounded bedtime in the quarters. During the cotton-picking season, the men sometimes ginned cotton until nine o'clock at night. For the hapless slaves on the sugar plantation, the work of boiling the sugar cane continued far into the night: they often worked eighteen hours a day during the harvest season; some sugar factories ran in shifts seven days and nights each week. The work, while varying in tempo, seemed almost endless. Cotton-planting started the last of March or first of April, cotton-picking lasted from August to Christmas and frequently until January or February. The corn was harvested after cotton-picking ended. During slack periods, the slaves cleared forest land, built fences, repaired the slave cabins, killed hogs, and engaged in a multitude of other tasks.

While the mass of slaves followed this routine, the domestic servants formed part of the plantation elite. They usually ate better food and wore better clothes than the field slaves because they received leftovers from the planter's larder and hand-me-downs from his wardrobe. In spite of this, their position was no sinecure. They ran errands, worked as part-time gardeners, cooked, served meals, cared for the horses, milked the cows,

spect," *Atlantic Monthly* CVII (March 1911), 363–69; Edwin A. Davis, "Bennett H. Barrow, Ante-Bellum Planter of the Felicianas," *Journal of Southern History* V (Nov. 1939), 431–46; Rosser H. Taylor, "The Gentry of Antebellum South Carolina," *North Carolina Historical Review* XVII (April 1940), 114–31; George C. Osborne, "Plantation Life in Central Mississippi as Revealed in the Clay Sharkey Papers," *Journal of Mississippi History* III (Oct. 1941), 277–88.

Figure 37. Field Hand

Figure 38.　Domestic Servant

sewed simple clothes, cared for the master's infant, wove, carded and spun wool, did the marketing, churned the milk, dusted the house, swept the yard, arranged the dining room, cut the shrubbery, and performed numerous other tasks. With the exception of the plantation cook each domestic servant was responsible not for one but for several of these tasks.[2]

At the beck and call of his master day and night, the domestic servant had no regular hours. Added to the long hours was the discomfiture of constantly being under the watchful eyes of the whites and being subject to their every capricious, vengeful, or sadistic whim. Domestic servants frequently had their ears boxed or were flogged for trifling mistakes, ignorance, delinquent work, "insolent" behavior, or simply for being within striking distance when the master was disgruntled. Lewis Clarke, who felt the domestic servants' lot was worse than that of the field slaves, described the problems which beset them:

> We were constantly exposed to the whims and passions of every member of the family; from the least to the greatest their anger was wreaked upon us. Nor was our life an easy one, in the hours of our toil or in the amount of labor performed. We were always required to sit up until all the family had retired; then we must be up at early dawn in summer, and before day in winter.[3]

The quantity, quality, and variety of food, clothing, housing, and medical care the slave received rarely satisfied him. The fact that another man determined how much and what kind of food, clothing, and shelter he needed to survive posed a serious problem for him. Equally serious was his dependence on the "average" amount of food and clothing his master decided was sufficient for *all* slaves. Obviously, an allotment of food or clothing sufficient for one man was not necessarily enough for another man. Most of the black autobiographers complained that they had at

2. Charles Ball, *Slavery in the United States . . .* (New York, 1849), 156–68, 245–300; Lewis G. Clarke, *Narrative of the Sufferings of Lewis Clarke . . .* (Boston, 1845), 10–22; Henry Watson, *Narrative of Henry Watson, a Fugitive Slave* (Boston, 1848), 5–17; Elizabeth Keckley, *Behind The Scenes* (New York, 1868), 17–28.

3. Clarke, *Sufferings,* 17.

least one owner who did not give them enough food. Sometimes, even when slaves generally received enough food, provisions ran low. When the slaves did not receive enough to eat, they stole food. James Watkins, Annie L. Burton, Andrew Jackson, Josiah Henson, and Peter Randolph reported that, in spite of the risks involved, the slaves on their plantations stole food when it was denied them. Other slaves trapped animals and fished at night and on Sundays in order to augment their meager diet.[4]

The slaves often complained bitterly about what their masters described as "adequate" housing. Most of the autobiographers reported that they lived in crudely built one-room log cabins with dirt floors and too many cracks in them to permit much comfort during the winter months. John Brown complained that in the log cabins: "The wind and rain will come in and the smoke will not go out." Austin Steward felt that the slave cabins were "not as good as many of our stables at the north."[5] Not only were the slave cabins uncomfortable, they were often crowded. Most of the cabins contained at least two families. The 260 slaves on Charles Ball's plantation shared 38 cabins, an average of 6.8 slaves per cabin. The 160 slaves on Louis Hughes's plantation lived in 18 cabins or an average of 8.8 slaves per cabin. Josiah Henson declared that from 10 to 12 people shared each cabin on his plantation. Some lived not in cabins but in sheds. William Green, for example, lived in a long low shed with 29 others. Some slaves, of course, lived in more spacious and comfortable cabins. Henry Watson's owner, for instance, had 27 cabins for his 100 slaves, an average of 3.7 slaves per cabin. Few slaves were as fortunate as Sam Aleckson whose master's slave cabins were not only neat and commodious, but also had flower gardens in front of them. Usually the slaves had to make what furniture and utensils they used. They built tables, beds, and benches and sometimes carved wooden spoons. Generally the cabins con-

4. James L. Smith, *Autobiography of James L. Smith* (Norwich, Conn., 1881), 1–9; John Brown, *Slave Life in Georgia* (London, 1855), 170–80; Austin Steward, *Twenty-Two Years a Slave, and Forty Years a Freeman* (Rochester, N.Y., 1861), 13–19; Annie L. Burton, *Memories of Childhood's Slavery Days* (Boston, 1909), 3–9; Josiah Henson, *The Life of Josiah Henson* (Boston, 1849), 6–7.

5. J. Brown, *Slave Life*, 191; Steward, *Twenty-Two Years*, 19.

tained beds made of straw covered boards, and tables of packing boxes. Some slaves slept on the ground or on mattresses of corn shucks without blankets.[6]

Whatever their treatment of slaves, most planters worked consistently to make them submissive and deferential. While the lash was the linchpin of his regime, the slaveholder adopted several practices to assure the slave's submissiveness. A master started early trying to impress upon the mind of the young black the awesome power of whiteness: he made the slave bow upon meeting him, stand in his presence, and accept floggings from his young children; he flogged the slave for fighting with young whites. The ritual of deference was required at every turn: the slave was flogged for disputing a white man's word, kicked for walking between two whites on a street, and not allowed to call his wife or mother "Mrs." [7] He had to approach the overseer or master with great humility. For example, on Charles Ball's plantation the slaves "were always obliged to approach the door of the mansion, in the most humble and supplicating manner, with our hats in our hands, and the most subdued and beseeching language in our mouths. . . ." [8]

Many masters tried first to demonstrate their own authority over the slave and then the superiority of all whites over blacks. They continually told the slave he was unfit for freedom, that every slave who attempted to escape was captured and sold further South, and that the black man must conform to the white man's every wish. The penalties for non-conformity were severe; the lessons uniformly pointed to one idea: the slave was a thing to be used by the "superior" race. Jermain Loguen, for instance,

6. J. Smith, *Autobiography*, 1–9; J. H. Banks, *A Narrative of Events of the Life of J. H. Banks* (Liverpool, 1861), 42–63; Allen Parker, *Recollections of Slavery Times* (Worcester, Mass., 1895), 7–20; James W. C. Pennington, *The Fugitive Blacksmith* (London, 1849), 66.

7. Ball, *Slavery*, 40–74; Watson, *Narrative*, 28–38; John Thompson, *The Life of John Thompson, A Fugitive Slave* (Worcester, Mass., 1856), 10–26; Sam Aleckson, *Before the War and After the Union* (Boston, 1929), 51–65; William Wells Brown, *Narrative of William W. Brown, A Fugitive Slave* (Boston, 1847), 95–98.

8. Ball, *Slavery*, 41.

wrote that he "had been taught, in the severest school, that he was a thing for others' uses, and that he must bend his head, body and mind in conformity to that idea, in the presence of a superior race. . . .' Likewise, Austin Steward had since his childhood "been taught to cower beneath the white man's frown, and bow at his bidding, or suffer all the rigor of the slave laws." [9]

Planters insisted that their slaves show no signs of dissatisfaction. Instead, they were to demonstrate their humility by cheerful performance of their tasks. Elizabeth Keckley's master, for instance, "never liked to see one of his slaves wear a sorrowful face, and those who offended in this particular way were always punished." Anxiously scanning the faces of his slaves, the master made them reflect, in their countenances, what he wanted rather than what they felt. Henry Watson asserted that "the slaveholder watches every move of the slave, and if he is downcast or sad,— in fact, if they are in any mood but laughing and singing, and manifesting symptoms of perfect content at heart,—they are said to have the devil in them. . . ." [10]

Lest the edifice he was building should fall, the master enlisted the aid of some black men to help him control the others. The most diligent slaves were rewarded and pointed to as models for the others to emulate. Black drivers were forced, on pain of punishment themselves, to keep the slaves at their tasks and to flog them for breaking the plantation rules. While the drivers provided part of the coercion necessary to keep the plantation machinery humming, the domestic servants often represented an extension of the master's eyes and ears: the plantation's secret police. Flattered and materially rewarded, the domestic servant kept the master informed of activities in the slave quarters. Trained to speak of his good treatment to Northern visitors and sometimes forced to spy on his fellows, the domestic servant was a valuable adjunct to the slaveholder's security and public relations staff.

9. Jermain Wesley Loguen, *The Rev. J. W. Loguen, as a Slave and as a Freedman* (Syracuse, N.Y., 1859), 165; Steward, *Twenty-Two Years*, 97–98.

10. Keckley, *Scenes*, 29; Watson, *Narrative*, 32.

Ritual deference and obedience to plantation rules could only be enforced by most planters by constant floggings. William Wells Brown spoke for many slaves when he wrote that on his plantation the whip was used "very frequently and freely, and a small offence on the part of a slave furnished an occasion for its use." [11] The slaves were flogged most frequently for running away and for failure to complete the tasks assigned them. Slaveholders often punished them for visiting their mates, learning to read, arguing or fighting with whites, working too slowly, stealing, fighting or quarreling with other slaves, drunkenness, or for trying to prevent the sale of their relatives. They were occasionally punished for impudence, asking their masters to sell them, claiming they were free men, breaking household articles, or for giving sexual favors to persons other than their masters.[12]

Nowhere does the irrationality of slavery appear as clearly as in the way that slaves were punished. While generally speaking a slaveholder had no desire to punish his slave so severely as to endanger his life, the master was only a man, subject, like most men, to miscalculations, to anger, to sadism, and to drink. When angry, masters frequently kicked, slapped, cuffed, or boxed the ears of domestic servants, sometimes flogged pregnant women, and often punished slaves so cruelly that it took them weeks to recover.[13] Many slaves reported that they were flogged severely, had iron weights with bells on them placed on their necks, or were shackled. Recalcitrant slaves received more stripes and were treated more cruelly by exasperated planters than were any other blacks. Moses Roper, an incorrigible runaway, regularly received 100 to 200 lashes from his owner. Once his master poured tar on his head and set it afire. On another occasion, after Roper had escaped from leg irons, his master had the nails on his fingers and toes beaten off. Since every white man considered himself the slave's policeman, the black also suffered at the hands of non-

11. W. W. Brown, *Narrative*, 15.

12. Ball, *Slavery*, pp. 160–68, 372–480; Thomas Jones, *The Experience of Thomas Jones, Who Was a Slave for Forty-Three Years* (Boston, 1850), 16–20; J. Brown, *Slave Life*, 21–30, 62–68, 127–36.

13. Steward, *Twenty-Two Years*, 22–30; W. W. Brown, *Narrative*, 37–41; Clarke, *Sufferings*, 14–20; J. Brown, *Slave Life*, 127–36; Watkins, *Narrative*, 9–10; Loguen, *Freedman*, 78–98.

slaveholders. Josiah Henson, for example, accidentally pushed a white man who later broke his arm and shoulder blades.[14]

Uncompromisingly harsh, the portrait which the slaves drew of cruel masters was filled with brutality and horror. On the plantations of these masters, strong black men suffered from overwork, abuse, and starvation; and the overseer's horn usually sounded before sleep could chase the fatigue of the last day's labor. Characteristically, stocks closed on hapless women and children, mothers cried for the infants torn cruelly from their arms, and whimpering black women fought vainly to preserve their virtue in the face of the lash or pleaded for mercy while blood flowed from their bare buttocks. A cacophony of horrendous sounds constantly reverberated throughout such plantations: nauseated black men vomited while strung up over slowly burning tobacco leaves, vicious dogs tore black flesh, black men moaned as they were hung up by the thumbs with the whip raising deep welts on their backs and as they were bent over barrels or tied down to stakes while paddles with holes in them broke blisters on their rumps. Frequently blacks called God's name in vain as they fainted from their master's hundredth stroke or as they had their brains blown out. The slaves described masters of this stripe as besotted, vicious, deceitful, coarse, licentious, bloodthirsty, heartless, and hypocritical Christians who were pitiless fiends.[15]

The first impulse of the historian is to reject the slave's portrait as too harsh. There is, however, a great deal of evidence in antebellum court records, newspapers, memoirs, and plantation diaries which suggests that this is not the case. However much it is denied by Southern romantics, there were many slaveholders who were moral degenerates and sadists. Quite frequently, even the most cultured of planters were so inured to brutality that they thought little about the punishment meted out to slaves. Floggings of 50 to 75 lashes were not uncommon. On numerous occasions, planters branded, stabbed, tarred and feathered, burned,

14. W. W. Brown, *Narrative*, 21–30; J. Brown, *Slave Life*, 21–30, 82–109; Loguen, *Freedman*, 122–36; Clarke, *Sufferings*, 22–30; Henson, *Life*, 15–18.

15. W. W. Brown, *Narrative*, 21–26; Clarke, *Sufferings*, 11–12; Steward, *Twenty-Two Years*, 91–93; Henson, *Life*, 15–18.

shackled, tortured, maimed, crippled, mutilated, and castrated their slaves. Thousands of slaves were flogged so severely that they were permanently scarred. In Mississippi a fiendish planter once administered 1,000 lashes to a slave.[16]

At the opposite extreme from the fiend was Dr. James Green Carson of Mississippi. Carson, although he inherited 200 slaves, early in life expressed an abhorrence of slavery on religious grounds. Unable to free his slaves because of Mississippi law, Carson felt a moral responsibility to treat them humanely. Consequently, he hired a plantation physician, paid white missionaries to preach to his slaves every Sunday, conducted prayer meetings in the quarters during the week, purchased labor saving machinery to lighten the slaves' work, punished his children for being discourteous to blacks, and never used the lash. James Carson was a rare man among Southern planters. Still, there were many others who were enough like him to be described as generally kind and humane in their treatment of slaves.[17]

According to antebellum whites there were many planters who dealt with their slaves in a humane fashion. Walter Peterson, for example, recalled that in Alabama "many slaveholders were kind masters." [18] Philip H. Jones of Louisiana asserted that "Many owners were humane and kind and provided well for them [slaves]." [19] According to Amanda Washington, among the planters *"Noblesse oblige* was recognized everywhere, and we felt bound to treat kindly the class dependent on us." [20]

16. Charles S. Sydnor, *Slavery in Mississippi* (Baton Rouge, 1966), 86–94; Kenneth Stampp, *The Peculiar Institution* (New York, 1956), 171–91.

17. Fletcher M. Green, ed., *Ferry Hill Plantation Journal, January 4, 1838–January 15, 1839* (Chapel Hill, 1961), vii–xxi; Osborne, "Plantation," 277–88; Anderson, "Carson," 243–67; Mary W. Highsaw, "A History of Zion Community in Maury County, 1806–1860," *Tennessee Historical Quarterly* V (June 1946), 111–40.

18. Walter F. Peterson, "Slavery in the 1850's: Recollections of an Alabama Unionist," *Alabama Historical Quarterly* XXX (Fall and Winter 1968), 221.

19. Philip H. Jones, "Reminiscences of Philip H. Jones," 4, Southern Historical Collection, University of North Carolina.

20. Amanda Washington, *How Beauty Was Saved* (New York, 1907), 64.

The testimony of the white witnesses is borne out by that of former slaves. A majority of the slaves, at one time, had one or two masters whom they considered kindly men. Josiah Henson described his master as a "kind-hearted, liberal, and jovial" man. Grimes felt that Dr. Collock of Savannah "was the best and most humane man I ever lived with, or worked under." Sam Aleckson's South Carolina master was "kind and generous." Isaac Jefferson recalled that his master, Thomas Jefferson, was of a similar stripe: "Old master [was] kind to servants." Elijah Marrs declared: "Our master was not hard on us." The slaveholders earned these encomiums in various ways. Sparing use of the lash, provision of adequate shelter, clothing, and food, and maintenance of the family unit all led the slaves to think of their masters as kindly men.[21]

However kind his master, the slave had no guarantee of benevolent treatment. The kindest masters were sometimes crotchety, often wreaking their anger on their slaves.[22] Austin Steward reported that his owner "was not a very hard master; but generally was kind and pleasant. Indulgent when in good humor, but like many of the southerners, terrible when in a passion." Grimes's master was of the same temperament. He was, according to Grimes, "a very kind master, but exceedingly severe when angry."[23]

Most masters were neither pitiless fiends nor saints in their relationships with slaves. Whenever possible, planters hired physicians for slaves when they were ill, gave them what the planter defined as "adequate" food, clothing, and shelter, and flogged them for lying, stealing, fighting, breaking tools, and numerous other "offenses." While ready to give the slave from 10 to 50 lashes for most offenses, the typical planter preferred to punish slaves in other ways (withholding passes, demotion, extra

---

21. Henson, *Life*, 2; Grimes, *Life*, 36–48; Aleckson, *Union*, 35; Isaac Jefferson, *Life of Isaac Jefferson of Petersburg, Virginia, Blacksmith* (Charlottesville, 1951), 23; Elijah P. Marrs, *Life and Histoy* (Louisville, Ky., 1885), 11.

22. Leonard Black, *The Life And Sufferings of Leonard Black, A Fugitive From Slavery* (New Bedford, 1847), 11; Pennington, *Blacksmith*, 9.

23. Steward, *Twenty-Two Years*, 33; Grimes, *Life*, 33.

work, humiliation, solitary confinement, etc.). Less violent means of punishment were preferred because they were not morally reprehensible, involved no physical harm to valuable property, and were often more effective in preserving discipline than floggings.[24]

In spite of the institutionally defined roles, the treatment of slaves varied from plantation to plantation. Differences in family life, childhood experiences, and religious beliefs caused the planters to treat their slaves in a great variety of ways. A few masters were so brutal and sadistic that they could crush the slaves' every manly instinct. Others were too humane, too lazy, or too stupid to make child-like dependents of their slaves. While the normal planter extracted all of the labor he could from blacks, there were several conflicting forces which made him at the same time callous toward the slaves' sufferings and impelled him to recognize their humanity.

One of the most important institutions which influenced the planter's treatment of the slave was the white family. The white child grew up in a society which stressed formalized courtship, romanticized women as angelic, made a fetish of the family, frowned on public displays of affection, encouraged prolific child-bearing, and promoted early marriages. The planter's family was patriarchal, deeply religious, and filio-pietistic. Males were given religious and moral lessons as well as being taught to be aggressive, proud, independent, courteous, courageous, chivalrous, honorable, and intelligent.[25]

Although fathers were venerated and children were frequently dependent on them until adulthood, rural isolation sometimes

24. J. Carlyle Sitterson, "The McCollams: A Planter Family of the Old and New South," *Journal of Southern History* VI (Aug. 1940), 347–67; Noah Davis, *A Narrative of the Life of Rev. Noah Davis, A Colored Man* (Baltimore, 1859), 1–14.

25. Susan Dabney Smedes, *Memorials of a Southern Planter* (Baltimore, 1887), 29, 108–15, 135–38; Edmund S. Morgan, *Virginians at Home* (Williamsburg, Va., 1952), 5–8, 36, 45–48; Julia Cherry Spruill, *Women's Life and Work in the Southern Colonies* (Chapel Hill, 1938), 43–50; Rosser H. Taylor, *Ante-Bellum South Carolina: A Social History* (Chapel Hill, 1942), 59–73; Arthur W. Calhoun, *A Social History of the American Family* (New York, 1960), II, 311–55.

promoted spontaneous and affectionate family relations. Discipline was unsystematic, and parents over-indulged their children. In spite of this, the formalized manners often militated against parents displaying deep affection for their children. Susan Dabney Smedes, for example, reported that her father "did not readily express his affections for his children . . ." [26] The child's relations with his mother were hedged in by his almost religious veneration of her as a genteel, delicate, saintly being. His father's circumspection in his contacts with white women reinforced the picture of her as an untouchable. The situation was complicated even more by the frequent remarriages of widows and widowers and the subsequent strains on their children.

One of the key figures in the white child's socialization was the ubiquitous black mammy to whom he frequently turned for love and security. It was the black mammy who often ran the household, interceded with his parents to protect him, punished him for misbehavior, nursed him, rocked him to sleep, told him fascinating stories, and in general served as his second, more attentive, more loving mother. The mammy's influence on her white charge's thought, behavior, language, and personality is inestimable. [27] One Englishman wrote that in the Carolinas: "Each child has its *Momma*, whose gestures and accent it will necessarily copy, for children, we all know, are imitative beings. It is not unusual to hear an elegant lady say, *Richard always grieves when Quasheehan is whipped, because she suckled him.*" [28] Often the child formed a deep and abiding love for his mammy and as an adult deferred to her demands and wishes.

Black childhood playmates had only a little less influence on the white child than the mammy. As a result of enduring friendships formed during their impressionable childhood, many white youngsters intervened to prevent the punishment or sale of their black favorites, demanded of them far less conformity to the slave role, or preferred the company of slaves to that of their

26. Smedes, *Memorials*, 115.
27. Smedes, *Memorials*, 20, 32–33, 116; Virginia Clay-Clopton, *A Belle of the Fifties* (New York, 1905), 4; Taylor, *South Carolina*, 22–34; Morgan, *Virginians*, 63–65; Calhoun, *Family*, II, 311–55.
28. Quoted in Spruill, *Women*, 56.

white neighbors.[29] William Wells Brown's master held Brown's father in such high esteem that he refused to sell the boy to New Orleans even after he had tried to escape. Similarly, William Green's mother prevented his separation from her by appealing to his young master whom she had nursed. Jacob Stroyer wrote that one intemperate white man terrorized his white neighbors but never abused his forty slaves because of the control his old mammy exercised over him. Rarely could a planter punish a slave with impunity if he were the favorite of his wife or children. The son of John Thompson's master, for instance, threatened to shoot an overseer for flogging the slave fiddler. The regard in which Andrew Jackson was held by his master's sons was so great that they refused to tell their father where he went when he escaped from Kentucky. Even if the slave were not a favorite, a member of the master's family might prevent unusually cruel treatment.[30]

The early association with blacks, and especially his black mammy, had a profound influence on the white Southerner. His constant exposure to the cruelties perpetrated upon slaves led to a sense of detachment which conflicted with his love and respect for his close black associates. Similarly, the demeanor of all slaves toward his parents and his parents' insistence that he demand deference from blacks taught the child to exercise authority. He soon observed that his strict moral code conflicted with the apparently more desirable loose morality, irresponsibility, and happiness of his black associates. He envied the slave his apparent freedom from social restraints and projected all of his own desires to break through these restraints onto the black. Often he internalized the love ideal of the black mammy but later learned that she was a hated, black thing. His intimate relation with the mammy, his observation of the casual sexual contacts among slaves, the idealization of white women and the

29. Smedes, *Memorials,* 116, 162; Taylor, *South Carolina,* 22–34.

30. Henry Box Brown, *Narrative of Henry Box Brown* (Boston, 1851), 1–21, 23–38; Samuel Hall, *47 Years A Slave* (Washington, Iowa, 1912), n.p.; Monroe F. Jamison, *Autobiography And Work of Bishop M. F. Jamison, D.D.* (Nashville, 1912), 17–23; Andrew Jackson, *Narrative and Writings of Andrew Jackson* (Syracuse, N.Y., 1847), 20–23.

pursuit of black women by white males, convinced him that sexual joy lay in the arms of a black paramour. The white male frequently resolved his love-hate complex by pursuing the allegedly passionate black woman. At the same time, he exaggerated the sexual prowess and desire of the black male for liaisons with angelic white women and reacted with extreme cruelty to any challenge to his monopoly of white women.[31]

The slaveholder's sadistic impulses were frequently restrained by the fear of public disapproval. Sympathetic whites often prevented the cruel punishment of slaves. An innkeeper once prevented Moses Roper's drunken master from flogging him. One of Charles Ball's masters never flogged him because he wanted to retain his public reputation as a benevolent slaveholder. Much to his embarrassment, Memphis city officials upbraided Louis Hughes's master when his overseer almost flogged a slave to death.[32] Frederick Douglass felt that public opinion was "an unfailing restraint upon the cruelty and barbarity of master, overseers, and slave-drivers, whenever and wherever it can reach them . . ."[33]

One of the strongest forces operating against cruel treatment of slaves was religion. Although it is impossible to determine how many slaveholders were deeply religious, it is obvious from the sources that a number of them tried to apply Christian principles in their relations with slaves. The important thing, however, is that ministers continually reminded masters of their duties to their slaves. One example of the interest in this subject was the response to an essay contest sponsored by the Baptist State Convention in Alabama. In 1849 forty men submitted essays on "The Duties of Christian Masters" in an effort to win the $200 prize the convention offered. Some of the essays went through several editions.

The relationship of the minister to the planter was a complex one. Frequently dependent on wealthy planters for his livelihood, the white minister almost never questioned the morality of the master-slave relationship. In fact, a majority of the min-

---

31. Grimes, *Life,* 15; Watson, *Narrative,* 5–17; Loguen, *Freedman,* 19–25; Charles Ball, *Slavery,* 238–300.
32. Ball, *Slavery,* 23–40; W. W. Brown, *Narrative,* 21–26.
33. Douglass, *Bondage,* 61.

isters insisted on slavery's divine origin and encouraged slaves to be obedient to their masters. Even so, in spite of the role of the minister played in preserving the peculiar institution and his refusal to castigate the planters for their treatment of slaves, he often preached about an ideal master-slave relationship and the duties and responsibilities planters had toward their slaves.

The first duty of the Christian master was to recognize the slave's humanity. This recognition entailed a respect for the feelings of the slave. Southern divines argued that the slave was also created in God's image. The Reverend J. H. Thornwell testified that

> the Negro is of one blood with ourselves—that he has sinned as we have, and that he has an equal interest with us in the great redemption. Science, falsely so called, may attempt to exclude him from the brotherhood of humanity . . . but the instinctive impulses of our nature, combined with the plainest declarations of the word of God, lead us to recognize in his form and lineaments—his moral, religious and intellectual nature—the same humanity in which we glory as the image of God. We are not ashamed to call him our brother.[34]

While the Reverend George W. Freeman was not as certain of the link between master and slave, he was more insistent on the necessity of respecting the black's feelings. Freeman exhorted masters, in their relations with slaves, "never forget that, as low as they are in the scale of humanity, they are yet *human beings, and have the feelings of human beings*—feelings too with many of them, as delicate and sensitive as your own, and which demand to be respected, and carefully preserved from outrage." [35]

Ministers quoted the Bible freely to prove the obligations masters had to their slaves. They reminded them that Paul had advised masters to forbear threatening slaves "knowing that your Master also is in Heaven; neither is there respect of persons with him" (Ephesians 6:9). The most frequently quoted Biblical

34. J. H. Thornwell, *The Rights and Duties of Masters, A Sermon Preached at the Dedication of a Church* (Charleston, S.C., 1850), 11.

35. George W. Freeman, *The Rights and Duties of Slave-Holders* (Charleston, 1837), 27.

admonition was Colossians 4:1: "Masters, give unto *your* servants that which is just and equal; knowing that ye also have a Master in heaven." How was the master to determine justice and equity? Most Southern divines translated the terms into the Golden Rule. The Reverend T. A. Holmes summed up the general view when he observed: "Equity pleads the right of humanity. . . . and, in the conscientious discharge of duty, prompts the master to such treatment of his servant as would be desired on his part, were their positions reversed." [36] Ministers asserted that cruel treatment of slaves would lead to Divine censure. The Reverend H. N. McTyeire of New Orleans declared, "As you treat your servants on earth, so will your Master in heaven treat you." [37] The Reverend T. A. Holmes was more direct. He cautioned slaveholders that "the exercise of right and authority on the part of the master, with reference only to his interest, uninfluenced by kindness to his servant, must incur the displeasure of Him with whom there is no respect of persons." [38]

According to the ministers, Christian masters had several duties to their slaves. They had to maintain the slaves properly, care for them in old age, require no more than a reasonable amount of labor from them, give them adequate leisure time, and respect their humanity. Many ministers repeated the question John Wesley asked slaveholders in 1774: "Have you tried what mildness and gentleness would do?" Holmes told planters that "the master should be the friend of his servant, and the servant should know it. Friendship implies good will, Kindness, a desire for the welfare of him for whom it is entertained." Freeman was just as insistent on mild treatment. He declared: "It is the duty of masters not only to be merciful to their servants, but to do everything in their power to make their situation comfortable, and to put forth all reasonable effort to render them contented and happy." [39]

36. H. N. McTyeire, *et al.*, *Duties of Masters of Servants: Three Premium Essays* (Charleston, S.C., 1851), 136.

37. H. N. McTyeire, *Duties of Christian Masters* (Nashville, 1859), 125–26.

38. McTyeire, *et al.*, *Essays*, 133.

39. McTyeire, *Duties*, 84; McTyeire, *et al.*, *Essays*, 143; Freeman, *Rights*, 25.

In addition to several personal and social forces which prevented planters from practicing the kind of cruelty necessary for the systematic extinction of every trace of manhood in the slave, there were certain features of the plantation that militated against abject docility on the part of slaves. Although legally the planter had absolute authority over the slave, there were many restraints on his use of that authority. Dependent on the slave's labor for his economic survival, the planter ordinarily could not afford to starve, torture, or work him to death. Whatever the regime on the plantation, the planter never had a supervisory staff which was large enough to extract the kind of labor that killed men in a few months. Consequently, in spite of the slave's constant labor, there was an absolute limit beyond which he was not pushed. The most important factor in this limitation was the size of most plantations and the consequent insurance of a low level of surveillance of many of the slave's activities. Since more than half of the slaves in 1860 lived on plantations containing twenty or more slaves, it is obvious that only a small minority of planters could personally supervise every detail of the work. Besides, many masters were too lazy, too stupid, or away too often visiting spas during the summer to maintain a strict surveillance over their slaves. The editor of the *Southern Quarterly Review* recognized this when he wrote that as a result of "the apathy of the master; his love of repose; his absence from his estates . . . the slave . . . acquires a thousand habits and desires all inconsistent with subordination, labour, decency, sobriety, and all virtues of regularity, humility and temperance." [40]

In order to insure regular labor and humility, most planters hired overseers to manage their slaves. The job of the overseer was unbelievably difficult.[41] One overseer indicated this plainly when he complained:

40. N.P.B., "The Treatment of Slaves In the Southern States," *Southern Quarterly Review* XXI (Jan. 1852), 212.

41. John E. Moore, ed., "Two Documents Relating to Plantation Overseers of the Vicksburg Region, 1831–1832," *Journal of Mississippi History* XVI (Jan. 1954), 31–36; Lucille Griffith, ed., "The Plantation Record Book of Brookdale Farm Amite County, 1856–57," *Journal of Mississippi History* VII (Jan. 1945), 25–31.

If there ever was or ever will be a calling in life as mean
and contemptible as that of an overseer—I would be right
down glad to know what it is, and where to be found. . . .
If there be . . . a favorable crop, the *master* makes a splen-
did crop; if any circumstances be unpropitious and an inferior crop is made, it is the overseer's fault, and if he flogs
[the slaves] to keep them at home, or locked up . . . he
is a brute and a tyrant. If no meat is made, the overseer
would plant too much cotton. . . . If hogs are taken good
care of the overseer is wasting corn, and "the most careless and thriftless creature alive." If he does not "turn out"
hands in time, he is *lazy;* if he "rousts" them out as your
dad and mine had to do, why he is a brute. . . .[42]

Planters insisted that the overseer spend all of his time on the
plantation, especially if the owner himself did not reside there.
George Washington was characteristic in this regard. He informed one of his overseers:

I do in explicit terms, enjoin it upon you to remain constantly at home, unless called off by unavoidable business,
or to attend divine worship, and to be constantly with your
people when there. There is no other sure way of getting
work well done, and quietly, by negroes; for when an over-
looker's back is turned, the most of them will slight their
work, or be idle altogether; in which case correction cannot
retrieve either, but often produces evils which are worse
than the disease. Nor is there any other mode than this to
prevent thieving and other disorders, the consequence of
opportunities.[43]

While constant surveillance of slaves was mandatory for successful management, this was one of the most onerous of the overseer's duties. One overseer complained in May 1858 that his
work was so time consuming that "I don't get time scarcely to

42. James C. Bonner, "The Plantation Overseer and Southern Na-
tionalism as Revealed in the Career of Garland D. Harmon," *Agricultural
History* XIX (Jan. 1945), 2.
43. William K. Scarborough, *The Overseer* (Baton Rouge, 1966), 73.

Figures 39, 40, 41, 42.   Cotton Plantation

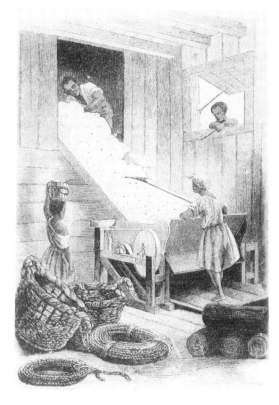

eat or sleep. I have not been off the plantation since the 3rd of Oct [.] . . . The truth is no man can begin to attend to such a business with any set of negros, without the strictest vigilance on his part." [44]

The disciplining of slaves was the major factor in the success or failure of an overseer. Expected to make a large crop while guarding the welfare of the slaves, the overseer often came into conflict with the planter. If the overseer used unusual force in driving the slaves, he incurred the wrath of the owner for damaging his property. On the other hand, if he were easy going, the planter might dismiss him for making a small crop. In fact, planters often dismissed overseers for cruelty, drunkenness, absenteeism, and lax discipline.

In order for the overseer to retain his job he had to be adept at managing slaves. There were many pitfalls in the endeavor. If on the one hand the overseer became too familiar with the slaves or had sexual relations with the black women, the slaves extracted favors from him and did little work. On the other hand, if the overseer was too cruel and hard driving, the slaves did everything they could to discredit him. It was often impossible for the overseer to find a happy medium between these two extremes. Whenever the slaves were dissatisfied with the overseer, they informed the owner of his transgressions, or ran away to escape heavy work or to avoid punishment. Often the slaves refused to return to work until they had spoken to their masters about their treatment. One harried overseer indicated the impact of this tactic when he complained that "if I donte please every negro on the place they run away rite strate." [45] If the overseer somehow managed to please the master *and* the slaves, he was guaranteed a long tenure on the plantation. For example, John B. Lamar wrote in 1844 that he was anxious to retain his overseer because "the negroes like him too." [46]

As the visible symbol of authority, the overseer was the most frequent target of rebellious slaves disgruntled over their work

44. Quoted in Scarborough, *Overseer*, 46.

45. John S. Bassett, *The Southern Plantation Overseer* (Northampton, Mass., 1925), 64.

46. Ulrich B. Philips, ed., *Plantation and Frontier* (2 vols., Cleveland, 1910), I, 170.

load, food allotment, or punishment. According to one observer, "An over-seer has to plan all the business and be with the negroes all the time. The negroes have great spite and hatred towards them and frequently fight them, when the over-seer pretends to whip them. The negroes think as meanly of the poor white people, as the rich white people do themselves and think anybody that is so poor as to be an overseer mean enough." [47] Hundreds of overseers were beaten, poisoned, stabbed, and shot by rebellious slaves. [48]

The overseer was the weakest link in the chain of plantation management. Whatever his character, it was impossible for the overseer to supervise every detail of the slave's life. Most men were unwilling to lead the kind of solitary life that plantation management demanded. Consequently, most overseers left the plantations periodically at night or on the weekends in order to find some recreation for themselves. Overwhelmed by a multitude of duties, the overseer could not be everywhere at once and consequently could not keep the slaves under constant surveillance. If he happened to be lazy, the level of surveillance was even lower. [49]

As a result of the differences in the characters of overseers and masters, many plantations deviated strikingly from the ideal outlined in the rules of management. According to the investigations of H. Herbemont of South Carolina, "there are very few planters who have anything like a regular system for either the moral or physical government of their slaves." A writer in the *American Farmer* agreed: "There is in fact little or no 'system' of management in regard to our slaves—they are insubordinate and *unmanageable*." [50]

Even when attempts were made to govern the slaves in some systematic fashion, the planters realized that since the slaves had

47. Martha Van Briesen, ed., *The Letters of Elijah Fletcher* (Charlottesville, 1965), 23.

48. Herbert Aptheker, *American Negro Slave Revolts* (New York, 1943); Philips, *Plantation*, II, 117–25.

49. Charles S. Sydnor, "A Slave Owner and His Overseers," *North Carolina Historical Review* XIV (Jan. 1937), 31–38.

50. *Southern Agriculturalist* IX (Feb. 1836), 71; *American Farmer*, II (March 16, 1821), 402.

Figures 43, 44, 45, 46.　Sugar Plantation

not internalized their ideals they had to make several compromises in order to maintain the façade of absolute control.[51] First, they recognized that their slaves differed in temperament and intelligence. For instance, one planter asserted: "In every servants' quarters there are the strong and the weak, the sagacious and the simple." Second, since they differed so much in character, all slaves could not be treated in the same manner. The most strong-willed and shrewdest slaves received better treatment than most others and were given positions of power in the plantation hierarchy. The intractable slave was either sold or never molested. Planters spotted him quickly, and inevitably, they were forced by him to be wary. There were certainly many masters who were cautious with slaves like Louis Manigault's Jack Savage. According to Manigault, Jack "was the only negro ever in our possession who I considered capable of murdering me or burning my dwelling at night or capable of committing any act." [52]

Planters often maintained the appearance of strict obedience by making it relatively easy for the slave to obey. Regardless of their desires, most masters realized that the slaves, like soldiers, were adept at "goldbricking." Once the slaves decided how much labor they were going to perform, they refused to work any harder. One slaveholder observed: "Experience has long since taught masters, that every attempt to force a slave beyond the limits that he fixes as a sufficient amount of labor to render his master, instead of extorting more work, only tends to make him unprofitable, unmanageable, a vexation and a curse." [53]

It was primarily because the planters recognized that slaves voluntarily limited their work that many of them set the standard of labor so low that every slave could meet it. Even when every allowance is made for different strains of certain crops, it is impossible to explain the variations in labor performed from plantation to plantation without recognition of the slave's role in restricting his output. Examine, for instance, the average amount of cotton picked per day by an adult slave. Between 1825 and

51. Brown, *Slave Life*, 82–109; Green, *Events*, 13.
52. *DeBow's Review* XXIX (Sept. 1860), 362; quoted in Taylor, *South Carolina*, 177.
53. "Negro Slavery at the South," *DeBow's Review* VII (Sept. 1849), 220.

Figures 47, 48.   Rice Plantation

1860 slaves in Mississippi generally picked between 130 and 150 pounds of cotton per day. On Charles Whitmore's delta plantation, however, few slaves picked more than 100 pounds of cotton daily. The slave's limitation on the labor he performed appears clearly in the results of races arranged by planters. In a race on a Mississippi plantation in 1830 fourteen slaves picked an average of 323 pounds of cotton, twice their normal average.[54] Many planters gave prizes to the best cotton pickers in an effort to speed up the work. While this was often effective, many slaves still refused to exert themselves.[55]

The slaveholder also kept up the pretense of absolute control by refusing to take note of every deviation from the rules. In effect, each planter had to learn to be selectively inattentive to rules infractions. A group of Alabama planters gave sound advice on this point: "Negroes lack the motive of self interest to make them careful and diligent, hence the necessity of great patience in the management of them. Do not, therefore, notice too many small omissions of duty." [56]

The personal relations between master and slave were strained. Rarely did their interests coincide. Because of this, the master used physical force to make the slave obedient. The personal relations on the plantation, however, were much more complicated than a simple relationship between subordinate and superordinate. In the first place, all masters did not demand ritual deference at all times to bolster their self-esteem. Second, the same obsequious behavior was not demanded of ordinary slaves and those in positions of trust. Sir Charles Lyell observed that the latter group of slaves were "involuntarily treated more as equals by the whites." Even when all slaves had to be deferential, whites did not require them to go through the ritual at all times. For example, Susan Dabney Smedes wrote that during

54. Mark Swearingen, "Thirty Years of a Mississippi Plantation: Charles Whitmore of Montpelier," *Journal of Southern History* I (May 1935), 198–211; Davis, "Barrow," 431–46; Kathryn T. Abbey, ed., "Documents Relating to El Destino and Chemonie Plantations, Middle Florida, 1828–1868," *Florida Historical Quarterly* VII (Jan. 1929), 179–213.

55. *American Farmer* VII (Jan. 13, 1826), 338.
56. *DeBow's Review* XVIII (June 1855), 718.

Christmas "there was an affectionate throwing off of the reserve and decorum of every-day life." [57]

While a planter could demand obedience, he could not always obtain the slaves's respect. Samuel Meredith complained in 1774 that one of his slaves had told a group of whites that "I am not worthy to be his Master." Sir Charles Lyell reported that frequently in conversing with an intelligent black driver, "This personage, conscious of his importance, would begin by enlarging, with much self-complacency, on the ignorance of his master. . . ." Such slaves gave deference only as a result of fear. They refused to identify with the planter's interest or to work unless they were watched. One of John B. Lamar's carpenters, Ned, was typical of this class. Lamar refused to send Ned off the plantation to construct buildings because of "his general character for intemperance, & disobedience, & quarrelsomeness. . . . He is an eye servant. If I was with him I could have the work done soon and cheap, but I am afraid to trust him off where there is no one he fears." [58]

The Southern white man's perceptions of slave behavior make one point quite clear: the planter recognized the variability of slave personality in his day-to-day relationships. In reality, he had to make several compromises in order to maintain the façade of absolute control. He often "bought off" the strongest slaves by placing them in the plantation hierarchy, was selectively inattentive to rules infractions, and accepted the slave's definition of how much labor he would perform. There was so little identification with the master's interest in the quarters that he frequently had to resort to coercion and to more and more oppressive laws. There were so many differences among slaveholders and the legal sanctions of slavery were applied in so many different ways that the regimen to which the slave was subjected varied considerably. If the masters' portrait of actual slave behavior is any guide, there was considerable variation in slave personalities.

57. Charles Lyell, *A Second Visit to the United States of North America* (2 vols., New York, 1850), II, 19–20; Smedes, *Memorials*, 162.

58. Quoted in Phillips, *Plantation*, II, 82; Lyell, *Second Visit*, II, 19.

7 Slave Personality Types

Blows and insults he bore, at the moment,
without resentment; deep but suppressed
emotion, rendered him insensible to their
sting; but it was afterward, when the memory
of them went seething through his brain,
breeding a fiery indignation at his injured
self-hood, that the resolve came to resist,
and the time fixed to resist, and the time
fixed when to resist, and the plot laid, how
to resist; and he always kept his self-pledged
word. In what he undertook, in this line, he
looked fate in the face, and had a cool, keen
look at the relation of means to ends.

James McCune Smith

The plantation was a battlefield where slaves fought masters
for physical and psychological survival. Although unlettered,
unarmed, and outnumbered, slaves fought in various ways to
preserve their manhood. Several factors exerted a powerful influence on this struggle. The slave's parents, relatives, conjurers,
religion, and the size of his master's plantation—all played some
role in the formation of his character and affected behavior in
the quarters.

In analyzing slave behavior, it is possible to utilize several
psychological theories. The most useful of them, however, is
Henry Stack Sullivan's "interpersonal theory." Sullivan argued
that the "significant others," or persons with most power to reward and punish, are primarily responsible for the way people
behave. Crucial to Sullivan's theory is the concept of the self
which he defined as "the content of consciousness at all times
when one is thoroughly comfortable about one's self-respect, the
prestige that one enjoys among one's fellows, and the respect

and deference which they pay one." [1] Interpersonal theorists argue that behavioral patterns are determined by the characteristics of the situation, how the person perceives them, and his behavioral dispositions at the time.[2] Despite the emphasis on variability, in interpersonal theory childhood is the most crucial of the personality eras. The general style of behavior adopted in childhood tends to be self-perpetuating. The person's first, most important, and enduring concept of himself develops during childhood as a result of his parents treating him as a unique, thoroughly lovable individual.

From the outset, the most important component of personality is self-esteem. Our sense of self-esteem is heightened or lowered by our perception of the images others have of us. Few adults, however, are solely dependent on the way others see them for their conception of themselves. In other words, one enters into every adult interpersonal relationship with some preconceived ideas of what kind of person he is. The most favorable aspect of this is the high opinion of ourselves which we have formed from interacting with our parents.[3] Sullivan, for example, observed that when everything else fails to preserve one's self-esteem, "membership in that family, which makes one unique and distinguishes one on the basis of the very early valuation, would be a treasured possession." [4]

Interpersonal behavior generally revolves around the dominant-submissive, hate-love axes. One form of behavior tends to elicit its complement: dominance leads to submission and vice versa. The extent of submissiveness often depends on the structure of the group to which the person belongs. The unique

1. H. S. Sullivan, "A Theory of Interpersonal Relations: The Illusion of Personal Individuality," in Hendrik M. Ruitenbeek, ed., *Varieties of Personality Theories* (New York, 1964), 140.

2. Robert C. Carson, *Interaction Concepts of Personality* (Chicago, 1969), 26; Ruitenbeek, *Varieties,* 139–40.

3. Carson, *Interaction,* 8–57; Michael Argyle, *The Psychology of Interpersonal Behavior* (Baltimore, 1967), 117–32; Peter B. Warr and Christopher Knapper, *The Perception of People and Events* (New York, 1968), 245–54.

4. Ruitenbeek, *Varieties,* 148.

norms or subculture of the group, its size, the spatial arrangements, frequency of interaction, and the superordinate's ability to observe the subordinates all affect the degree of submission. In institutions there is a formal pattern for exercising authority (tone of voice, facial expressions, phrases, physical violence) and giving deference (obsequious behavior, bowing, tipping hat, downcast look, etc.). Studies of industrial organizations have shown that members of smaller groups tend to internalize more of the expectations of those in power and to comply more fully with their demands than members of larger ones. Behavior in these organizations varies from friendly to aggressive dominance, and from hostile submissiveness to docility. A person may identify with the dominant person either because of affection or fear. In the latter case the identification or internalization of the ideals of the dominant person is directed toward avoiding punishment and is on a rather shallow level.

The extent of surveillance is the key to internalization. If the superordinate feels that the subordinate has internalized the submissive role, he feels no compulsion to continue surveillance beyond the initial stage ("Though I'm not around my daughter will not drink because I have taught her to abstain from alcoholic beverages"). On the other hand, if the superordinate believes that the subordinate has not internalized the role, he is compelled to continue surveillance indefinitely.[5]

The same pattern holds for the exercise of coercive power. Initially the superordinate threatens and punishes the subordinate to insure behavioral conformity to the submissive role. If the subordinate internalizes the submissive role in the initial stages, the superordinate does not have to rely on threats and punishments later. In other words, the frequent resort to coercion in interpersonal relations indicates that the low power person has not fully accepted his submissive role. Peter Blau noted this when he declared that "coercive force, which can hardly be

5. Stanley Milgram, "Behavioral Study of Obedience," in Warren G. Bennis, *et al.*, eds., *Interpersonal Dynamics* (Homewood, Illinois, 1964), 110; Abraham Zaleznik and David Moment, *The Dynamics of Interpersonal Behavior* (New York, 1964), 179–213, 256–86; Carson, *Interaction*, 57–92, 122–71; Erving Goffman, *Interaction Ritual: Essays on Face-To-Face Behavior* (Garden City, New York, 1967), 60.

resisted, is important as a last resort for exercising power over individuals who cannot otherwise be made to yield." [6] An illustration of this appears in the parent-child relationship. Parents frequently punish their young children for lying and stealing but later, when the parental value of honesty has been internalized, they no longer have to rely on coercive power. But, if the values have not been internalized, the parents have to threaten and punish the child continually to insure behavioral conformity.[7] Such a situation reveals a diminution in power. Blau clearly demonstrates this:

> If an individual has much power over others, which means that they are obligated to and dependent on him for greatly needed benefits, they will be eager to do his bidding and anticipate his wishes in order to maintain his good will, particularly if there are still others who compete for the benefits he supplies them. If an individual has little power over others, however, they will be less concerned with pleasing him, and he may even have to remind them that they owe it to him to follow his requests. Such reminders demonstrate to them that he really needs the services they render him, just as they need his services, which implies that the relation between him and them is not one of unequal power but one of egalitarian exchange. Great inequality of power typically obviates the need for such reminders. . . .[8]

While psychologists have found that a superordinate's reliance on coercive power (threats and violent punishment) generally

6. Peter M. Blau, *Exchange and Power in Social Life* (New York, 1967), 125.

7. Herbert C. Kelman, "Compliance, Identification, and Internalization: Three Processes of Attitude Change," in Harold Proshansky and Bernard Seidenberg, eds., *Basic Studies in Social Psychology* (New York, 1965), 140–48; Amitai Etzioni, "Organization Dimensions and Their Interrelationships: A Theory of Compliance," in Bernard P. Indik and F. Kenneth Berrien, eds., *People, Groups, and Organizations* (New York, 1968), 94–109; Rose Laub Coser, "Insulation From Observability and Types of Social Conformity," *American Sociological Review* XXVI (Feb. 1969), 28–39.

8. Blau, *Exchange*, 134–35.

leads to the subordinate's compliance, they have been unable to show that compliant behavior is necessarily an indication of internalization or of inner feelings. Feelings and attitudes, of course, are private and only partially communicable. Still, most powerless individuals comply with the demands of the powerful persons with whom they interact (parent-child, boss-employee). The need to internalize the submissive role, however, may be limited by several factors. First, the superordinate may be more interested in the behavior than in the inner feelings of the subordinate ("I don't care what you think as long as you do as I tell you"). Second, and most important, if the subordinate is not kept under constant surveillance, he can "play at" the role during the superordinate's rare direct observations and, when free of surveillance, behave in a decidedly different manner.

The subordinate may give deference at no emotional cost. He may, for instance, truly believe the superordinate worthy of his respect. If not, he may feign respect through the ritual of deference in spite of his low opinion of the superordinate. The subordinate is able to practice this deception because the superordinate frequently demands submission and deferential behavior more for an audience than for himself. For this reason, and often to maintain his belief in himself as a person worthy of respect, the superordinate may read more into a deferential act than the subordinate means to convey (misperception) or overlook minor lapses (selective inattention) in the submissive role played by the subordinate.[9] Taking advantage of the superordinate's misperception, the subordinate may overact, being very submissive and deferential, to deceive or to show his inner contempt for the superordinate and to preserve his own autonomy.[10] In this regard, Erving Goffman argues: "By easily showing a

9. Goffman, *Ritual*, 5–95; Richard M. Emerson, "Power-Dependence Relations," *American Sociological Review* XXVII (Feb. 1962), 31–41; Edgar F. Borgatta, "Role-Playing Specification, Personality and Performance," *Sociometry* XXIV (Sept. 1961), 218–33; R. D. Laing, H. Phillipson, and A. R. Lee, *Interpersonal Perception* (New York, 1966), 3–8.

10. Emerson, "Power-Dependence Relations," 31–41; Carl W. Backman and Paul F. Secord, "Liking, Selective Interaction, and Misperception in Congruent Interpersonal Relations," *Sociometry* XXV (Dec. 1962), 321–35.

regard that he does not have, the actor (subordinate) can feel that he is preserving a kind of inner autonomy." The rituals of deference are fleeting, highly formalized, almost unconscious acts which are often performed without too much psychological cost to the subordinate. This is especially true in institutions. Goffman asserts: "Where ceremonial practices (of deference) are thoroughly institutionalized . . . it would appear easy to be a person." [11]

The subordinate, often having to curb or repress his anger, may become excessively submissive, or he may focus his hostile feelings on a scapegoat, or make jokes which express his aggressive feelings toward the superordinate to avoid total dependency. Throughout this discussion, it must be remembered that every individual, however submissive he may be in one interpersonal relationship, interacts with other people where he is the dominant one. The greater the number of the latter, the less impact any one submissive stance makes on his personality.[12] In this regard, Sullivan has correctly observed that "every human being has as many personalities as he has interpersonal relations. . . ." [13]

In practically all interpersonal relationships, the subordinate has some independence, some power, some resources as long as he possesses something valued by the superordinate, whether it be labor or deference. McCall and Simmons noted this fact in their study of social interaction: "there are always some resources and choices open even to the most abject slave." [14]

In order to understand the resources and choices theoretically open to Southern slaves, it is necessary to examine "total" institutions. A total institution is a complex organization in which permanent or semi-permanent personal relationships are determined primarily by the demands, rules, and objectives of the organization, institutional roles are reinforced by ritual defer-

11. Goffman, *Ritual*, 58, 91.

12. Carson, *Interaction*, 93–171; Zaleznik and Moment, *Behavior*, 173–372; Bruce J. Biddle and Edwin J. Thomas, *Role Theory: Concepts and Research* (New York, 1966), 144–48, 195–200, 282–87, 313–17.

13. Ruitenbeek, *Varieties*, 143.

14. George J. McCall and J. L. Simmons, *Identities and Interactions* (New York, 1966), 157.

ence, rewards, and punishments, most of the needs of members are satisfied, and members are set apart (spatially and socially) in various ways from non-members. Psychological studies of compliance in such total institutions as concentration camps, prisons, and armies have shown that there is a close relationship between the kind of coercion, pain, torture, or threat of bodily harm that men are exposed to and their ability to resist the institutional norms. On the one hand, the "cruel" treatment (starvation, daily torture, and murder) that concentration camp inmates received caused them to be extremely submissive, infantile, and docile. On the other, the "mild" treatment (relatively adequate food and rare punishment) of prisoners and soldiers led them to be deferential toward their superordinates while rejecting their norms and participating in underground resistance to them. In fact, in institutions where superordinates are not so devoid of moral sense and so free of societal restraints that they can frequently kill subordinates, it would appear virtually impossible to crush all dissent, insubordination, rebellion, independence, and manhood in the organization's members. When the plantation is viewed as a total institution, it is obvious that the slave's personality was intimately bound up with the use of coercive power by his master.[15]

According to the black autobiographers, one of the most important factors affecting their struggle for personal autonomy was the frequency and the nature of the punishment meted out by masters and overseers. In his lifetime a slave usually had several owners; the black autobiographers included in this study had an average of three. While eight of the autobiographers had only one master, Charles Ball and William Grimes had eight and Moses Roper a phenomenal fourteen. As a consequence of having an average of three masters, the slaves were extremely conscious of the differences in human character and contended

15. Paul de Berker, ed., *Interaction: Human Groups in Community and Institution* (Oxford, England, 1969), 7–30; Amitai Etzioni, *A Comparative Analysis of Complex Organizations* (New York, 1961); Erving Goffman, *Asylums* (Garden City, N.Y., 1961), 1–74; see appendix.

that there was great variety among slaveholders. Henry Clay Bruce was typical. He wrote that his experience with many slaveholders: "taught him that all masters were not cruel. . . . While some masters cruelly whipped, half fed and overworked their slaves, there were many others who provided for their slaves with fatherly care, saw that they were well fed and clothed, would neither whip them themselves, nor permit others to do so." [16] Differences in severity of treatment affected behavior on the plantation in the same way that they determined the degree of docility and infantilism in prisons, armies, and concentration camps. Cruel masters caused one kind of behavioral pattern while kind or benevolent masters caused another in the quarters.

The slaves reacted in various ways to humane treatment. Generally, the master's kindness, confidence, and trust was repaid by faithful work on the part of the slave.[17] Bruce argued that a good master made slaves industrious and trustworthy: "The master who treated his slaves humanely had less trouble, got better service from them, and could depend upon their doing his work faithfully, even in his absence, having his interest in view always." [18] Robert Anderson agreed; on his plantation the slaves "were willing to put our best into the tasks when we were treated humanely." [19] Often the slaves were content with such masters. William Grimes demonstrated this clearly when he asserted: "Those slaves who have kind masters are, perhaps, as happy as the generality of mankind. They are not aware that

16. Henry Clay Bruce, *The New Man. Twenty-Nine Years A Slave. Twenty-Nine Years A Free Man* (York, Pa., 1895), iii.

17. Samuel Hall, *47 Years a Slave* (Washington, Iowa, 1912), n.p.; Solomon Northrup, *Twelve Years a Slave* (London, 1853), 78–104; Charles Ball, *Slavery in the United States: a Narrative of the Life and Adventures of Charles Ball* (Lewiston, Pa., 1836), 250–300; Jermain Wesley Loguen, *The Rev. J. W. Loguen, as a Slave and as A Freedman* (Syracuse, N.Y., 1859), 136–62, 178–211; William Wells Brown, *Narrative of William W. Brown, A Fugitive Slave* (London, 1893), 102–3; John Brown, *Slave Life in Georgia* (London, 1855), 158.

18. Bruce, *New Man*, 88.

19. Robert Anderson, *From Slavery to Affluence* (Hemingford, Nebraska, 1927), 32.

their condition can be better, and I don't know as it can. . . ." [20]

Many slaves identified their own interests with that of a kind master and worked diligently for him. They respected him and refused to steal from him or to lie to him. Lucius H. Holsey exemplified the slave's sense of identity with a kind master. His last owner was very kind, he wrote, and "had great confidence in me and trusted me with money and other valuables. In all things I was honest and true to him and his interests. Though young, I felt as much interest in his well being as I have felt since in my own. . . . I made a special point never to lie to him or deceive him in any way." [21]

Slaves identified with their owners for several reasons. Many, for example, worked faithfully for their masters because they expected to be freed at some future date. They were sometimes loyal because masters catered to their vanity or desire to stand out from the mass of slaves. With house servants this was often a matter of receiving fancy clothes. Louis Hughes, for instance, declared when his master gave him some new clothes, "I had known no comforts, and had been so cowered and broken in spirits, by cruel lashings, that I really felt light-hearted at this improvement in my personal appearance, although it was merely for the gratification of my master's pride; and I thought I would do all I could to please Boss." [22] One of the most frequent reasons for the slave's industriousness was the feeling that he had a stake in the successful completion of his work. Many slaves developed this feeling because the planters promised them money, gifts, dinners, and dances if they labored faithfully. [23]

Simple kindness did much to engender respect. John Mercer Langston's father, for instance, "gained the respect and confidence of all, and might very well trust his people, as was his

20. William Grimes, *Life of William Grimes The Runaway Slave, Brought Down to The Present Time* (New Haven, Conn., 1855), 36–48.

21. Lucius H. Holsey, *Autobiography, Sermons, Addresses, And Essays* (Atlanta, 1898), 10.

22. Louis Hughes, *Thirty Years a Slave* (Milwaukee, 1897), 63–64.

23. Ball, *Slavery*, 112–56; Henry Box Brown, *Narrative of Henry Box Brown* (Boston, 1851), 23–38; Hughes, *Thirty Years*, 39–58.

habit, to govern and direct, largely, their own movements." [24] Robert Anderson recalled that his master "was a very easy going man, kind and generous, and loved by all the plantation people. We colored folks did what he ask us to because we liked him." [25] On plantations where they were treated humanely, the slaves sometimes looked upon their master almost as a kindly father. Richard Allen described his master as "more like a father to his slaves than anything else. He was a very tender, humane man."[26] W. H. Robinson asserted that one of his masters "was a very kind, fatherly acting man." [27] One of Frederick Douglass's mistresses was so "kind, gentle and cheerful" that he "soon learned to regard her as something more akin to a mother, than a slave-holding mistress." [28]

Rarely did the slave identify with a master who frequently flogged and abused him. Even so, on plantations where masters and overseers were almost as morally insensitive, cruel, and sadistic as the guards in the German concentration camps, many of the slaves became docile, submissive, and Sambo-like. At the same time, unless the slave belonged to a planter who was mentally deranged, he had more elbow room than the German concentration camp inmates. In contrast to the camp inmate, the slave had greater freedom from the threat of death and had less need for abject servility in order to avoid it. Besides, unlike the camp inmate, the slave's life was worth considerably more than a bullet. Ultimately, this fact set limits on the amount of cruelty to which a slave was subjected. Within these limits, however, on many plantations abuse, constant floggings, cruelty, overwork, and short rations were part of the slave's daily life.

Faced with unrelenting cruelty and depressed at every turn,

24. John Mercer Langston, *From the Virginia Plantation To The National Capitol* (Hartford, Conn., 1894), 17.

25. Anderson, *From Slavery*, 19.

26. Richard Allen, *The Life, Experience, And Gospel Labors of the Rt. Rev. Richard Allen . . .* (Philadelphia, 1887), 6.

27. W. H. Robinson, *From Log Cabin To The Pulpit* (Eau Claire, Wis., 1913), 73.

28. Frederick Douglass, *My Bondage and My Freedom* (New York, 1855), 142.

Figure 49. Frederick Douglass

many of the slaves despaired of resisting abuse, lived in deadly fear of all whites, and soon lost all feeling of independence, self-respect, and sympathy for others.[29] Henry Bibb spoke for many when he declared that "It is useless for a poor helpless slave to resist a white man in a slaveholding state." The slave, subjected to the will of others "in all respects whatsoever," had, he declared, a feeling "of utter helplessness."[30] After describing an

29. Elizabeth Keckley, *Behind The Scenes* (New York, 1868), 29–38; Moses Roper, *A Narrative of the Adventures and Escape of Moses Roper From American Slavery* (London, 1840), 56–61,·70–99; Austin Steward, *Twenty-Two Years a Slave, and Forty Years a Freeman* (Rochester, N.Y., 1861), 13–19; James Watkins, *Narrative of the Life of James Watkins* (Bolton, England, 1852), 12–18.

30. Henry Bibb, *Narrative of the Life and Adventures of Henry Bibb, An American Slave* (New York, 1849), 317–19.

Figure 50. Austin Steward

extremely cruel beating, Thomas Jones asked: "Is it any wonder that the spirit of self-respect of the poor, ignorant slave is broken down by such treatment of unsparing and persevering cruelty?" [31]

The lash, frequently applied, was an awesomely successful fear-inducing instrument. James Mars received many floggings from his master of whom he "thought a great deal," but he also "stood greatly in fear of him and dreaded his displeasure, for I did not like the lash." [32] Henry Watson testified that all of his fellow slaves feared his mistress because of her frequent use of the lash, and, "as for myself, I was perfectly terrified when she

31. Thomas Jones, *The Experience of Thomas Jones, Who Was a Slave for Forty-Three Years* (Boston, 1850), 17.
32. James Mars, *Life of James Mars, A Slave Born and Sold in Connecticut* (Hartford, 1864), 21–22.

approached." [33] Frederick Douglass asserted that slaves were "accustomed from childhood and through life to cower before a driver's lash." [34] Sometimes the fear of punishment became unbearable. Lewis Clarke reported that he was so afraid of being flogged that he often walked in his sleep. Other slaves mutilated themselves or committed suicide rather than submit to painful floggings.[35]

Unremitting cruelty often subdued the slave and broke his will to resist. Charles Ball saw one slave whose spirit was so broken by the lash "that he was ready to suffer and to bear all his hardships; not indeed without complaining, but without attempting to resist his oppressors, or to escape from their power." The lash, frequently applied, often drained every ounce of manhood, of resistance, of self-respect, and of independence from the slave. Six months under a Negro breaker, Frederick Douglass declared, "succeeded in breaking me. I was broken in body, soul and spirit." William Wells Brown saw one proud black turned into a "degraded and spirit-crushed" man by three months of daily floggings and unremitting labor. Austin Steward contended that slavery was such a cruel institution that it "crushes and brutalizes the wretched slave." Josiah Henson argued that the slaveholders' tyrannical treatment turned "the slave into the cringing, treacherous, false, and thieving victim of tyranny." [36]

Often when his own punishment or the flogging of his fellows was practically an everyday occurrence, the slave grew indifferent to human sufferings. Sometimes he taunted those slaves who made unsuccessful attempts to escape or who were punished. Henry Watson, after years of service under cruel masters, finally reached the point where "his heart began to grow less feeling for the sufferings of others, and even indifferent to my own

33. Henry Watson, *Narrative of Henry Watson, A Fugitive Slave* (Boston, 1848), 23.

34. Douglass, *Bondage*, 120.

35. Ball, *Slavery*, 40–74, 245–58; Keckley, *Scenes*, 29–34; Grimes, *Life*, 24–33; Lewis G. Clarke, *Narrative of the Sufferings of Lewis Clarke* (Boston, 1845), 107–22.

36. Ball, *Slavery*, 89; Douglass, *Bondage*, 219; W. H. Brown, *Narrative*, 29; Steward, *Twenty-Two Years*, 26; Josiah Henson, *The Life of Josiah Henson* (Boston, 1849), 5.

punishment." [37] Jermain Loguen gave a perfect description of the slave's lot under a cruel master. Under his master, he

> had been driven along from day to day by dread of physical suffering, and the hope of escape from it. His affections were not allowed a moment's repose. It was ever a fearful looking for outrage of some kind, attended by an impractical determination not to bear it. His highest aim was to dodge the lash of a tyrant—his daily prayer, that his mother, sisters and brothers might not be subjects of new wrongs. So habited was he to wrongs, that he met them without disappointment, and endured them without complaint. [38]

Added to the slave's fear of the lash was the dread of being separated from loved ones. To be sold away from his relatives or stand by and see a mother, a sister, a brother, a wife, or a child torn away from him was easily the most traumatic event of his life. Strong men pleaded, with tears in their eyes, for their master to spare their loved ones. Mothers screamed and clung grimly to their children only to be kicked away by the slave trader. Others lost their heads and ran off with their children or vainly tried to fight off overseer, master, and slave trader. Angry, despondent, and overcome by grief, the slaves frequently never recovered from the shock of separation. Many became morose and indifferent to their work. Others went insane, talked to themselves, and had hallucinations about their loved ones. A few slaves developed suicidal tendencies. William Wells Brown described one slave woman who was so despondent over being forced to leave her husband that she drowned herself. Separation in many cases caused the slave to decide to run away and obtain his freedom. For most of the slaves, however, there was no recourse but to accept the inevitable. [39] Samuel Hall's reaction

37. Watson, *Narrative*, 32.
38. Loguen, *Freedman*, 162.
39. John Quincy Adams, *Narrative of the Life of John Quincy Adams, When in Slavery, and Now as a Freeman* (Harrisburg, Pa., 1872), 22–30; John Anderson, *The Story of the Life of John Anderson, A Fugitive Slave* (London, 1863), 8–20; William Green, *Narrative of Events in the Life of William Green* (Springfield, 1863), 6–8; Peter Randolph, *Sketches of Slave Life* (Boston, 1855), 16–19; Jacob Stroyer, *My Life in the South* (Salem, 1890), 41–44.

Figure 51. Solomon Northrup

was probably typical. When he was sold away from his wife and children, he wrote that "His soul rebelled against such subservience to men who called themselves masters and his temper was aroused to such a pitch that he was like a wild animal in a cage, conscious, in a way, of the hopelessness of his situation, but none the less tamed, or willing to admit that he was justly restrained." [40]

The cruel separations and constant floggings created a sense of despair among many of the slaves that was all consuming. They saw no hope of improving their condition. As a young

40. Hall, 47 *Years*, n.p.

man, Frederick Douglass wrote: "To my bondage I saw no end. It was a terrible reality, and I shall never be able to tell how sadly that thought chafed my young spirit." Feeling that even God had forgotten them, the slaves tried to resign themselves to their bleak fate. Certainly many of them must have felt what Jermain Loguen expressed: "no day dawns for the slave, nor is it looked for. It is all night—night forever." [41]

A number of the slaves were so oppressed that they accepted their master's claims about the rightness, the power, and the sanctity of whiteness and the degradation, the powerlessness, and the shame of blackness. As a result, some blacks wished passionately that they were white. James Watkins was treated so cruelly by his master that eventually, he declared: "I felt as though I had been unfortunate in being born black, and wished that I could by any means change my skin into a white one, feeling certain that I should then be free." [42]

The idea of the superiority of whites was etched into the slave's consciousness by the lash and the ritual respect he was forced to give to every white man. The impact of the planter's credo is revealed in the slave's reaction to kind and egalitarian treatment from whites. Jermain Loguen, who cried the first time he heard kindly words from whites, could not bear the thought of interacting with them on equal terms. Asked to play blind man's bluff with a white girl, he was horrified: "Under any circumstances he could not address Alice but as a superior being. For so humble and degraded a thing as he, purposely to put his hand on her person, seemed to him like trespassing on an angel." Many others were uncomfortable interacting with whites on terms of equality. The first time this occurred it was especially traumatic for the slave. Famished John Brown was unable to eat the delicious meal offered to him by a Quaker family when he escaped from slavery because they insisted that he eat at the table with them: "I was so completely abashed, and felt so out of my element, that I had no eyes, no ears, no understanding. I was quite bewildered. As to eating, it was out of the question." [43]

41. Douglass, *Bondage*, 156, 329.
42. Watkins, *Narrative*, 11.
43. Loguen, *Freedman*, 187; J. Brown, *Slave Life*, 158.

Regardless of how the slave felt about white supremacy, he reacted to cues from whites. He had to be a lifelong student of the white man's moods, ideas, and actions and then conduct himself according to the changes in the white man's behavior. John Brown reported that as a slave he "had been forced to watch the changes of my master's physiognomy, as well as those of the parties he associated with, so as to frame my conduct in accordance with what I had reason to believe was their prevailing mood at any given time." Jermain Loguen felt that all whites believed in maintaining the rituals of white supremacy, but "Whether they did or did not, it was all the same—for they ever acted upon that absurdity, and he was compelled to shape his life to it." [44]

Some slaves were compelled to shape their behavior so completely to the white man's moods that they became Sambos. Nowhere was Sambo more ubiquitous than among house servants and slaves on small plantations who lived in almost constant contact with whites. Because of the continual surveillance, these slaves had to go through the ritual of deference so often that they frequently internalized the submissive role. Often the master and slave lived and worked together on such intimate terms that they developed an affection for each other, and the slave identified completely with his master. Even if the slave initially had no affection for his master, the uninterrupted surveillance led so often to swift punishment for the smallest deviation from the submissive role that the domestic servant became extremely deferential and obsequious.

It is no accident that the Sambo of Southern novels and plays was usually a house servant. Because the planters often had little contact with field hands, in white autobiographies it is almost always the house servant who is portrayed as the epitome of loyalty. While the personal history of a number of house servants appears in white autobiographies, the field slaves are usually portrayed as an anonymous mass. One reflection of the faithfulness of house servants and the low level of contact between field hands and whites is that, in an overwhelming ma-

44. J. Brown, *Slave Life,* 106; Loguen, *Freedman,* 165.

jority of the cases where masters manumitted individual slaves, they were house servants.[45]

Unlike the house servant, the typical field slave was sullenly obedient and hostilely submissive. He escaped from total dependency, infantilism, and abject docility, however, because the plantation, unlike the German concentration camp, was not a rationally organized institution capable of crushing all discontent, guaranteeing identification of the subordinate with superordinates, completely abolishing family life and alternative referents of self-esteem to those provided by the institution. Whatever stance the slave was forced to adopt, his master could not watch him all of the time or control his thoughts. Having a variety of relationships, besides that with his master, the slave was able to preserve his self-esteem in spite of the cruel punishment he received. The docility of the slave was a sham, a mask to hide his true feelings and personality traits. Since masters recognized the contradiction between how they wanted the slaves to act and the slaves' true personalities, they often resorted to coercion to obtain the semblance of submission. Rarely did this coercion cause the slaves to identify with their masters. Whatever his behavior, the slave did not passively accept the portrait whites painted of him.

In spite of the ritual deference they gave to whites, the slaves frequently rejected the arguments of the Negro's inferiority and tried to prove that they were false. As a young slave, Austin Steward felt such charges were "utterly false." Jermain Loguen constantly heard claims about white superiority, but "Of course, he never believed in anything of the sort. . . ." Some blacks, distressed by the allegations of the Negro's dishonesty, stupidity, and indolence, tried to counter the charges by their own actions. Noah Davis was characteristic of many: "Nothing would mortify me as much, as to hear it said, 'A Negro can't be trusted.' This

45. Letitia M. Burwell, *Plantation Reminiscences* (Owensboro, Ky., 1878), 4, 37, 159–61; J. G. Clinkscales, *On the Old Plantation* (Spartanburg, S.C., 1916), 8, 40–41; James Stirling, *Letters from the Slave States* (London, 1857), 287–88; Kemp P. Battle, *Memories of an Old-Time Tar Heel* (Chapel Hill, 1945), 125–31; George Lewis, *Impressions of America* (Edinburgh, 1845), 129, 144, 160.

Figure 52. Moses Roper   Figure 53. Josiah Henson

saying would always nerve me with a determination *to be trustworthy*."[46]

The nature of Southern society prevented the slave's acceptance of all whites as superior beings. The poor whites, looked down upon and treated with contempt by the slaveholders, were viewed by the slave as lower in the scale of humanity than he was. Belonging to wealthy masters themselves, and frequently better fed, housed, and clothed than the poor whites, the slaves considered them far from superior beings. Instead, poor whites were the objects of ridicule, pity, and scorn in the quarters.[47] Henry Bibb felt that they were "generally ignorant, intemperate, licentious, and profane." Robinson reported that they were as illiterate and as oppressed as the Negroes: "When they went before their employer they put their hats under their arms, as any Negro would do, and usually they were as afraid of him as the Negro was of the overseer." Douglass declared that the poor whites were "the laughing stock" of the slaves. Robert Anderson wrote that in the quarters "the colored person who would asso-

46. Steward, *Twenty-Two Years*, 21; Loguen, *Freedman*, 165; Noah Davis, *A Narrative of the Life of Rev. Noah Davis, A Colored Man* (Baltimore, 1859), 16.

47. J. Brown, *Slave Life*, 62–68; R. Anderson, *From Slavery*, 26–30; Bibb, *Adventures*, 20–24; Steward, *Twenty-Two Years*, 101–2; Robinson, *Pulpit*, 21–26; J. H. Banks, *A Narrative of Events of the Life of J. H. Banks* (Liverpool, 1861), 16.

Figure 54.   J. W. C. Pennington   Figure 55.   Henry Bibb

ciate with the 'po' white trash' were practically outcasts, and held in very great contempt." Henry Clay Bruce revealed the depth of this contempt when he slapped the son of a poor white, to whom he had been hired, for "saucing" him and then refused to let the man flog him. Many years later he wrote: "I would be ashamed of myself, even now, had I allowed that poor white man to whip me." [48]

Some slaves did not have to look to the poor whites to discover the false base of the white supremacy argument; they found it, instead, in the ignorance, indolence, and dissolution of their masters. Josiah Henson, for example, frequently carried his drunken master home "with the pride of conscious superiority" and increasingly, as he ran the plantation practically unaided, he came to feel that his master was "absolutely dependent upon his slave." [49]

Several factors prevented the slaves from regressing to infantilism and abject docility. First of all, most of them lived on plantations containing twenty or more slaves. On such plantations it was impossible for the planters or their overseers to supervise every detail of slave life, and many of the slaves on these plantations had few personal contacts with whites as long as their work was generally satisfactory. Consequently, these slaves

48. Bibb, *Adventures,* 24; Robinson, *Pulpit,* 21; Douglass, *Bondage,* 344; R. Anderson, *From Slavery,* 29; Bruce, *New Man,* 66.
49. Henson, *Life,* 15, 21.

(especially field hands) rarely had to go through the ritual of deference. Even when planters spent all of their time on the plantations they only saw the field slaves at work.[50]

Often slaves did not have to be docile because it was more important to a planter that they adhere strictly to the rules of deference when other whites were around than when he was alone with them. Henry Clay Bruce reported that his owner, for instance, was a kind master who rarely required his slaves to assume a deferential posture. Yet, "he tried to appear to his neighbors what he was not, a hard master . . . in the presence of a neighbor he always scolded more, acted more crabbed, and he was harder to please than when alone with us, for as soon as the neighbor left, we could get along with him very well." [51]

It is obvious that many of the slaves recognized the customary deferential act for what it was, a ritual. It was so customary for many of them that they thought little about it. Since it was a habitual mode of behavior, many did not view the deferential act as a symbol of their degradation. Sometimes, in fact, they viewed it as one means of influencing their masters. Charles Ball, for example, reported that the slaves always had to approach their masters humbly, "but, in return, we generally received words of kindness, and very often a redress of our grievances." When Israel Campbell thought that his master was going to punish him, he became very humble. "I knew," he wrote, "that the best way to get around master was to be very humble . . . I set my wits to work to find out something that would please him." [52]

Another factor which sometimes contributed to the slave's self-esteem was his relationship with whites other than his master. Even when he had a cruel master, he might associate with other whites who treated him with kindness. Such associations elevated his self-respect and confidence.[53] While working in his

50. Stirling, *Letters*, 288; Mackay, *World*, I, 282–87; Margaret Devereux, *Plantation Sketches* (Cambridge, 1906), 9–10, 34.

51. Bruce, *New Man*, 84.

52. Ball, *Slavery*, 41; Israel Campbell, *An Autobiography* (Philadelphia, 1861), 62.

53. H. B. Brown, *Narrative*, 23–38; Loguen, *Freedman*, 149–64; Jones, *Experience*, 8–15.

Figure 56.
Isaac Jefferson

master's store, Thomas Jones developed a very close relationship with one of the white clerks. "I seemed to be lifted up by this noble friend at times, from the dark despair which settled down upon my life, and to be joined once more to a living hope of future improvement in my sad lot." Jermain Loguen's employment by an unusually egalitarian white family, he wrote, "cultivated my self-respect—brought forth the manly qualities of his nature— . . . refined his manners—elevated his aspirations. . . ."[54]

Many of the slaves survived almost indescribable cruelties because they were resigned to their fate. They simply had to make the best of the situation in which they found themselves. Henry Clay Bruce contended that there were many slaves, "who,

54. Jones, *Experience,* 12; Loguen, *Freedman,* 157.

though they knew they suffered a great wrong in their enslavement, gave their best services to their masters, realizing, philo-
sophically, that the wisest course was to make the best of their
unfortunate situation." Such slaves were determined to survive
however cruel their masters were. They were brutally realistic.
Frederick Douglass spoke for many of them when he asserted:
"A man's troubles are always half disposed of when he finds
endurance his only remedy." William Grimes indicated the brutal realism and the will to survive of many slaves when he declared that slavery was a cruel institution, "but being placed in
that situation, to repine is useless; we must submit to our fate,
and bear up, as well as we can, under the cruel treatment of
our despotic tyrants." [55]

One of the primary reasons the slaves were able to survive
the cruelty they faced was that their behavior was not totally
dependent on their masters. The slave had many other referents
for self-esteem, for instance, than his master. In religion, a slave
exercised his own independence of conscience. Convinced that
God watched over him, the slave bore his earthly afflictions in
order to earn a heavenly reward. Often he disobeyed his earthly
master's rules to keep his Heavenly Master's commandments
because he had greater fear for his immortal soul than for the
pain which could be inflicted on his body. Religious faith gave
an ultimate purpose to his life, a sense of communal fellowship
and personal worth, and reduced suffering from fear and anxiety.
In short, religion helped him to preserve his mental health.
Trust in God was conducive to psychic health insofar as it excluded all anxiety-producing preoccupations by the recognition
of a loving Providence. [56]

In the quarters the slave was rarely under the direct surveillance of his master. Here, he could be a man. He could express
his true feelings and gain respect and sympathy in his family

55. Bruce, *New Man,* iii; Douglass, *Bondage,* 65; Grimes, *Life,* 35.
56. Seward Hiltner, "The Contributions of Religion to Mental
Health," *Mental Hygiene* XXIV (July 1940), 366–67; P. E. Johnson,
"Religious Psychology and Health," *Mental Hygiene* XXXI (Oct. 1947),
556–66; "Symposium on Relationships Between Religion and Mental
Health," *American Psychologist* XIII (Oct. 1958), 565–79; Chapter 2.

circle. Friendship, love, sexual gratification, fun, and values which differed from those of the master were all found in the quarters.

Many were able to maintain their self-esteem because of their status in the quarters. This status was based on several factors. Generally, those slaves who held some important post in the plantation hierarchy were ascribed higher status in the quarters than the mass of slaves. The slaves also gained status and self-esteem by adding bright new clothes to the coarse, ill-fitting wardrobe that most slaves had, or because they were strong, intelligent, or comely.[57] The wealth of his owner enhanced the slave's status when dealing with whites and other slaves outside the plantation because it allegedly assured him better food, clothing, housing, and treatment. Then, too, whites were less likely to mistreat the slaves of wealthy than of poor planters.

The few slaves who learned to read gained immeasurable status in the quarters because they had a secret mirror on the outside world and could keep the others informed of events which were transpiring there. Henry Clay Bruce, for instance, wrote that among the slaves: "A Colored man who could read was a very important fellow." In addition, education elevated the slave's sense of personal worth in the midst of his afflictions. After Thomas Jones started learning to read secretly, he wrote that, "I felt at night, as I went to my rest, that I was really beginning to be a *man,* preparing myself for a condition in life better and higher and happier than could belong to the ignorant *slave."* [58] Since whites put so many restrictions upon slaves obtaining an education, the slaves themselves invested it with almost magical qualities.

So few slaves learned how to read and write that they had to develop other skills to maintain their personal autonomy. Most did this by carefully masking their true personality traits from whites, while adopting "sham" characteristics when interacting with them. According to Lucy Ann Delaney, slaves lived behind

57. Ball, *Slavery,* 15; J. Anderson, *Story,* 29–30; Hughes, *Thirty Years,* 59–63.
58. Bruce, *New Man,* 86; Jones, *Experience,* 18.

an "impenetrable mask . . . how much of joy, of sorrow, of misery and anguish have they hidden from their tormentors!" [59] On innumerable occasions the slaves' public behavior contradicted their private attitudes. For instance, they frequently pretended to love their cruel masters. Lewis Clarke argued that this was "the hardest work that slaves have to do. When any stranger is present we have to love them very much . . . [But when they were sick or dying] Then they all look glad, and go to the cabin with a merry heart." Austin Steward discovered the same practice among his fellow slaves when his mistress died: "The slaves were all deeply affected by the scene; some doubtless truly lamented the death of their mistress; others rejoiced that she was no more. . . . One of them I remember went to the pump and wet his face, so as to appear to weep with the rest." Similarly, when Jacob Stroyer's cruel master died, the slaves shed false tears: "Of course the most of them were glad that he was dead . . . [and some said,] 'Thank God, massa gone home to hell.' " [60]

The slaves dissembled, they feigned ignorance and humility. If their masters expected them to be fools, they would play the fool's role. Frederick Douglass described this trait of the slave. He asserted: "as the master studies to keep the slave ignorant, the slave is cunning enough to make the master think he succeeds." The slave frequently pretended to be much more humble than he actually was. When Jermain Loguen returned after an absence of several months to his rather despicable master, for example, he pretended to be happy. He wrote that he "went through the ceremony of servile bows and counterfeit smiles to his master and mistress and other false expressions of gladness." Later, Loguen fought with his master. [61]

The more the slaves yearned for freedom, the more passionately did they show disdain for it. They walked circumspectly for fear of arousing the wrath of the whites. Lunsford Lane re-

59. Lucy Ann Delaney, *From The Darkness Cometh The Light: Or Struggles for Freedom* (St. Louis, n.d.), 18.

60. Clarke, *Sufferings*, 113; Steward, *Twenty-Two Years*, 86; Stroyer, *My Life*, 31.

61. Douglass, *Bondage*, 81; Loguen, *Freedman*, 226.

vealed how the slave balanced on a tight rope between revealing his true character and incurring the anger of whites and masking his feelings and surviving:

> Even after I entertained the first idea of being free, I had endeavored so to conduct myself as not to become obnoxious to the white inhabitants, knowing as I did their power, and their hostility to the colored people. . . . First, I had made no display of the little property or money I possessed. . . . Second, I had never appeared to be even so intelligent as I really was. This all colored people at the south, free and slaves, find it peculiarly necessary for their own comfort and safety to observe.[62]

Often the slaves had to mask their feelings in their relations with their masters because of their attitudes toward whites. Most slaves hated and were suspicious of all whites. William Wells Brown contended: "The slave is brought up to look upon every white man as an enemy to him and his race. . . ." The treatment the slave received verified this suspicion and left him angry. For example, upon conversing with one group of regularly flogged and continuously mistreated slaves, William Webb "saw there was great anger among them about the way they were treated."[63]

Many slaves tried to drown their anger in the whiskey bottle,[64] and if not drowned, the anger welling up was translated into many other forms. Sometimes the slave projected his aggression onto his fellow slaves: he might beat up, stab, or kill one of his fellow sufferers. Generally, however, he expressed his resentment in rebellious language in the quarters. William Webb, for instance, frequently heard the slaves talking about wreaking vengeance on their masters, killing them, and appropriating their homes, food, clothes, and women. In addition to their empty

62. Lunsford Lane, *The Narrative of Lunsford Lane* (Boston, 1848), 31.

63. W. W. Brown, *Narrative,* 95–96; William Webb, *The History of William Webb* (Detroit, 1873), 21.

64. Douglass, *Bondage,* 251–56; Allen Parker, *Recollections of Slavery Times* (Worcester, Mass., 1895), 65.

threats of vengeance, the slaves customarily gave contemptible nicknames to their masters.[65]

Since the slave viewed all whites as enemies, his master as a tyrant, and himself as being without protection before the law, he generally developed a strong sense of loyalty to all blacks. Douglass wrote that the slaves on his plantation: "were as true as steel, and no band of brothers could have been more loving. There were no mean advantages taken of each other, as is sometimes the case where slaves are situated as we were, no tattling; no giving each other bad names . . . ; and no elevating one at the expense of the other. . . . We were generally a unit, and moved together." [66]

The code, of course, was not perfect; some blacks, especially house servants, could not be trusted. Those who violated the code, while currying the favor of their masters, became outcasts in the quarters and faced retaliation from their fellows. Consequently, often the elite slaves—drivers and house servants—were, in spite of the part they played in policing the plantation, extremely effective in protecting their fellows from the rigors of bondage. Domestic servants were the field slave's most important windows on the outside world and aides in trying to fathom the planter's psyche. Although forced to flog his fellows, a driver frequently allowed them to rest when the overseer was not around, or made his whip create more sound than pain. If he were especially trusted by his master, he doled out much more food than the master or overseer did.

Group solidarity in the quarters enabled the slaves to unite in their struggle against their masters.[67] The ideals in the quarters dictated hostility to and contempt for cruel masters and overseers. The slaves refused to work diligently when cruel masters and overseers were not watching them. Under the lash, the slave became an "eye servant." Robert Anderson asserted that when an overseer treated the slaves cruelly: "we . . . used our wits

65. James W. C. Pennington, *The Fugitive Blacksmith* (London, 1849), 72; Campbell, *Autobiography*, 31, 41, 67.

66. Douglass, *Bondage*, 269.

67. Northrup, *Twelve Years*, 223–62; Henson, *Life*, 15–25; J. Brown, *Slave Life*, 137–70.

to escape from all the work we could, and would lag behind, or shirk when he was not looking." Bruce declared that cruel treatment caused the slaves to work against the planter's best interests: "a mean and cruel master made shiftless, careless, and indolent slaves, who, being used to the lash as a remedy for every offense, had no fears of it, and would not go without it." They schemed to get revenge on their masters without incurring the risk of death. Their offensive weapons included the slowdown, riding their master's horses to death, stealing from him, and breaking his plows and hoes. They tried to avoid the lash by being inconspicuous: working neither too fast nor too slow, acting neither too intelligent nor too stupid. The relationship between master and slave was one continual tug of war. According to Allen Parker, "There was always a kind of strife between master and slave, the master on the one hand trying to get all the work he possibly could out of the slaves . . . and the slaves . . . trying to get out of all the work they could, and to take every possible advantage of their master. . . ." As a result of this strife, most slaves grudgingly labored for their masters and tried to repress their anger. They were at least restrained by the lash.[68]

Strong-willed blacks were restrained, but were not broken by the lash. William H. Heard declared that in spite of the cruel treatment meted out to the slaves, "many of them were never conquered." Rather than cower before the overseer's lash, they often cursed the man who inflicted the pain on them. Frederick Douglass reported that one slave woman, after being flogged severely: "was not subdued, for she continued to denounce the overseer, and to call him every vile name. He had bruised her flesh, but had left her invincible spirit undaunted." On many occasions the slaves proved their indomitability by refusing to cry out under the lash. Elizabeth Keckley, for instance, resisted the effort of her master to flog her and when he succeeded in doing so, she recalled that it was agonizing but did not break her spirit: "Oh God! I can feel the torture now—the terrible, ex-

68. R. Anderson, *From Slavery,* 32; Bruce, *New Man,* 41; Parker, *Recollections,* 62.

cruciating agony of those moments. I did not scream; I was too proud to let my tormentor know what I was suffering." [69]

In spite of the slave's general submissiveness, he might at any time resist his master or overseer. In every daily confrontation with his master violence threatened to erupt. Any spark could set off the reaction: carping criticisms for work the slave knew had been done well, or a clearly unjustified flogging, or almost anything else. The slave might submit to any and all abuse for years, then, suddenly fed up, fight any man who attempted to punish him. In many instances the slaves fought with or killed their masters and overseers when their temporary anger overcame their customary caution.

Many of the strongest, most industrious and intelligent slaves refused to submit passively to floggings. [70] Approaching the master or overseer directly, the slaves informed them that they would do the labor required of them, but that no man would whip them. William Wells Brown recalled that there was one strong and valuable slave on his plantation who had never been flogged and had often declared: "that no white man should ever whip him—that he would die first." With such slaves, the gun was an effective and necessary instrument of discipline. Young W. H. Robinson, for instance, wrote that although he wanted to obey his father's admonition that he "never pull off your shirt to be whipped," the sight of a gun in his master's hand, "knocked all of the manhood out of me." Generally, one white man could not whip such a slave. [71]

The relationship of the planters and overseers to the recalcitrant slave was a strange one. Generally, they feared him, particularly if he were noted for his strength. On innumerable occasions they refused to punish such a slave unless they could get him drunk, surprise him, or get other slaves or whites to

69. William H. Heard, *From Slavery To the Bishopric In the AME Church: An Autobiography* (Philadelphia, 1924), 26; Douglass, *Bondage*, 95; Keckley, *Scenes*, 34.

70. R. Anderson, *From Slavery*, 17–23; Bruce, *New Man*, 32–35, 88–96; Randolph, *Sketches*, 16–19; Isaac Mason, *Life of Isaac Mason as a Slave* (Worcester, Mass., 1893), 13–18; James Mars, *Life of James Mars, A Slave Born and Sold in Connecticut* (Hartford, 1864), 1–13.

71. W. H. Brown, *Narrative*, 18; Robinson, *Pulpit*, 25, 40.

overpower him. In most cases the masters tried to avoid trouble with the intractable slave because of his value as a worker. The only way he could be punished was to shoot him. Realizing this, many slaves parlayed it into better treatment: they threatened to run away, to fight, or to stop work if they were flogged. William Green, after fighting his master to a standstill when the latter tried to flog him for disobedience, declared that no man would whip him and if he were flogged, he would cease work. His master relented, Green declared, and "after this we made up and got along very well for almost a year." James Mars wrote that he refused to permit his master to flog him when he was sixteen, and from that time until he was twenty-one he had no more trouble with his master: "I do not remember that he ever gave me an unpleasant word or look." [72] Similarly, when Samuel Hall, Solomon Northrup, and Jermain Loguen fought rather than permit their owners to whip them their masters let them alone.[73] Frederick Douglass asserted that after he fought the Negro breaker, Covey, to prevent a flogging: "During the whole six months that I lived with Covey after this transaction, he never laid on me the weight of his finger in anger." According to Douglass, when a man resisted a flogging "Such floggings are seldom repeated by the same overseer. They prefer to whip those who are most easily whipped . . . and that slave who has the courage to stand up for himself against the overseer . . . becomes, in the end, a freeman, even though he sustain the formal relation of a slave." [74]

It is obvious from the discussion above that there was great variety in slave behavior. Some slaves were always docile; others were docile most of the time and rebellious at other times. Likewise, some resisted bondage throughout their lives in various ways, while others, generally docile, might be rebellious only once. In other words, the slave was no different in most ways from most men. The same range of personality types existed in the quarters as in the mansion. The slaves, it is true, were generally submissive and obedient in most of their relations with

72. Green, *Events*, 13; Mars, *Life*, 24.
73. Loguen, *Freedman*, 230–43; Northrup, *Twelve Years*, 105–61; Hall, *47 Years*, n.p.
74. Douglass, *Bondage*, 95, 246.

whites. Obviously, slavery could not have survived had it been otherwise.

While slaves were generally submissive, they did not regress to the infantile dependency, extreme obsequiousness, unquestioning obedience, and abject docility of the concentration camp inmate primarily because they were not treated as harshly as the inmates. Whatever the cruelty inherent in slavery, the slaves were not systematically starved, forced to stand naked for hours in freezing weather, worked eighteen hours daily, and customarily tortured and murdered as the concentration camp inmates were. While the German camp was such an efficient instrument of destruction that the monthly mortality rate was often 20 per cent and less than one per cent of the inmates in some camps survived, there was a natural *increase* in the slave population in the South. However much the black slave was overworked and underfed, he was not systematically starved and worked to death: Between 1830 and 1860 there was a 23 per cent natural increase in the slave population every decade. Because masters had a greater sense of morality and a greater interest in protecting their laborers than camp guards had toward inmates, the slave did not live in the shadow of death and did not have to center all of his energies on and tailor all of his behavior toward survival.

The important fact which emerges from the black autobiographies is that the master-slave relationship was not the only factor that determined the slave's behavior. Even when it was crucial, this relationship varied from master to master. The slave's behavior, attitudes, and degree of self-esteem also changed as he changed hands. Frequently, since he changed masters often and the behavior expected of him also changed, the impression that an individual owner made on his personality was minimal. In the end, the slave's personality was a composite of the effects on him of cruel and kind owners, of those who demanded ritual deference at all times and of those who demanded it occasionally, and of several other factors. Most slaves lived on such large plantations, had such little contact with their masters and overseers, or went through the ritual of deference so infrequently, that no master made an important impression on their personalities.

While the slave was customarily obedient and deferential to his master, this was not necessarily an innate character trait. He went through the ritual of deference in some cases because he recognized that it was mandatory for his survival. In most cases, he went through the ritual the way that most men perform habitual acts: with little thought about their symbolic significance. Besides, the deferential posture was not the only one the slave assumed. At the same time that he was deferential to his master, he also interacted with other human beings on other levels: he viewed poor whites with contempt, enjoyed the love, respect, and companionship of his family; thought of himself as superior to besotted, licentious masters; won praise, inspired admiration, acquired status, found companionship, obtained sexual gratification, dominated others, and played and relaxed in the quarters. Most importantly, he had a great deal of time free from observation by whites.

The resiliency of the slave was such that the infrequent occasions when he went through the ritual of deference were not sufficient to blot out the numerous other roles he played. Because of this there was a great variety of personality types among slaves. Henry Clay Bruce summed up this phenomenon perfectly:

> There were different kinds of slaves, the lazy fellow, who would not work at all unless forced to do so, and required to be watched, the good man, who patiently submitted to everything . . . and then there was the one who would not yield to punishment of any kind. . . . Then there was the unruly slave, whom no master particularly wanted for several reasons: first, he would not submit to any kind of corporal punishment; second, it was hard to determine which was the master or which the slave; third, he worked when he pleased to do so. . . . This class of slaves were usually industrious, but very impudent. There were thousands of that class, who spent their lives in their master's service doing his work undisturbed, because the master understood the slave . . . there were thousands of high-toned and high spirited slaves, who had as much self-respect as their masters, and who were industrious, reliable, and truth-

ful, and could be depended on by their masters in all cases.
. . . These slaves knew their own helpless condition. . . .
But . . . they did not give up in abject servility. . . .[75]

The typical slave used his wits to escape from work and punishment, preserved his manhood in the quarters, feigned humility, identified with masters and worked industriously only when he was treated humanely, simulated deference, was hostilely submissive and occasionally obstinate, ungovernable, and rebellious.

75. Bruce, *New Man,* 36–37.

Appendix:
Comparative
Examination
of Total Institutions

A comparison of such total institutions as armies, prisons, and concentration camps suggests several ways of examining slave behavior and the range of options open to the slave. From the comparison, it would appear that there is no deterministic relationship between institutional sanctions, roles, and subordinate status and submissiveness. Authorities in total institutions often maintain the façade of absolute control by setting behavioral standards so low that everyone can meet them, ignoring breaches of rules, and accommodating the strongest members of the subordinate group with better treatment. Those officials in closest contact with the subordinate group rarely apply the sanctions rigidly. Consequently, large numbers of individuals pretend to be submissive while preserving their own personalities. While authorities are misled by the outward pattern of deference, group conformity is based on fear rather than internalization of the institutional roles. Subordinate members are able to reject institutional expectations when they hold rigid religious beliefs, expect or accept their treatment as a sign of martyrdom, or can turn to their peer group or subculture for self-esteem, or values and expectations which differ from those of the institution.

The degree to which the members of institutions are able to avoid becoming abjectly docile is dependent on the kinds of power exercised, the level of surveillance, and the frequency of interaction. The ways in which these and other factors operate in large institutions similar to the plantation can be seen by examining armies, prisons, and concentration camps.

Scholarly studies of the army show that it is a closed, highly stratified, authoritarian, neo-feudal, paternalistic institution providing all the biological and psychological needs of its members except sex and family life. Rules control every aspect of the highly routinized existence and failure to obey all rules leads to punishment. Although the army uses the sanctions of personal humiliation, physical abuse, imprisonment, and death to enforce the rules, it tries to make its members internalize them. The most powerful group in the army consists of the aristocratic officers who expect deference, honor, and obedience from enlisted men and use their power to maintain status and to obtain special privileges. The non-commissioned officer, second in the army hierarchy, serves as an intermediary between officers and men, a channel of communications, and helps to enforce rules. At the bottom of the army hierarchy stands the enlisted man.[1]

Army life for the common soldier is a succession of deprivations and frustrations. This begins with the "shock" of basic training, his first weeks in the army. The new recruit is a helpless, insecure, scared, lone individual in a complex, bewildering new environment. One recruit asserted that in basic training "The recruit is warned and threatened, shouted at and sworn at, punished and promised further punishments, with such frequency and from so many sides that he gets to be like the rat in the neurosis production experiment."[2] Exploited by veterans, physically exhausted, constantly repeating his actions, the recruit often loses his initiative and develops a sense of infantile dependency and personal degradation. He soon fears the army and internalizes some of its rules.[3]

1. Hugh Mullian, "The Regular-Service Myth," *American Journal of Sociology* LIII (January 1948), 276–81; Samuel Andrew Stouffer, *et al.,* *The American Soldier: Adjustment During Army Life* (4 vols., Princeton, N.J., 1949), I, 54–57; Arnold Rose, "The Social Structure of the Army," *American Journal of Sociology,* LI (March 1946), 361–64; "Life in the U.S. Army; Fantasy-Land, Peace-Time Variety," *Commentary* XXVI (September 1958), 227–38.

2. Stouffer, *Soldier,* I, 412.

3. Stouffer, I, 410–413; August B. Hollingshead, "Adjustment to Military Life," *American Journal of Sociology* LI (March 1946), 439–50; "Life in the U.S. Army," 227–37; Howard Brotz and Everett Wilson, "Characteristics of Military Society," *American Journal of Sociology* LI (March 1946), 371–75.

Although the soldier internalizes some of the ideals of the army, fear of punishment is the primary inducement to obedience. Moreover, there is general contempt for the soldier who lives by the rules. The average soldier tries to be inconspicuous. He "goldbricks," doing just enough of the boring, nonsensical tasks to avoid punishment. He deprecates but bitterly accepts authority while rejecting the army's degrading image of himself.

Psychologist Dearborn Spindler argued that American society does not prepare young American males for the strict obedience demanded in the army. In fact, he asserted, the female-dominated American family leads to an "inflation of the growing child's ego, to the extent that he may always be reluctant to surrender it to any group or interest not for his direct personal benefit or be placed in a subordinate position." [4] Whatever the reason, enlisted men do not completely accept the army as a substitute parent. Instead, during his free time the soldier asserts his independence and seeks to regain his pride through rebellious language, drinking, bragging, cursing his officers, and uninhibited sexual exploits. In spite of frequent turnover in personnel, face-to-face contacts, common grievances, and a special language bind the enlisted men together in their underground resistance to the formal control of the officers. According to one sociologist, "The informal social group of enlisted men may supplement, interpret, or even effectively negate the directives of the formal social organization." [5] The norms of the soldier's peer group are often more important than those of his officers.[6] Contrary to army ideals, these norms, according to Samuel Stouffer, may require him "to curb his desire to be industrious or efficient,

4. G. Dearborn Spindler, "American Character As Revealed in the Military," *Psychiatry* XI (August 1948), 280.

5. "Informal Social Organization in the Army," *American Journal of Sociology* LI (March 1946), 365.

6. Frederick Elkin, "The Soldier's Language," *American Journal of Sociology* LI (March 1946), 414–22; Stouffer, *Soldier*, I, 413–29; "Informal Social Organization in the Army," *American Journal of Sociology* LI (March 1946), 365–70; Spindler, "Character," 275–78; Henry Elkin, "Aggressive and Erotic Tendencies in Army Life," *American Journal of Sociology* LI (March 1946), 408–13; Douglas Scott, "The Negro and the Enlisted Man: An Analogy," *Harper's Magazine* CCXXV (October 1962), 19, 21.

desire to compete or get ahead, from fear of his fellows. . . ." [7]
Officers neither communicate with the soldiers nor understand how they feel. The great social distance between the two groups frequently causes the officers to misinterpret the troops' actions. For instance, officers almost uniformly grossly overestimate the respect enlisted men have for them.[8] Samuel Stouffer concluded in his four-year study of the army: "Officers could easily be misled by the rituals of deference exacted from all enlisted men.

. . . It is easy to understand how during the course of time they could come to mistake these compulsory outward symbols of deference for voluntary respect and fail to perceive underlying hostilities and resentments." [9] Similarly, the non-com, subjected to the resentment and pressure of the enlisted men with whom he socializes and shares the inequalities of army life, also misleads the officers. He conforms to the soldiers' demand for sympathy behind a façade of strict obedience to his officers.[10]

Another total institution is the prison. Subject to absolute authority, playing a restricted number of roles, physically isolated from loved ones, uncertain about the future, prisoners sometimes lose their initiative, show extreme dependency, and are indifferent to other prisoners. Life is routinized and impersonalized. Prisoners are often described as lazy and stupid.[11]

Although theoretically prisoners are under absolute control, the institution, according to an anthropologist who served two years in prison, is divided into two "enemy camps [that] coexist in an atmosphere of mutual fear and hostility." Consequently, there is "the appearance of conformity within the official system, and an underground pattern of nonconformity by which the individual inmate tries to live by his own codes, preserving as

7. Stouffer, *Soldier*, I, 413.
8. Stouffer, I, 391–95; Spindler, "Character," pp. 275–81; Arnold Rose, "The Social Structure of the Army," *American Journal of Sociology* LI (March 1946), 361–64.
9. Stouffer, I, 396.
10. Stouffer, I, 401–10; anonymous, "Informal Social Oganization in the Army," *American Journal of Sociology* LI (March 1946), 365–70.
11. A. J. W. Taylor, "Social Isolation and Imprisonment," *Psychiatry* XXVI (November 1961), 373–76.

best he can his personal preferences and habits." [12] The inmate's personal adjustment is bolstered by group acceptance. The code of the group dictates hostility to the administration, rejection of the administration's myths of justice and equality, and places high values on group loyalty, courage, and power.[13]

The officials recognize the higher status of some prisoners by giving them better jobs as a means of control. Two prison officials, McCorkle and Korn, report that in giving the best jobs to the most powerful inmates "the institution buys peace with the system by avoiding battle with it." [14] This same pattern of avoidance is reflected in the euphemistic "hard labor" of prisons. Generally inmates not only refuse to work more than the prison tradition requires, but take reprisals on prisoners who do more work than others.[15]

Among total institutions, the German concentration camp stands in stark contrast to armies and prisons. First, the inmates went through the "shock" of arrest and imprisonment for unknown reasons and under the most painful and bewildering conditions. Jammed into railroad cars and transported hundreds of miles often in freezing weather, they were forced to stand sometimes for seventeen hours without food or water, and systematically whipped, shot, and bayonetted. Totally isolated from their usual cultural surroundings, family, and the opposite sex, the inmates worked from twelve to eighteen hours daily. There was no privacy and they were under the constant surveillance of the guards. Prisoners were deliberately degraded, starved, tortured, and exterminated. One of the strongest forces ruling them was the anarchy of accident: they could be suddenly killed

12. M. Arc, "The Prison 'Culture'—From the Inside," *New York Times Magazine* (February 28, 1965), p. 52.

13. Lloyd W. McCorkle and Richard Korn, "Resocialization Within Walls," *Annals of the American Academy of Political and Social Science* CCXCIII (May 1954), 88–98; Donald Clemmer, *The Prison Community* (New York, 1965 [1940]), 83–133; Robert C. Atchley and M. Patrick McCabe, "Socialization in Correctional Communities: A Replication," *American Sociological Review* XXXIII (October 1968), 774–85; Arc, "Prison 'Culture,'" 52–63.

14. McCorkle and Korn, "Walls," 91.

15. McCorkle and Korn, "Walls," 91–92.

for doing or not doing almost anything; punishment was completely arbitrary. As a result of the torture, physical deprivation, and unremitting labor, 75 per cent of the new prisoners died within six months; the monthly mortality rate was about 20 per cent; and in some camps the survival rate was less than one per cent.[16]

The objectives of the camps were to make inmates docile, to train the Gestapo in the best terror-producing devices, and to exterminate an "undesirable" population group. The prisoners received the kind of punishment from the guards that helpless children receive from cruel fathers and led an extremely routinized existence. According to one survivor, Bruno Bettelheim, "Every single moment of their lives was strictly regulated and supervised."[17] The guards aimed at a total regression of the inmate to infantilism. In the process they played on cultural determinants of disgust and guilt. While German culture placed a high value on cleanliness, filth was the enforced norm in the camps. Prisoners were often tortured or forced to fight each other for food. Sometimes they had to drink water or eat their food from toilet bowls.

With death and starvation as their constant companions, the prisoners naturally centered practically all of their energies on self-preservation. The concentration camp, rationally organized by a powerful national government as an instrument of pain and death, systematically tried to crush the inmate's will. As a result, many prisoners became child-like, boastful, and dishonest; they identified with their oppressors, developed a sense of detachment to the cruelties inflicted on fellow prisoners, lost control of bodily functions, did not resist their guards, and had no

16. Peter Phillips, *The Tragedy of Nazi Germany* (London, 1969), 185–205; Christopher Burney, *The Dungeon Democracy* (London, 1945); Leon Szalet, *Experiment "E"* (New York, 1945); David Rousset, *The Other Kingdom* (New York, 1947); Elie Cohen, *Human Behavior in the Concentration Camp* (New York, 1953); Olga Lengyel, *Five Chimneys: The Story of Auschwitz* (Chicago, 1947), 7–22; Eugen Kogon, *The Theory and Practice of Hell* (New York, 1946), 66–90.

17. Bruno Bettelheim, "Individual and Mass Behavior in Extreme Situations," *Journal of Abnormal Psychology* XXXVIII (October 1943), 417.

hatred for their oppressors after liberation. The inmate's sole interest was apparently in self-preservation. Not only was there practically no concern with sex, but as a result of starvation, fatigue, trauma, and fear of death, males became impotent, women stopped menstruating, and the beginning of menstruation was delayed several years for most young girls. The psychical shock of the concentration camp experience was so great that many previous physiological and psychosomatic diseases became dormant.[18]

In spite of the barbaric treatment they received, the reaction of the German concentration camp inmates was not simply submission. Often living with the daily odors from the crematoria, many prisoners lost their fear of death. According to Bettelheim, because of the arbitrary punishment of the inmates "all rules were broken." [19] Losing their status, suffering from lack of affection, unable to leave the camp, the inmates envied, hated, and were contemptuous of the guards. Hatred sometimes led to intra-group fights, insubordination, and a few rebellions and attempts to escape.

Among the old prisoners, and especially criminals, a number accepted the guards as father figures and identified with them. The highest ranking inmates (prominents) in the camp hierarchy were more likely to accept the values of the guards and copy their verbal and physical aggressions than were other prisoners. The number of ordinary prisoners who identified com-

18. Bruno Bettelheim, *The Informed Heart* (Glencoe, Illinois, 1960); Peter Oswald and Egon Bittner, "Life Adjustment After Severe Persecution," *American Journal of Psychiatry* CV (February 1949), 601–5; Wolfgang Lederer, "Persecutions and Compensations," *Archives of General Psychiarty* XII (May 1965), 464–74; V. A. Kral, "Psychiatric Observation Under Severe Chronic Stress," *American Journal of Psychiatry* CVIII (September 1951), 185–92; G. W. Allport, J. S. Bruner, E. M. Jandorff, "Personality Under Social Catastrophe: Ninety Life Histories of the Nazi Revolution," *Character and Personality* X (September 1941), 1–22; Curt Bondy, "Problems of Internment Camps," *Journal of Abnormal Psychology* XXXVIII (October 1943), 453–75; Paul Friedman, "Some Aspects of Concentration Camp Psychology," *American Journal of Psychiatry* CV (February 1949), 601–5; *Commentary* XXV (January 1958), 80–83.

19. Bettelheim, "Individual," 422.

pletely with their aggressors, however, was small. Hilde Bluhm's study of a large number of the narratives of concentration camp inmates confirms this fact.[20] Those individuals who had a prior love object with whom they identified strongly were least likely to identify with the guards. Even among the old inmates, the identification was apparently not complete. Bettelheim observed in his camp that "these same old prisoners who identified with the Gestapo at other moments defied it, demonstrating courage in doing so." [21]

As Bluhm has observed, it is easy to explain death and infantilism among the camp inmates. The difficult thing is to explain how some of them survived psychologically. The degree of psychological damage depended on the physical stamina of the inmate, his nationality, his social position in the camp, food, kind of work, and condition of the camp. The duration and brutality of imprisonment also strongly affected behavioral patterns. It must be remembered that the German camps ranged from forced labor to extermination centers. Several investigators noted that the degree of regression to childhood depended on the kind of treatment (frequency and nature of torture, amount of food, etc.) that the inmates received. While the very old and the very young fared worse physically and psychologically, children and adolescents were not as deeply affected by the camp experience. Women adjusted more easily than men and very religious people had a higher psychological survival rate than non-religious ones.[22]

Those persons who belonged to groups with ideals differing greatly from those of the Nazis survived with their prior personalities relatively intact. The Jehovah's Witnesses, Gypsies, political prisoners, non-Germans, and members of primary groups who had been imprisoned at the same time cooperated to protect

20. Hilde O. Bluhm, "How Did They Survive? Mechanisms of Defense in Nazi Concentration Camps," *American Journal of Psychotherapy* II (January 1948), 25.

21. Bettelheim, "Individual," 451.

22. Kral, "Stress," 185–92; Bundy, "Problems," 453–75; Bettelheim, "Individual," 417–22; Cohen, *Camp*, 115–210; Szalet, *Experiment*, 69–73; Rousset, *Kingdom*, 52–62.

each other and refused to abandon entirely the prior cultural determinants of their status and behavior. In fact, members of these groups regarded themselves as martyrs, gained some esteem because they had been considered dangerous enough to be imprisoned, and considered themselves superior to their oppressors. The individual's previous character, group consciousness, and sense of responsibility often prevented personality disintegration. The earlier in life one's struggle for survival had begun, the easier it was to withstand the trauma of the camp experience. Those persons, for instance, who had some previous experience with prisons adjusted better than non-criminals because they had some idea of what to expect. Those inmates with prior referents of self-esteem suffered less than middle class prisoners. For example, in spite of the fact that one's previous status had no relationship to status inside the camp, upper class persons often developed a greater sense of superiority after being imprisoned.[23]

In comparing the behavioral patterns of concentration camp inmates, prisoners, and soldiers, it would appear that the most important factor in causing infantilism, total dependency, and docility in the camps was the real threat of death which left few, if any, alternatives for the inmates. Undoubtedly, the fact that soldiers and prisoners were not systematically starved or worked until they were totally exhausted left them with enough energy to engage in covert resistance and group practices which were at variance with institutional norms.[24] In other words, it is easier to maintain personal autonomy in organizations where deviations from the institutionally defined behavioral patterns are not met swiftly and invariably by brutal punishment, torture, and death than in organizations where inmates are continuously faced with cruel and inhuman treatment and with death. Without the frequent use of coercive power, it is impos-

23. See footnote 22, Bluhm, "Survive," 3–32; Allport, "Catastrophe," 1–22; Burney, *Dungeon*, 36–49.

24. One important difference among total institutions was that the soldiers and prisoners are often "attached" to them for a short time. Certainly the behavior of soldiers might also be affected by their sense of patriotism.

sible to force the subordinate to regress to infantile dependency, where his sole concern is to insure his self-preservation through abject docility. Placed on a continuum of total institutions, the concentration camp is far removed from the Southern plantation. Still, an examination of the camp is useful for it illustrates several things. Based on the analysis of the camp experience, it is obvious that a rationally planned, relatively fully staffed twentieth-century organization utilizing all of the scientific knowledge available, could make helpless, child-like dependents of large numbers of people through a variety of techniques. In contrast, the plantation was irrationally organized and understaffed with bureaucrats and guards; it was not aimed at the extermination of its laborers, it emerged when the science of psychology was in its infancy, and could not keep its laborers under constant surveillance, could not survive if it systematically tortured, starved, or exterminated its inmates; it permitted some form of sex and family life to inmates who performed a valuable service and did not live with the daily smell of death. While the concentration camp differed significantly from the plantation, it illustrates how, even under the most extreme conditions, persecuted individuals can maintain their psychical balance because of group solidarity, prior experience in similar institutions, religious ideals, a culture differing greatly from that of their oppressors, prior referents for self-esteem, and physical stamina. If some men could escape infantilism in a murderous institution like the concentration camp, it may have been possible for the slave to avoid becoming abjectly docile in a much more benign institution like the plantation.

Critical Essay on Sources

Sources left by slaves, and especially the autobiography, have been utilized more heavily in this study than others primarily because there is no better way to investigate the slave's personality than through his personal records. Since slaves have left so few letters and diaries, the autobiography provides the interested observer with the largest body of personal material dealing with the intimate details of their lives. If historians seek to provide some understanding of the past experiences of slaves, then the autobiography must be their point of departure; in the autobiography, more clearly than in any other source, we learn what went on in the minds of black men. It gives us a window into the "inside half" of the slave's life which never appears in the commentaries of "outsiders." Autobiographers are generally so preoccupied with conflict, those things blocking their hopes and dreams, that their works give a freshness and vitality to history which is often missing in other sources.

Autobiographies are especially important in any study of the slave's personality development. There is generally so much ego involvement in the autobiographies that they are invaluable for studies of black self-concepts. Since these works focus on the mental life of the authors (fear, love, pain, dreams, insecurity, frustrations), they provide the scholar with numerous insights into the nature of interpersonal relations during slavery. At the same time, such works place the general conditions under which slaves existed in America in the context where they have the most meaning, their personal lives. While other sources are important in any general description of the institution of slavery, they rarely tell us much about how blacks *perceived* their experiences. Yet, psychologists have constantly pointed out that how people perceive objective conditions is, under most circumstances, more important in determining their attitudes and how they act than the "reality" of the situation. The chief value of the autobiography lies in the fact that it is subjective, that it tells us a great deal about how blacks felt about the conditions under which they lived. Since no other large body of material written by blacks is so profoundly introspective, and since no one can know as much about blacks as they themselves knew, black autobiographies are crucial for an understanding of the slave experience.

There are, of course, several problems involved in the use of them. Even so, it is possible to examine autobiographies systematically by applying the rules of evidence rigidly. Four works which are especially helpful in establishing a framework for using autobiographies are: Ernest S. Bates, *Inside Out: An Introduction to Autobiography* (1936), G. W. Allport, *The Use of Personal Documents in Psychological Science* (1942), Roy Pascal, *Design and Truth in Autobiography* (1960), and John H. Wigmore, *The Principles of Judicial Proof* (1931).

One of the major shortcomings of autobiographies (though common to other sources) is that few men are able to tell the *whole* truth about themselves. Almost inevitably they exaggerate the difficulties they faced and make themselves more heroic than they were in real life. The unconscious plays tricks on the conscious; some things are either too painful to recall or to reveal to others. Undoubtedly this was a serious problem for black men as they contemplated the hostile audience to which they were addressing themselves. Could they really strip themselves bare before white America? Even if they had been able to overcome these problems, however, the black autobiographers were confined by the conventions of the genre they were using. In nineteenth-century autobiographies, a discussion of sex was taboo and family secrets were too sacred to reveal. For those accustomed to twentieth-century canons of literary taste, these limitations would almost rule out analysis altogether. While they certainly make the task more difficult, the problems are not insurmountable. Some men, of course, violated the conventions; and when they did not, an unguarded slip of the pen here and an innuendo there often provide clues to topics not explored in depth.

The usefulness of any autobiography is affected by the objectives, age, and memory of the author. Generally speaking, the black autobiographies were written to leave records for relatives and historians, to raise money, and as polemical attacks on the institution of slavery. With the objectives clearly stated, it is usually possible to separate fact from opinion, myth, and propaganda. On the other hand, it is often impossible to determine the impact of the age of the author on the reliability of his autobiography. While it is true that old age distorts memory, psychologists have found that old people tend to have far less difficulty in recalling events which occurred in the remote than the recent past. Then, too, the aging process operates differently in different individuals; some eighty-year-old men have more vivid memories than some fifty-year-old men. Consequently, every autobiography must be evaluated on its own merit. At the same time, it is obvious that if a majority of the authors in a sample of autobiographies were senile, the chances of error and distortion would be great. In regard to the black autobiographers included in this study, it would appear that they wrote their accounts long before the age at which senility usually occurs: 41 per cent published their books before they reached the age of fifty, and 71 per cent before they were sixty. The average age of the authors when they published their accounts was fifty-two years.

Because an autobiography is the record of what one person has seen and experienced, the stories of the men and women included in this study have been verified by investigating several independent sources. Since the autobiographies were often concerned with things which rarely, if ever, appeared in other sources, however, it was often impossible to check the experiences of an individual narrator against independent records. Consequently, it was generally more fruitful to compare the experiences of one autobiographer with those of others, and to accept exceptional events as truthful if everything else in the individual's account appeared to be true.

The inevitable question which arises in connection with autobiographies is: "Are they representative?" It must be admitted, of course, that the black autobiographers were unique in that they were either literate enough to describe their experiences or lucky enough to get sympathetic whites to do so. While recognizing this fact, it must be remembered that this is not peculiar to this genre. Autobiographies are just as representative as other kinds of literary material (perhaps more so). Any historian who deals with such material is forced to ignore the illiterate masses and recognize that many of these sources have been preserved only by accident. Probably no historian, for example, will ever know how much our portrayal of Southern society would have been altered if small planters and poor whites had left as many records as the large planters have. In a sense, all studies based on literary records are selective, the people they describe are "atypical," their generalizations apply only to that small percentage of the population which has left written records.

Like most personal documents, the autobiography provides a window to the larger world. In this sense, the slave writers present a participant observer's comments on the larger slave society. As an eye-witness, the autobiographer brings the historian into contact with almost all kinds of slaves. When the autobiographies are accepted both as records of the unique experiences of each individual author and as eyewitness accounts of several slave communities, they are clearly "representative."

The crux of the matter, of course, is what is meant by "representative." Whether explicit or implicit, the representative slave for many Americans is a composite of myths long perpetuated by historians and the white man's stereotypes of blacks. Since blacks have been the invisible men of American scholarship, certainly real black men have as much claim to representativeness as the mythological slave. This is especially true because the historian has ignored blacks for so long that we have few objective facts to use to construct a profile of the "average" or representative slave. Rather than testing the autobiographers against the mythological average slave, it may be better to reverse the procedure. Historians must use autobiographies the same way they have used other kinds of literary sources, recognizing both their uniqueness and their representativeness.

A more serious question than representativeness is the reliability of that which is revealed in the autobiography. This is especially true in regard to the autobiographies of fugitive slaves. Many historians refuse to use these accounts because they have felt the fugitive, as the primary sufferer in the institution, was unable to give an objective account of bondage. This is obviously true. At the same time, most historians realize that few individuals are able to give completely objective accounts of things and persons with whom they were associated intimately. Inasmuch as all commentators were prejudiced in some way, slaves cannot be dismissed because of their biases. Historians can no longer discount the narratives while using other material from even more biased witnesses. Stanley Elkins, for example, in his study of slavery illogically rejected the slaves' accounts because of their alleged bias while relying heavily on Bruno Bettelheim's concentration camp narrative which several American psychological journals rejected because it lacked objectivity. Significantly, Bettelheim's answer to his critics was that in regard to the concentration camps "the persons most able to discuss them are former prisoners, who obviously are more interested in what happened to them than why it happened." (Bruno Bettelheim, "Individual and Mass Behavior in Extreme Situations," *Journal of Abnormal Psychology* XXXVIII [October 1943], 418; Bruno Bettelheim, *The Informed Heart* [1960], p. 118.) Instead of rejecting the narratives *in toto,* investigators must use those which pass the tests commonly applied to historical documents. The slave, like the master, gave *his* view of the institution. Both distorted reality as they viewed the world through their respective lenses. In a sense, their views represent two sides of a coin. The distortions cancel themselves out and we are left, if we study both views, with a clear impression of the institution. If nothing else, both views reveal how the participants felt about the institution.

One cannot concede, however, that there is no validity in the slave narratives. Most of them have the ring of truth. Many of the writers, for instance, analyzed slavery in relatively dispassionate terms. The portrait of the institution of slavery which emerges from the narratives is not the simple picture of hell on earth that most historians have led us to believe they contain. Instead, the fugitives' plantations are peopled with the same range of heroes and villains, black and white, which one generally finds in the human race. The narratives add an important dimension to the story of slavery: the black's life within, and reaction to, the institution. There is, of course, no better way to explore this important facet of bondage than through the words of the slave himself.

Many historians refuse to accept the narratives as the actual words of the slaves. They point to the well-known fact that some of the fugitives had abolitionist amanuenses as sufficient reason to discount the narratives. Unfortunately, since they have not read many of the narratives, these historians have no way of knowing what percentage of them were, in fact, edited by the abolitionists. Many of the fugitives had received enough education and had associated long enough with educated whites to have written their *own* stories. On the other hand, such narratives as those of Solomon Bayley, G. W. Offley, and Andrew Jackson are so lacking in style, so woefully ungrammatical, and so straightforward that they could only have been written by relatively uneducated men. In other instances, a check of the narrative against other writings of the fugitives reveals unmistakable similarities in style. I have compared, for example, the narratives with numerous antebellum letters, speeches, sermons, and books published by such fugitives as James W. C. Pennington, Henry Bibb, and Jermain Loguen.

Probably a little more than half of the fugitive slave narratives were written by abolitionists. Often these were not distorted, but rather written as dictated by the fugitive or copied from court and church records. Believing that truth alone could destroy slavery, many of the editors felt no need to embellish the story. Fabrications, of course, would not help the anti-slavery cause. The abolitionists were seriously embarrassed, for instance, when a Negro, passing himself off as a fugitive, manufactured a story and tricked John Greenleaf Whittier into editing it for him—the slaveholders had a field day exposing the fraudulent *Narrative of James Williams*. It is significant that the abolitionists checked the authenticity of the other accounts so thoroughly that there were no comparable exposés during the antebellum period. Instead of exaggerating the horrors of slavery, it is clear in some instances that the editors toned down the accounts. The editor of Charles Ball's narrative, for example, asserted that he had excluded the slave's bitterness and that "Many of his opinions have been cautiously omitted" (p. ii).

There were, of course, some narratives which were edited heavily by the abolitionists. These, however, can be identified relatively easily. In fact, one can often discover the points in the narratives where the editor interpolated his own views. His literary flourish, sweeping condemnation, and stirring appeals generally contrast sharply with the monotonous details of daily routine supplied by the slave. The most heavily edited narratives are generally very short, stress generalization rather than details, focus on the escape from, rather than the routine of, slavery, and are diatribes on unbelievably fiendish masters who terrorized the perfectly angelic slave. These furnished little evidence for this study.

It is perhaps even easier to detect the fictional and largely fictional slave narratives than the heavily edited ones. Richard Hildreth's *Archy Moore: Or the White Slave* (1836), and Peter Nielson's *The Life of Zamba* (1850), for example, were among the best antebellum fictional narratives. While Hildreth almost knew enough about slavery to palm off his novel as a true account of a fugitive slave, none of the other novels approach the verisimilitude of the real narratives. Frequently, for instance, the novelists had their heroes engaging in practices almost totally foreign to slavery. The best example of this is the story of a fugitive slave written by the Englishman, Charles Lee. In the story, purportedly narrated by Francis Fedric, *Slave Life in Virginia and Kentucky* (1863), all of the slaves are chaste, cunning, and courageous. The reader begins to question the validity of the account when Lee records the slaves frequently shaking hands with slaveholders, talking about running off to Canada in the presence of their masters, using such expressions as "fie" and "bid you fare you well," and offering high opinions of Great Britain and of Englishmen.

In some of the fictional accounts, the major character may have been a real fugitive, but the narrative of his life is probably false. *Aunt Sally: Or the Cross the Way to Freedom* (1858), distributed by the American Reform Tract and Book Society as a Sunday School reader for children, is a good example of the type. Aunt Sally is so Christ-like, suffers so patiently all of the horrors of slavery, draws a religious moral from so many of her sufferings, and speaks so directly to the children, that only children could have believed her account. Similarly, in spite of Lydia Maria Child's insistence that she had only revised the manuscript of Harriet Jacobs "mainly for purpose of condensation and orderly arrangement," the work is not credible. In the first place, *Incidents in the Life of a Slave Girl* (1861), is too orderly; too many of the major characters meet providentially after years of separation. Then, too, the story is too melodramatic: miscegenation and cruelty, outraged virtue, unrequited love, and planter licentiousness appear on practically every page. The virtuous Harriet sympathizes with her wretched mistress who has to look on all of the mulattoes fathered by her husband, she refuses to bow to the lascivious demands of her master, bears two children for another white man, and then runs away and hides in a garret in her grandmother's cabin for seven years until she is able to escape to New York. In the meantime, her white lover has acknowledged his paternity of her children, purchased their freedom, and been elected to Congress. In the end, all live happily ever after.

Fortunately, historians do not have to rely solely on internal evidence to determine the validity of the narratives. A number of scholars have investigated plantation records, manuscript census returns, diaries and letters of whites, local records, newspapers, and city directories in an effort to determine if the slave narratives were true. Joseph Logsdon and Sue Eakin's painstaking check of Solomon Northrup's story, and Paul Edward's investigation of the narrative of Gustavus Vassa are just two examples of successful efforts to verify the slave narratives.

Frequently, one autobiography which was undoubtedly true confirmed the validity of others of less credibility. The paths of the fugitive slaves, for example, often crossed those of free Negroes and of those men and women who wrote their autobiographies after the Civil War. For instance, Henry Box Brown's account of his escape from bondage in a small box appears at first glance to be a tall tale. Yet Brown was able to demonstrate to a group of Englishmen how he did this. The most convincing evidence, however, was supplied by Miflin Gibbs, a free Negro who was at the Philadelphia railroad depot when the box containing Brown arrived.

Even if one is unable to untangle the question of the validity of the fugitive slave narratives, it is still possible to present the Negro's view of bondage. Many Negroes who were born in slavery either purchased their freedom, or were manumitted by their owners, or emancipated by the Civil War, and later wrote their autobiographies. Seventy-six of the black autobiographies included in this study were written by slaves or by black men or women who had direct knowledge of the institution. Twenty of these accounts were written by slaves who were manumitted by their masters, or who purchased their freedom. Thirty-four of these autobiographies were written before 1860 and forty-two after 1860. Only twenty-six of them were written by fugitive slaves. Consequently, the description of slavery in this volume rests primarily upon the accounts of men and women who had no abolitionist amanuenses. The diversity in the descriptions of slavery in the autobiographies is, perhaps, the greatest testament to their validity. The most informative of the autobiographies were those written by Louis Hughes, Henry Clay Bruce, Jermain Loguen, William Wells Brown, Robert Anderson, Frederick Douglass, Sam Aleckson, Jacob Stroyer, Austin Steward, Solomon Northrup, Elizabeth Keckley, and Henry Bibb.

However important traditional records are in delineating the Southern white man's political, social, economic, and racial ideology, they are inferior to the slave narratives in explaining slave behavior. Traditional sources (plantation records, newspapers, letters, travel accounts) have been used in this study primarily to verify some details of the narratives, to amplify topics not explored in depth by the black writers, and to analyze the master's perception of interpersonal relations on the plantation. In regard to the latter point, the autobiographies written by antebellum Southern whites, and especially the manuscript ones, were most helpful. Among the more revealing ones were those written by Rebecca Felton, Susan Smedes, Robert Q. Mallard, Jane Swisshelm, J. G. Clinkscales, Virginia Clayton, Letitia Burwell, Philip H. Jones, Norman Woods, Charles Hutson, Elizabeth Pringle, and Walter F. Peterson.

Travel accounts were among the most important sources used in this study. Xenophobia, class and race bias, age, sex, intelligence, routes, mode of travel, and numerous other things have to be considered in reading the travel accounts. By and large, the travelers' observations are much more trustworthy in regard to' the attitudes of whites than their opinions of slaves. Even so, many of the accounts are extremely illuminating if they are used cautiously. The most reliable accounts were written by business-men, soldiers, scientists, journalists, teachers, and persons who either spent several months in one location or several years in one or more states, recorded their observations soon after the trip, and habitually gave detailed descriptions of people and in-stitutions. A number of the more famous travelers have not been included in the bibliography because they were so long on generalization and so short on details.

Many historians have been so preoccupied with the attitudes of travelers toward slavery that they have not considered the accounts on their merits. Often profoundly ignorant of American institutions, many foreign travelers made facile generalizations about the plantations based on data gathered in fashionable salons and from gossip. Others rarely left their steamboat, train, or stagecoach and yet spoke with great "authority" on the South. The most misleading of the lot, however, were those gullible travelers who reported as fact whatever the planters told them, or judged the institution of slavery from what they saw of the relationship between house servants and slaveholders.

If one discounts the haphazardly formed generalizations and studies instead the descriptions of events the travelers actually saw, the accounts can be extremely useful. This is especially true because much of what the traveler saw was new to him. Consequently, he was much more likely to comment on things which resident whites accepted as commonplace (religious serv-ices, singing, dancing, dress, and language patterns in the quarters) than natives. Viewed from this perspective, even the most rabid abolitionist or pro-slavery zealot provides the investi-gator with some useful information. The most illuminating ac-counts were written by Oscar Comettant, Timothy Flint, Charles Lyell, Charles Lanman, Francis and Theresa Pulszky, Mathilda Houston, George Lewis, Frederick Law Olmstead, Basil Hall, Fredrika Bremer, S. A. O'Ferrall, Thomas Nichols, James K. Paulding, and Robert Sutcliff.

Secondary works on slavery are numerous. Several of them formed an indispensable part of my background reading. Three studies of slave narratives, Charles Nichols, *Many Thousand Gone* (1969), Stanley Feldstein, *Once A Slave* (1971), and Marion W. Starling, "The Slave Narrative: Its Place in American Literary History" (PhD., New York University, 1946), although primarily literary analyses or compendiums, contain good bibliographies. The most extensive treatment of the masters appears in Ulrich B. Phillips, *American Negro Slavery* (1918) and *Life and Labor in the Old South* (1929). Eugene Genovese's *The Political Economy of Slavery* (1965) reiterates many of the points Phillips made and places the plantation economy within a Marxian framework. Kenneth Stampp's *Peculiar Institution* (1956), free of the racial antipathy of Phillips, presents the clearest picture of the slave laborer and planter exploitation. Stanley Elkins' *Slavery* (1959) contains some interesting hypotheses about slave personality development. Since this pioneering book is not based on primary sources and many of its weaknesses are well known, I did not feel that it was necessary to write a critique. Instead, I have accepted the book the way that Elkins hoped that it would be received, as a "proposal," or series of hypotheses to be tested. For the most part this meant a refinement of or additions to Elkins' questions with new answers. Ann Lane's *Slavery* (1971) contains a good collection of essays critical of Elkins' hypotheses. The most perceptive comments on the slave appear in such studies of slavery as Charles Sydnor, *Slavery in Mississippi* (1933); Orville Taylor, *Negro Slavery in Arkansas* (1958); and James B. Sellers, *Slavery in Alabama* (1950). All of the secondary accounts should be supplemented with sophisticated articles on specific topics in the *Journal of Negro History, Phylon, North Carolina Historical Review, Journal of Southern History, Journal of Mississippi History, Louisiana Historical Quarterly* and the *Georgia Historical Quarterly*. James C. Bonner, "Plantation and Farm: The Agricultural South," and Bennett H. Wall, "African Slavery," in Arthur S. Link and Rembert W. Patrick, eds., *Writing Southern History* (Baton Rouge, 1965), are good historiographical essays on plantation slavery.

A good introduction to theories of personality development can be found in Henry Clay Lindgren, ed., *Contemporary Research in Social Psychology* (1969) and Hendrik M. Ruitenbeek, ed.,

Varieties of Personality Theories (1964). The most important works, however, are the monographs and reports of experiments which appear in such journals as *Sociometry* and the *American Journal of Psychiatry*. Erving Goffman's *Asylums* (1961) and Amitai Etzioni's *A Comparative Analysis of Complex Organizations* (1961) contain the best analyses of total institutions.

Select Bibliography

I *Primary Sources, Unpublished*

Louisiana State University

Bond, Priscilla, Diary
De Clouet, Alexandre, Papers
Hephzibah Church Books, 1813–1840
McKinney, Jeptha, Papers
Pugh, Alexander F., Plantation Diaries, 1850–65
Risley, Alice C., Diary
Ryland, Robert H., Journals
Tibbetts, John C., Correspondence
Town, Clarissa, Diary

National Archives

Records of the Bureau of Freedmen and Abandoned Lands, Record Group 105

University of North Carolina

Aiken, David Wyatt, Autobiography
Allan, William, Memoirs
Asbury, Samuel E., Papers
Bateman, Mary E., Diary
Bayne, Hugh A., Memoirs
Berry, Mrs. John, Reminiscences
Blanchard, Elizabeth, Papers
Bondurant, Emily M., Reminiscences
Boyd, John, Diary
Bradbury, Charles W., Papers
Broidrick, Annie L., Recollections
Burnley, Edwina and Bertha, Recollections
Carmouche, Annie Jeter, Papers
Chotard, Eliza W., Autobiography
Clitherall, Eliza B., Diary
Colcock, William F., Autobiography
Comer, John Fletcher, Farm Journal
Foster, Elmina, Reminiscences
Gale and Polk Family Papers
Grimball, Meta M., Journal
Hardaway, Robert A., Book
Herbert, Hilary A., Reminiscences
Hutson, Charles W., Reminiscences
Jones, Philip H., Reminiscences
Killebrew, Joseph B., Autobiography
King, William Henry, Papers
Lawton, Alexander Robert, Diary
Mallet, Peter, Papers
Mayo, Peter H., Recollections
Meriwether, Elizabeth A., Recollections
Miller, Letitia D., Recollections
Milner Papers
Morrison, Columbus, Autobiography
Pharr, Louise Taylor, Book
Pilsbury, Rebecca, Diary
Polk, George W., Reminiscences
Rainey-Wren Papers
Ramsey, James Gettys, Autobiography
Stuart, James R., Recollections
Tazewell, Littleton Waller, Book
Wilson, Thomas B., Reminiscences

II   *Primary Sources, Published*

A. Black Autobiographies and Memoirs

Adams, John Quincy, *Narrative of The Life of John Quincy Adams, When in Slavery, and Now as a Freeman* (Harrisburg, Pa., 1872)

Aleckson, Sam, *Before the War, and After The Union* (Boston, 1929)

Allen, Richard, *The Life, Experience, And Gospel Labors of the Rt. Rev. Richard Allen . . .* (Philadelphia, 1887)

Anderson, John, *The Story of the Life of John Anderson, A Fugitive Slave* (London, 1863)

Anderson, Robert, *From Slavery To Affluence* (Hemingford, Nebraska, 1927)

Arter, Jared M., *Echoes From A Pioneer Life* (Atlanta, 1922)

Ball, Charles, *Slavery in the United States: A Narrative of the Life and Adventures of Charles Ball* (Lewistown, Pa., 1836)

Banks, J. H., *A Narrative of Events Of The Life of J. H. Banks* (Liverpool, 1861)

Bayley, Solomon, *A Narrative of Some Remarkable Incidents, In the Life of Solomon Bayley, Formerly A Slave* (London, 1825)

Bibb, Henry, *Narrative of the Life and Adventures of Henry Bibb, An American Slave* (New York, 1849)

Black, Leonard, *The Life And Sufferings Of Leonard Black, A Fugitive From Slavery* (New Bedford, 1847)

Brown, Henry Box, *Narrative of Henry Box Brown* (Boston, 1851)

Brown, John, *Slave Life in Georgia* (London, 1855)

Brown, William Wells, *Narrative of William W. Brown, A Fugitive Slave* (Boston, 1847)

———, *My Southern Home* (Boston, 1880)

Bruce, Henry Clay, *The New Man. Twenty-Nine Years A Slave. Twenty-Nine Years A Free Man* (York, Pa., 1895)

Burton, Annie L. *Memories of Childhood's Slavery Days* (Boston, 1909)

Campbell, Israel, *An Autobiography* (Philadelphia, 1861)

Clarke, Lewis G., *Narrative of the Sufferings of Lewis Clarke . . .* (Boston, 1845)

Craft, William, *Running A Thousand Miles For Freedom: Or The Escape of William and Ellen Craft From Slavery* (London, 1860)

Davis, Noah, *A Narrative of The Life of Rev. Noah Davis, A Colored Man* (Baltimore, 1859)

Delaney, Lucy Ann, *From The Darkness Cometh The Light: Or Struggles For Freedom* (St. Louis, Mo., n.d.)

Douglass, Frederick, *My Bondage and My Freedom* (New York, 1855)

Grandy, Moses, *Narrative of The Life of Moses Grandy* (London, 1843)

Green, Elisha W., *Life Of The Rev. Elisha W. Green* (Maysville, Ky., 1888)

Green, William, *Narrative Of Events In The Life Of William Green* (Springfield, 1853)

Grimes, William, *Life of William Grimes, The Runaway Slave, Brought Down To The Present Time* (New Haven, Conn., 1855)

Hall, Samuel, *47 Years A Slave* (Washington, Iowa, 1912)

Heard, William H., *From Slavery To The Bishopric In The A.M.E. Church: An Autobiography* (Philadelphia, 1924)

Henson, Josiah, *The Life of Josiah Henson* (Boston, 1849)

———, *Father Henson's Story of His Own Life* (New York, 1962 [1858])

Holsey, Lucius H., *Autobiography, Sermons, Addresses, And Essays* (Atlanta, 1898)

Hughes, Louis, *Thirty Years A Slave* (Milwaukee, 1897)

Jackson, Andrew, *Narrative and Writings of Andrew Jackson* (Syracuse, N.Y., 1847)

Jamison, Monroe F., *Autobiography and Work of Bishop M. F. Jamison, D.D.* (Nashville, 1912)

Jefferson, Isaac, *Life of Isaac Jefferson of Petersburg, Virginia, Blacksmith* (Charlottesville, 1951)

Johnson, Thomas L., *Twenty-Eight Years A Slave: Or The Story of My Life In Three Continents* (London, 1909)

Jones, Thomas, *The Experience of Thomas Jones, Who Was a Slave For Forty-Three Years* (Boston, 1850)

Keckley, Elizabeth, *Behind The Scenes* (New York, 1868)

Lane, Isaac, *Autobiography* (Nashville, 1916)

Lane, Lunsford, *The Narrative of Lunsford Lane* (Boston, 1848)

Langston, John Mercer, *From The Virginia Plantation To The National Capital* (Hartford, Conn., 1894)

Lewis, J. Vance, *Out of the Ditch* (Houston, Texas, 1910)

Loguen, Jermain Wesley, *The Rev. J. W. Loguen, As A Slave And As A Freedman* (Syracuse, N.Y., 1859)

Lowery, I. E., *Life on the Old Plantation in Ante-Bellum Days: Or A Story Based on Facts* (Columbia, S.C., 1911)

Marrs, Elijah P., *Life and History* (Louisville, Ky., 1885)

Mason, Isaac, *Life Of Isaac Mason As A Slave* (Worcester, Mass., 1893)

Newton, A. H., *Out of the Briars* (Philadelphia, 1910)

Northrup, Solomon, *Twenty Years A Slave* (London, 1853)

Offley, G. W., *A Narrative of the Life and Labors of the Rev. G. W. Offley, A Colored Man* (Hartford, Conn., 1860)

O'Neal, William, *Life and History of William O'Neal* (St. Louis, 1896)

Parker, Allen, *Recollections of Slavery Times* (Worcester, Mass., 1895)

Pennington, James W. C., *The Fugitive Blacksmith* (London, 1849)

Randolph, Peter, *Sketches of Slave Life* (Boston, 1855)

Roberts, James, *The Narrative of James Roberts* (Hattiesburg, Miss., 1945 [1858])

Robinson, W. H., *From Log Cabin To The Pulpit* (Eau Clare, Wis., 1913)

Roper, Moses, *A Narrative of the Adventures and Escape of Moses Roper from American Slavery* (London, 1840)

Smith, Amanda, *An Autobiography* (Chicago, 1893)

Smith, James L., *Autobiography of James L. Smith* (Norwich, Conn., 1881)

Smith, Venture, *A Narrative of the Life and Adventures of Venture, A Native of Africa* (New London, Conn., 1798)

Steward, Austin, *Twenty-Two Years A Slave, And Forty Years A Freeman* (Rochester, N.Y., 1861)

Stroyer, Jacob, *My Life in the South* (Salem, 1890)

Thompson, John, *The Life of John Thompson, A Fugitive Slave* (Worcester, Mass., 1856)

Vassa, Gustavus, *The Interesting Narrative of the Life of Olaudah Equiano, or Gustavus Vassa, The African* (London, 1794)

Veney, Bethany, *The Narrative of Bethany Veney, A Slave Woman* (Worcester, Mass., 1889)

Washington, Booker T., *Up From Slavery* (Cambridge, 1928)

Watkins, James, *Narrative of the Life of James Watkins* (Bolton, England, 1852)

Watson, Henry, *Narrative of Henry Watson, A Fugitive Slave* (Boston, 1848)

Webb, William, *The History of William Webb* (Detroit, 1873)

White, George, *A Brief Account Of The Life, Experience, Travels and Gospel Labours Of George White, An African* (New York, 1810)

Wilkerson, James, *Wilkerson's History of His Travels & Labors, In the United States* (Columbus, Ohio, 1861)

Williams, Isaac D., *Sunshine and Shadow of Slave Life* (East Saginaw, Mich., 1885)

B. White Autobiographies and Memoirs

Andrews, Garnett, *Reminiscences of an old Georgia Lawyer* (Atlanta, 1870)

Avirett, James Battle, *The Old Plantation: How We Lived in Great House and Cabin before the War* (New York, 1901)

Bailey, Robert, *The Life and Adventures of Robert Bailey* (Richmond, 1822)

Banks, Mary Ross, *Bright Days in Old Plantation Times* (Boston, 1882)

Battle, Kemp P., *Memories of an Old-Time Tar Heel* (Chapel Hill, 1945)

Brackenridge, H. M., *Recollections of Persons and Places in the West* (Philadelphia, 1868)

Burke, Emily P., *Reminiscences of Georgia* (Oberlin, 1850)

Burwell, Letitia M., *Plantation Reminiscences*, by Page Thacker, Pseud. ([Owensboro?, Kentucky], 1878)

Candler, Mrytil Lon, "Reminiscences of Life in Georgia During the 1850's and 1860's," *Georgia Historical Quarterly* XXXIII (June 1949), 110–23

Chester, Samuel, *Pioneer Days in Arkansas* (Richmond, 1927)

Clayton, Victoria Virginia, *White and Black Under the Old Regime* (Milwaukee, 1899)

Clinkscales, J. G., *On the Old Plantation* (Spartanburg, S.C., 1916)

De Saussure, Mrs. Nancy (Bostick), *Old Plantation Days, Being Recollections of Southern Life before the Civil War* (New York, 1909)

Devereux, Mrs. Margaret, *Plantation Sketches* (Cambridge, 1906)

Drake, Daniel, *Pioneer Life in Kentucky 1795–1800* (New York, 1948)

DuBose, John W., "Recollections of the Plantations," *Alabama Historical Quarterly* I (Spring 1930), 63–75, (Summer 1930), 107–18

Duke, Basil W., *Reminiscences of General Basil W. Duke, CSA* (Garden City, New York, 1911)

Etzenhouser, Elder R., *From Palmyra, N.Y., 1830, to Independence, Mo., 1894* (Independence, Mo., 1894)

Felton, Rebecca Latimer, *Country Life in Georgia in the Days of my Youth* (Atlanta, 1919)

Fulkerson, H. S., *Random Recollections of Early Days in Mississippi* (Vicksburg, 1885)

Gilmer, George R., *Sketches of Some of the First Settlers of Upper Georgia, of the Cherokees, and the Author* (New York, 1855)

Hallum, John, *Diary of an old Lawyer* (Nashville, 1895)

Joyce, John A., *A Checkered Life* (Chicago, 1883)

Kemble, Francis A., *Journal of a Residence on a Georgian Plantation in 1838–1839* (New York, 1863)

Le Conte, Joseph, *The Autobiography of Joseph Le Conte* (New York, 1903)

Macon, T. J., *Life's Gleanings* (Richmond, 1913)

Mallard, Robert Q., *Plantation Life Before Emancipation* (Richmond, 1892)

Maury, Dabney H., *Recollections of a Virginian* (New York, 1894)

Meade, Anna Hardeman, *When I Was a Little Girl: The Year's Round on the Old Plantation* (Los Angeles [1916])

Meek, A. B., *Romantic Passages in Southwestern History* (Mobile, 1857)

Michaux, R. R., *Sketches of Life in North Carolina* (Cutler, N.C., 1894)

Morton, Marmaduke B., *Kentuckians Are Different* (Louisville, 1938)

Paschal, George W., *Ninety-Four Years—Agnes Paschal* (Washington, D.C., 1871)

Pendleton, James M., *Reminiscences of a Long Life* (Louisville, 1891)

Peterson, Walter F., "Slavery in the 1850's: The Recollections of an Alabama Unionist," *Alabama Historical Quarterly* (Fall and Winter 1968), 219–27

Redd, John, "Reminiscences of Western Virginia, 1770–1790," *Virginia Magazine of History and Biography* VI (April 1899), 337–46

Shaler, Nathaniel Southgate, *Autobiography* (Boston, 1909)

Sims, J. Marion, *The Story of My Life* (New York, 1884)

Smedes, Susan Dabney, *Memorials of a Southern Planter* (Baltimore, 1887)

Stafford, G. M., ed., "The Autobiography of George Mason Graham," *Louisiana Historical Quarterly* XX (Jan. 1937), 43–57

Stoney, Samuel G., ed., "The Memoirs of Frederick Augustus Porcher," *South Carolina Historical and Genealogical Magazine* XLIV (July 1943), 135–47, XLV (April 1944), 80–98

Swisshelm, Jane Grey, *Half a Century* (Chicago, 1880)

Torian, Sarah H., ed., "Ante-Bellum and War Memories of Mrs. Telfair Hodgson," *Georgia Historical Quarterly* XXVII (December 1943), 350–56

Washington, Amanda, *How Beauty Was Saved* (New York, 1907)

Wilkinson, Eliza, *Letters of Eliza Wilkinson* (New York, 1839)

Wood, Norman B., *The White Side of a Black Subject* (Chicago, 1894)

C. Travel Accounts

"A St. Joseph Diary of 1839," *Florida Historical Quarterly* XVII (Oct. 1938), 132–51

Alexander, James Edward, *Transatlantic Sketches* (2 vols., London, 1833)

Anburey, Thomas, *Travels Through the Interior Parts of America* (London, 1789)

Arfwedson, Carl D., *The United States and Canada in 1832, 1833 and 1834* (2 vols., London, 1834)

Ashworth, Henry, *A Tour in the United States . . .* (London, 1861)

Baxter, W. E., *America and the Americans* (London, 1855)

Benwell, J., *An Englishman's Travels in America* (London, 1853)

Berquin-Duvallon, *Vue de colonie espagnole du Mississippi* (Paris, 1803)

Birkbeck, Morris, *Notes on a Journey to America* (Philadelphia, 1817)

Boucher, Jonathan, *Reminiscences* (Boston, 1923)

Bremer, Fredrika, *The Homes of the New World* (2 vols., New York, 1853)

Brickell, John, *The Natural History of North Carolina* (Dublin, 1737)

Bryant, William C., *Letters of a Traveller* (London, 1850)

Buni, Andrew, ed., "Rambles Among the Virginia Mountains: The Journal of Mary Jane Boggs, June 1851," *Virginia Magazine of History and Biography* LXXVII (Jan. 1969), 78–111

Candler, Isaac, *A Summary View of America* (London, 1824)

Chastellux, François Jean, *Travels in North America in the Years 1780, 1781 and 1782* (Chapel Hill, 1963)

Comettant, Jean Pierre O., *Trois Ans aux Etats-Unis* (Paris, 1857)

———, *L'Amerique telle qu'elle est* (Paris, 1864)

Cresswell, Nicholas, *The Journal of Nicholas Cresswell, 1774–1777* (New York, 1924)

Daubeny, Charles, *Journal of A Tour Through The United States, and Canada, Made During the Years 1837–38* (Oxford, 1843)

Davis, John, *Travels in the United States of America, 1798 to 1802* (Boston, 1910)

De Montulé, Edouard, *Travels In America, 1816–1817* (Bloomington, Ind., 1950)

Denny, Collins, ed., "Diary of John Early, Bishop of the Methodist Episcopal Church, South," *Virginia Historical Magazine* XXXIII (April 1925), 166–74

Descourtilz, Miguel Esteban, *Voyages d'un Naturaliste* (3 vols., Paris, 1809)

Drayton, John, *A View of South Carolina* (1802)

Dureau, Jean Baptiste, *Les Etats-Unis en 1850* (Paris, 1891)

Du Roi, August, *Journal of Du Roi the Elder* (Philadelphia, 1911)

Easterby, J. H., ed., "South Carolina Through New England Eyes: Almira Coffin's Visit to the Low Country in 1851," *South Carolina Historical and Genealogical Magazine* XLV (July 1944), 127–36

Eddis, William, *Letters from America, Historical and Descriptive Comprising Occurrences from 1769 to 1777, Inclusive* (London, 1792)

Evarts, Jeremiah, *Through the South and West* (Lewisburg, Pa., 1956)

Faux, W[illiam], *Memorable Days in America* (London, 1823)

Feltman, William, *The Journal of Lieut. William Feltman, of the First Pennsylvania Regiment, 1781–82* (Philadelphia, 1853)

Ferguson, William, *America by River and Rail* (London, 1856)

Finch, John, *Travels in the United States of America and Canada* (London, 1833)

Fithian, Philip V., *Journal and Letters of Philip Vickers Fithian, 1773–1774* (Williamsburg, Va., 1943)

Flint, Timothy, *Recollections of the Last Ten Years, Passed in Occasional Residence and Journeying in the Valley of the Mississippi* (New York, 1968)

Flower, Richard, *Letters from Lexington and Illinois* (London, 1819)

Fontaine, Jaques, *Memoirs of a Hugenot Family* (New York, 1853)

Glen, James, *A Description of South Carolina* (London, 1761) in B. R. Carrol, ed., *Historical Collection of South Carolina* (2 vols., New York, 1836)

Glover, Thomas, *An Account of Virginia* (Oxford, 1907)

Hall, Basil, *Travels in North America in the Years 1827 and 1828* (3 vols., Philadelphia, 1829)

Hall, Francis, *Travels in Canada and the United States in 1816 and 1817* (London, 1818)

Hamilton, Thomas, *Men and Manners in America* (2 vols., Philadelphia, 1833)

Harris, William T., *Remarks made during a Tour through the United States of America in the years 1817, 1818, and 1819* (London, 1821)

Hartwell, Henry, *The Present State of Virginia* (London, 1727)

Herz, Henri, *Mes Voyages en Amerique* (Paris, 1866)

Hewatt, Alexander, *An Historical Account of the Rise and Progress of the Colonies of South Carolina and Georgia* (2 vols., 1779) in B. R. Carrol, ed., *Historical Collection of South Carolina* (2 vols., New York, 1836)

Hinke, William J., ed., "Report of the Journey of Francis Louis Michel from Berne, Switzerland, to Virginia, October, 1701–December 1, 1702," *Virginia Magazine of History and Biography* XXIV (April 1916), 113–41

Hodgson, Adam, *Letters from North America, written during a Tour of the United States and Canada* (2 vols., London, 1824)

Ingraham, Joseph Holt, *The South-West: By a Yankee* (2 vols., New York, 1835)

Irving, John B., *A Day on Cooper River* (Charleston, 1842)

Johnston, Gideon, *Carolina Chronicle* (Berkeley, 1946)

Jones, Hugh, *The Present State of Virginia* (Chapel Hill, 1956)

Kellar, Herbert A., ed., "A Journey Through the South in 1836: Diary of James D. Davidson," *Journal of Southern History* I (Aug. 1935), 345–77

Knight, Henry C., *Letters from the South and West* (Boston, 1824)

Lanman, Charles, *Haw-He-Noo: Or Records of a Tourist* (Philadelphia, 1850)

Latrobe, Charles J., *The Rambler in North America 1832–33* (2 vols., New York, 1835)

Lawson, John, *A New Voyage to Caroline* (Chapel Hill, 1967)

Lewis, George, *Impressions of America* (Edinburgh, 1845)

Lyell, Charles, *Travels in North America, Canada, and Nova Scotia* (2 vols., London, 1845)

———, *A Second Visit to the United States of North America* (2 vols., New York, 1850)

Martineau, Harriet, *Society in America* (3 vols., London, 1837)

———, *Retrospect of Western Travel* (3 vols., London, 1838)

Mackay, Alexander, *The Western World: Or Travels in the United States in 1846–47* (3 vols., Philadelphia, 1849)

Mead, Whitman, *Travels in North America* (New York, 1820)

Moffatt, L. G., and J. M. Carriere, eds., "A Frenchman visits Norfolk, Fredericksburg and Orange County, 1816," *Virginia Magazine of History and Biography* LIII (July 1945), 197–214

Murat, Achille, *America and the Americans* (New York, 1849)

Murray, Amelia, *Letters from the United States, Cuba and Canada* (New York, 1856)

Murray, James, *Letters of James Murray* (Boston, 1901)

Nairne, Thomas, *A Letter from South Carolina* (London, 1732)

Nichols, Thomas Low, *Forty Years of American Life, 1821–1861* (New York, 1937)

O'Connor, John, *Wanderings of a Vagabond* (New York, 1873)

O'Ferrall, S. A., *A Ramble of Six Thousand Miles Through the United States of America* (London, 1832)

Padgett, James A., ed., "A Yankee School Teacher in Louisiana, 1835–1837: The Diary of Caroline B. Poole," *Louisiana Historical Quarterly* XX (July 1937), 651–79

Paine, Lewis, *Six Years in a Georgia Prison* (New York, 1951)

Palliser, John, *Solitary Rambles* (London, 1853)

Paulding, James K., *Letters from the South Written During an Excursion in the Summer of 1816* (New York, 1817)

Power, Tyrone, *Impressions of America, During the Years 1833, 1834, and 1835* (London, 1836)

Pulszky, Francis and Theresa, *White, Red and Black* (3 vols., London, 1853)

Perrin du Lac, François Marie, *Voyage dans les deux Louisianes* (Lyon, 1805)

Robinson, Solon, *Solon Robinson, Pioneer and Agriculturalist* (2 vols., Indianapolis, 1936)

Rogers, George, *Memoranda of the Experience, Labors, and Travels of a Universalist Preacher* (Cincinnati, 1845)

Romans, Bernard, *A Concise Natural History of East and West Florida* (New York, 1775)

Rugbaean, A., *Transatlantic Rambles* (London, 1851)

Sealsfield, Charles, *The Americans as They Are, Described in a Tour through the Valley of the Mississippi* (London, 1828)

Shelley, Fred., ed., "The Journal of Ebeneezer Hazard in Virginia, 1777," *Virginia Magazine of History and Biography* LXII (Oct. 1954), 400–423

Stewart, Catherine, *New Homes in the West* (Nashville, 1843)

Stirling, James, *Letters from the Slave States* (London, 1857)

Stoddard, Amos, *Sketches, Historical and Descriptive of Louisiana* (Philadelphia, 1812)

Story, Thomas, *A Journal of the Life of Thomas Story* (Newcastle-upon-Tyne, 1747)

Stuart-Wortley, *Travels in the United States, Etc., During 1849 and 1850* (3 vols., London, 1851)

Sutcliff, Robert, *Travels in Some Parts of North America in the Years 1804, 1805, & 1806* (York, England, 1811)

Tasistro, Louis F., *Random Shots and Southern Breezes* (2 vols., New York, 1842)

Thomson, William, *A Tradesman's Travels* (Edinburgh, 1842)

Tixier, Victor, *Travels on the Osage Prairies* (Norman, Oklahoma, 1940)

Watson, Elkanah, *Men and Times of the Revolution* (New York, 1857)

Whipple, Henry B., *Bishop Whipple's Southern Diary* (Minneapolis, 1937)

Woolman, John, *A Journal of Life* (Dublin, 1776)
Younger, Edward, ed., "A Yankee Reports on Virginia, 1842–1843: Letters from John Adam Kasson," *Virginia Magazine of History and Biography* LVI (Oct. 1948), 408–30

D. Miscellaneous

Abbey, Kathryn T., ed., "Documents Relating to El Destino and Chemonie Plantations, Middle Florida, 1828–1868," *Florida Historical Society Quarterly* VII (Jan. 1929), 179–213
Arrowood, Mary D. and Thomas H. Hamilton, "Nine Negro Spirituals, 1850–61, From Lower South Carolina," *Journal of American Folklore* XLI (Oct.–Dec. 1928), 579–84
Bacon, A. M., "Conjuring and Conjure Doctors," *Southern Workman* XXIV (Nov. 1895), 193–94, (Dec. 1895), 209–11
Brown, John Mason, "Songs of the Slave," *Lippincott's Magazine* II (Dec. 1868), 617–23
Cable, George Washington, "Creole Slave Songs," *Century Magazine* XXXI (April 1886), 807–28
Catterall, Helen, ed., *Judicial Cases Concerning American Slavery and the Negro* (5 vols., Washington, D.C., 1926–37)
Dayrell, Elphistone, *Folk Stories From Southern Nigeria, West Africa* (London, 1910)
"Diary of Col. William Bolling of Bolling Hall," *Virginia Magazine of History and Biography* XLIII (Oct. 1935), 330–42
Donnan, Elizabeth, ed., *Documents Illustrative of the History of the Slave Trade in America* (4 vols., Washington, 1930–35)
Easterby, J. H., ed., "Charles Cotesworth Pinckney's Plantation Diary, April 6–December 15, 1818," *South Carolina Historical and Genealogical Magazine* XLI (Oct. 1940), 135–50
"Eighteenth Century Slaves as Advertized by their Masters," *Journal of Negro History* I (April 1916), 163–216
Ennis, Merlin, ed., *Umbundu: Folk Tales From Angola* (Boston, 1962)
Evans, Gladys C., and Theodora B. Marshall, eds., "Plantation Report From the Papers of Levin R. Marshall of 'Richmond,' Natchez, Mississippi," *Journal of Mississippi History* III (Jan. 1941), 45–55
Fortier, Alcée, *Louisiana Folk-Tales* (Boston, 1895)
Freeman, George W., *The Rights and Duties of Slave-Holders* (Charleston, 1837)
Green, Fletcher M., ed., *Ferry Hill Plantation Journal, January 4, 1838–January 15, 1839* (Chapel Hill, 1961)
Griffith, Benjamin W., "Longer Version of 'Guinea Negro Song,' From a Georgia Frontier Songster," *Southern Folklore Quarterly* XXVIII (June 1964), 117–18
Griffith, Lucille, ed., "The Plantation Record Book of Brookdale Farm, Amite County, 1856–57," *Journal of Mississippi History* VII (Jan. 1945), 23–31

Itgayemi, Phebean, and P. Gurney, eds., *Folk Tales and Fables* (London, 1953)

Jablow, Alta, ed., *An Anthology of West African Folklore* (n.p., 1962)

Jones, Charles Colcock, *The Religious Instruction of the Negroes in the United States* (Savannah, Ga., 1842)

"Journal of Col. James Gordon," *William and Mary Quarterly* 1st. ser., XII (July 1903), 1–12

"Journal of John Barnwell," *Virginia Magazine of History and Biography* VI (July 1898), 42–55

McKim, J. M., "Negro Songs," *Dwight's Journal of Music* XXI (Aug. 9, 1862), 148–49

McKim, Lucy, "Songs of the Port Royal Contrabands," *Dwight's Journal of Music* XXI (Nov. 8, 1862), 254–55

McTyeire, H. N., *et al., Duties of Masters of Servants: Three Premium Essays* (Charleston, S.C., 1851)

————, H. N. *Duties of Christian Masters* (Nashville, 1859)

Moore, John H., ed., "Two Documents Relating to Plantation Overseers of the Vicksburg Region, 1831–32," *Journal of Mississippi History* XVI (Jan. 1954), 31–36

Morton, Louis, ed., "The Daybook of Robert Wormeley Carter of Sabine Hall, 1766," *Virginia Magazine of History and Biography* LXVIII (July 1960), 301–16

Salley, A. S., ed., "Journal of General Peter Horry," *South Carolina Historical and Genealogical Magazine* XXXIX (Oct. 1938), 157–59, XL (July 1939), 91–96, XLI (Jan. 1940), 15–18

Thornwell, J. H., *The Rights and Duties of Masters: A Sermon Preached at the Dedication of a Church* (Charleston, S.C., 1850)

III   *Secondary Sources*

A. Books

Abrahamson, Mark, *Interpersonal Accommodation* (New York, 1966)

Argyle, Michael, *The Psychology of Interpersonal Behavior* (Baltimore, 1967)

Bennis, Warren G., *et al.*, eds., *Interpersonal Dynamics* (Homewood, Illinois, 1964)

Ballagh, J. C., *A History of Slavery in Virginia* (Baltimore, 1902)

Bassett, John S., *History of Slavery in North Carolina* (Baltimore, 1899)

Berken, Paul de, ed., *Interaction: Human Groups in Community and Institutions* (Oxford, Eng., 1969)

Berkowitz, Leonard, ed., *Advances in Experimental Social Psychology* (2 vols., New York, 1965)

Berrien, F. Kenneth and Bernard P. Indik, eds., *People, Groups, and Organizations* (New York, 1968)

Biddle, Bruce J., and Edwin J. Thomas, eds. *Role Theory: Concepts and Research* (New York, 1966)

Bjerstedt, Ake, *Glimpses from the World of the School Child* (Lund, Sweden, 1960)

Blau, Peter M., *Exchange and Power in Social Life* (New York, 1967)

Botkin, B. A., ed., *Lay My Burden Down* (Chicago, 1945)

Brackett, Jeffrey R., *The Negro in Maryland* (Baltimore, 1889)

Burney, Christopher, *The Dungeon Democracy* (London, 1945)

Carson, Robert C., *Interaction Concepts of Personality* (Chicago, 1969)

Clemmer, Donald, *The Prison Community* (New York, 1965)

Cohen, Elie A., *Human Behavior in the Concentration Camp* (New York, 1953)

Craven, Wesley Frank, *White, Red, and Black: The Seventeenth Century Virginian* (Charlottesville, 1971)

Davis, Charles S., *The Cotton Kingdom in Alabama* (Montgomery, 1939)

Davis, David B., *The Problem of Slavery in Western Culture* (Ithaca, New York, 1966)

Degler, Carl, *Neither Black nor White* (New York, 1971)

Elkins, Stanley, *Slavery: A Problem in American Institutional and Intellectual Life* (Chicago, 1959)

Fisher, Miles Mark, *Negro Slave Songs in the United States* (Ithaca, New York, 1953)

Flanders, Ralph B., *Plantation Slavery in Georgia* (Chapel Hill, 1933)

Freyre, Gilberto, *The Masters and the Slaves* (New York, 1946)

Genovese, Eugene D., *The Political Economy of Slavery* (New York, 1965)

Goffman, Erving, *Interaction Ritual: Essays on Face-To-Face Behavior* (Garden City, New York, 1967)

Gray, Louis C., *History of Agriculture in the Southern United States to 1860* (2 vols., Washington, 1933)

Hare, A. Paul, *et al.*, eds., *Small Groups: Studies in Social Interaction* (New York, 1965)

Harris, Marvin, *Patterns of Race in the Americas* (New York, 1964)

Hereven, Tamara K., ed., *Anonymous Americans* (Englewood Cliffs, New Jersey, 1971)

Herskovits, Melville, *The Myth of the Negro Past* (New York, 1941)

Ichheiser, Gustav, *Appearances and Realities* (San Francisco, 1970)

Johnson, Guion Griffis, *Ante-Bellum North Carolina: A Social History* (Chapel Hill, 1937)

Johnson, Guy B., *Folk Culture on St. Helena Island, South Carolina* (Chapel Hill, 1930)

Jordan, Winthrop D., *White over Black* (Chapel Hill, 1968)

Kardiner, Abram and Lionel Ovesey, *The Mark of Oppression* (New York, 1951)

Knapper, Christopher and Peter B. Warr, *The Perception of People and Events* (New York, 1968)

Knight, Franklin W., *Slave Society in Cuba During the Nineteenth Century* (Madison, 1970)

Kogon, Eugen, *The Theory and Practice of Hell* (New York, 1946)

Laing, R. D., H. Phillipson, and A. R. Lee, *Interpersonal Perception* (New York, 1966)

Lane, Ann, ed., *The Debate Over Slavery* (Urbana, Ill., 1971)

Lindgren, Henry Clay, ed., *Contemporary Research in Social Psychology* (New York, 1969)

Lengyel, Olga, *Five Chimneys: The Story of Auschwitz* (Chicago, 1947)

McCall, George J., and J. L. Simmons, *Identities and Interactions* (New York, 1966)

Moment, David and Abraham Zaleznik, *The Dynamics of Interpersonal Behavior* (New York, 1964)

Mooney, Chase C., *Slavery in Tennessee* (Bloomington, 1957)

Mullin, Gerald W., *Flight and Rebellion: Slave Resistance in Eighteenth Century Virginia* (New York, 1972)

Newcomb, Theodore M., *Social Psychology* (New York, 1950)

Nichols, Charles H., *Many Thousand Gone* (Leiden, 1963)

Oraison, Marc, *Being Together: Our Relationships with Other People* (Garden City, New York, 1970)

Owsley, Frank L., *Plain Folk of the Old South* (Baton Rouge, La., 1949)

Pepitone, Albert, *Attraction and Hostility* (New York, 1964)

Phillips, Peter, *The Tragedy of Nazi Germany* (London, 1969)

Phillips, Ulrich B., *American Negro Slavery* (New York, 1918)

———, *Life and Labor in the Old South* (Boston, 1929)

Postell, William D., *The Health of Slaves on Southern Plantations* (Baton Rouge, 1951)

Proshansky, Harold and Bernard Seidenberg, eds., *Basic Studies in Social Psychology* (New York, 1965)

Ruitenbeek, Hendrik, ed., *Varieties of Personality Theories* (New York, 1964)

Rousset, David, *The Other Kingdom* (New York, 1947)

Sampson, Edward E., ed., *Approaches, Contexts, and Problems in Social Psychology* (Englewood Cliffs, New Jersey, 1964)

Scarborough, William K., *The Overseer* (Baton Rouge, 1966)

Schutz, William C., *The Interpersonal Underworld* (Palo Alto, California, 1966)

Sellers, James B., *Slavery in Alabama* (University, Alabama, 1950)

Stampp, Kenneth, *The Peculiar Institution* (New York, 1956)

Stein, Stanley, *Vassouras* (Cambridge, 1957)

Stouffer, Samuel A., *et al.*, eds., *The American Soldier: Adjustment During Army Life* (4 vols., Princeton, New Jersey, 1949)

Sydnor, Charles S., *Slavery in Mississippi* (New York, 1933)

Tannenbaum, Frank, *Slave and Citizen* (New York, 1947)

B. Articles

Abel, Theodore, "The Sociology of Concentration Camps," *Social Forces* XXX (Dec. 1951), 150–55

Adler, H. G., "Ideas toward a Sociology of the Concentration Camp," *American Journal of Sociology* LXIII (March 1958), 513–22

Anderson, Ronald E., "Status Structures in Coalition Bargaining Games," *Sociometry* XXX (Dec. 1967), 393–403

Arc, M., "The Prison 'Culture'—From the Inside," *New York Times Magazine* (Feb. 28, 1965), pp. 52–63

Backman, Carl W., Paul F. Secord, and Jerry R. Pierce, "Resistance to Change in the Self-Concept as a Function of Consensus Among Significant Others," *Sociometry* XXVI (March 1953), 102–11

Backman, Carl W., and Paul F. Secord, "Liking, Selective Interaction, and Misperception in Congruent Interpersonal Relations," *Sociometry* XXV (Dec. 1962), 321–35

Bauer, Raymond A. and Alice H. Bauer, "Day to Day Resistance to Slavery," *Journal of Negro History* XXVII (Oct. 1942), 388–419

Bendix, Reinhard, "Compliant Behavior and Individual Personality," *American Journal of Sociology* LVIII (Nov. 1952), 290–303

Bettelheim, Bruno, "Individual and Mass Behavior in Extreme Situations," *Journal of Abnormal Psychology* XXXVIII (Oct. 1943), 417–52

Bloch, Herbert A., "The Personality of Inmates of Concentration Camps," *American Journal of Sociology* LII (Jan. 1947), 335–41

Bluhm, H. O., "How Did They Survive?" *American Journal of Psychotherapy* II (Jan. 1948), 3–32

Bondy, Curt, "Problems of Internment Camps," *Journal of Abnormal Psychology* XXXVIII (Oct. 1943), 453–75

Brotz, Howard, and Everett Wilson, "Characteristics of Military Society," *American Journal of Sociology* II (March 1946), 371–75

Cade, John B., "Out of the Mouths of Slaves," *Journal of Negro History* XX (July 1935), 294–337

Corlew, Robert E., "Some Aspects of Slavery in Dickson County," *Tennessee Historical Quarterly* X (Sept. 1931), 224–48

Coser, Rose Laub, "Insulation From Observability and Types of Social Conformity," *American Sociological Review* XXVI (Feb. 1969), 28–39

Couch, Carl J., and John S. Murray, "Significant Others and Evaluation," *Sociometry* XXVII (Dec. 1964), 502–9

Elkin, Frederick, "The Soldier's Language," *American Journal of Sociology* II (March 1946), 414–22

Elkin, Henry, "Aggressive and Erotic Tendencies in Army Life," *American Journal of Sociology* II (March 1946), 408–13

Emerson, Richard M., "Power-Dependence Relations," *American Sociological Review* XXVII (Feb. 1962), 31–41

Friedman, Paul, "Some Aspects of Concentration Camp Psychology," *American Journal of Psychiatry* CV (Feb. 1949), 601–5

Galtung, Johan, "The Social Functions of a Prison," *Social Problems* VI (Fall 1958), 127–40

Harvey, O. J., "Personality Factors in Resolution of Conceptual Incongruities," *Sociometry* XXV (Dec. 1962), 336–52

Hayner, Norman S., and Ellis Ash, "The Prison as a Community," *American Sociological Review* V (Aug. 1940), 577–83

Hollingshead, August B., "Adjustment to Military Life," *American Journal of Sociology* LI (March 1946), 439–47

Jackson, Luther P., "Religious Development of the Negro in Virginia from 1790 to 1860," *Journal of Negro History* XVI (April 1931), 168–239

Jeltz, Wyatt F., "The Relations of Negroes and Choctaw and Chickasaw Indians," *Journal of Negro History* XXXIII (Jan. 1948), 24–37

Jernegan, Marcus W., "Slavery and Conversion in the American Colonies," *American Historical Review* (April 1916), 504–27

Johnson, Hosmer H., "Some Effects of Discrepancy Level on Responses to Negative Information About One's Self," *Sociometry* XXIX (March 1966), 52–66

Johnson, Hosmer H., and Ivan D. Steiner, "The Effects of Source on Responses to Negative Information About One's Self," *Journal of Social Psychology* LXXIV (April 1968), 215–24

Jordan, Weymouth T., "The Elisha F. King Family, Planters of the Alabama Black Belt," *Agricultural History* XIX (July 1945), 152–63

Knoff, William F., "Roles: A Concept Linking Society and Personality," *American Journal of Psychiatry* CXVII (May 1961), 1010–15

Korn, Richard, and Lloyd W. McCorkle, "Resocialization Within the Walls," *Annals of the American Academy of Political and Social Science* CCXCIII (May 1954), 88–98

Kral, V. A., "Psychiatric Observations under Severe Chronic Stress," *American Journal of Psychiatry* CVIII (Sept. 1951), 185–92

Lederer, Wolfgang, "Persecutions and Compensation," *Archives of General Psychiatry* XII (May 1965), 464–74

Perkins, Haven P., "Religion for Slaves: Difficulties and Methods," *Church History* X (Sept. 1941), 228–45

Porter, Kenneth W., "Negroes on the Southern Frontier, 1670–1763," *Journal of Negro History* XXXIII (Jan. 1948), 53–78

Postell, Paul E., "John Hampton Randolph, A Louisiana Planter," *Louisiana Historical Quarterly* XXV (Jan. 1942), 149–223

Read, Allen W., "Bilingualism in the Middle Colonies, 1725–1775," *American Speech* XII (April 1937), 93–99

Rose, Arnold, "The Social Structure of the Army," *American Journal of Sociology* LI (March 1946), 361–64

Sides, Susan D., "Southern Women and Slavery," *History Today* XX (Jan. 1970), 54–60, (Feb. 1970), 124–30

Scott, Douglass, "The Negro and the Enlisted Man: An Analogy," *Harper's Magazine* CCXXV (Oct. 1962), 19, 21

Sitterson, J. Carlyle, "The McCollams": A Planter Family of the Old and New South," *Journal of Southern History* VI (Aug. 1940), 347–67

Southall, Eugene P., "Negroes in Florida Prior to the Civil War," *Journal of Negro History* XIX (Jan. 1934), 77–86

Spindler, G. Dearborn, "American Character as Revealed in the Military," *Psychiatry* XI (Aug. 1948), 275–81

Sullivan, Henry Stack, "Toward A Psychiatry of Peoples," *Psychiatry* XI (May 1948), 105–16

Sykes, Gresham M., "Men, Merchants, and Toughs: A Study of Reaction to Imprisonment," *Social Problems* IV (Oct. 1956), 130–38

Thorpe, Earle, "Chattel Slavery and Concentration Camps," *Negro History Bulletin* XXV (May 1962), 171–76

Vibert, Faith, "The Society for the Propagation of the Gospel in Foreign Parts: Its Work for the Negroes in North America before 1783," *Journal of Negro History* XVIII (April 1933), 171–212

Weinberg, S. Kirson, "Aspects of the Prison's Social Structure," *American Journal of Sociology* XLVII (March 1942), 717–26

White, Alice P., "The Plantation Experience of Joseph and Lavinia Erwin, 1807–1836," *Louisiana Historical Quarterly* XXVII (April 1944), 343–478

Whittington, G. P., "Dr. John Sibley of Nachitoches, 1757–1837," *Louisiana Historical Quarterly* X (Oct. 1927), 468–521

Index

Abolitionists:
  literature barred from mails, 141;
  mob violence against, 141; Southern writers and, 138–39
Abraham, 123
Acculturation, 17
Adultery:
  among slaves, 82, 88–89; among
  whites, 82–85
Africa:
  culture, 3, 17–21; origins of slaves,
  2–3; reminiscences of, 10–17; slave
  trade and, 1–9
African survivals:
  dance, 19–20; factors affecting, 39;
  folktales, 20–21, 25–27; in U.S.
  and Latin America, 39; language,
  21–24; music, 19, 27–32; religion,
  17–18, 32–35
Aggression, slave:
  patterns of, 209–13; projection,
  209; repression, 211; verbal, 56–59,
  210
Aleckson, Sam, 96, 98, 159, 165, 235
Allain, Helen, 31
Allen, Richard, 61, 193
Allen, William F., 74
Allport, Gordon W., 288
Anderson, John, 86
Anderson, Robert, 43, 56, 64, 191ff,
  235
Arada, 2
Army:
  as total institution, 189–90, 218–
  20; compared to plantation, 189–
  90
Arson, by slaves, 209
Ashantee, 2, 26
Assignation:
  black men and white women, 84–
  85; white men and black women,
  82–83, 168–69
Autobiography:
  fictional, 233–34; use, 227–35

Bakongo, 2

Ball, Charles, 24, 25, 92, 98, 102,
  159–60, 169, 190ff, 232
Bambara, 2
Barbados, 15
Bates, Ernest S., 228
Bayley, Solomon, 232
Behavior:
  and personality, 188; factors affect-
  ing slave, 190–213; of planters,
  160–72
Bell, John, 23
Benin, 12
Bettelheim, Bruno, 222ff, 231
Biafada, 2
Bibb, Henry, 48, 83, 86, 87, 88, 232,
  235
Biddell, Hosea, 91
Bilingualism of slaves, 21–24
Blau, Peter, 186ff
Bluhm, Hilde, 224
Bonner, James C., 237
Brazil:
  literary stereotypes of slaves, 137–
  38; sex ratio of slaves, 77
Bremer, Fredrika, 236
Brewer, John Mason, 57
Brown, Henry Box, 159, 199ff
Brown, William Wells, 49, 62, 70,
  82, 98, 102, 162, 168, 196ff, 235
Bruce, Henry Clay, 48, 66, 191ff, 235
Burton, Annie L., 159
Burwell, Letitia, 235

Call and response:
  in African songs, 19; in slave mu-
  sic, 67–68
Campbell, Israel, 204
Carson, James Green, 164
Cartwright, Samuel A., 136
Castration of slaves, 141
Catterall, Helen T., 107
Chickasaws, 121
Child, Lydia Maria, 73, 234
Childhood:
  of planters, 166–68; of slaves, 94–
  102; racial equality during, 95–96

Children, slaves:
  and masters, 96–97, 160; and parents, 98–103; infant mortality of, 94; socialization, 94–102; unaware of status, 95–96
Choctaws, 121
Christian, Ella, 68
Christian masters:
  duties, 170; ministers and; 169–70
Church, slave:
  desire for freedom, 66–75; preachers, 64–66; theology, 61–64, 66
Church, white:
  and slave marriages, 81; restrict planter cruelty, 169–70
Clarke, Lewis, 158, 196, 208
Clayton, Virginia, 235
Clinkscales, J. G., 235
Clothing:
  and self-esteem, 192; slave, 158
Comettant, Oscar, 236
Community, slave:
  and self-esteem, 203–8; folktales and, 49–50, 56–59; quarters and, 210; rules, 210–11; slave driver and, 161; socialization, 94–103
Compliance:
  and coercion, 162–64, 193–97; and identification with masters, 186, 191–93; and surveillance, 186
Concentration camp:
  as total institution, 189–90, 221–25; behavior in, 222–25; compared to plantation, 189–90, 225–26; factors promoting psychological survival in, 224–25; infantilism in, 222–23; resistance in, 223
Conjurer:
  African roots, 32–33; and slave resistance, 48; effect on whites, 49; impact on slaves, 45–48; role on plantation, 45–48
Conrad, Robert, 77
Corn songs, 52–53
Cotton plantation:
  cultivation, 155; Labor requirements, 180
Cowley, Malcolm, 8
Cresswell, Nicholas, 50

Cuba:
  rebellion in, 124–25; sex ratio of slaves in, 77
Culture:
  affect of on slave behavior, 41–42; African, 3, 17–21; and self esteem, 41–42; elements of slave, 41

Dahomey, 2
Dambala, 33
Dances:
  African, 19–20; slave, 44–45
Davis, David B., 137
Davis, Hugh, 80
Davis, Noah, 92, 201
Decoration of graves, 33–34
Deference:
  and personality, 185–89; ritual, 160–62; slave, 193–201, 204
Delaney, Lucy Ann, 207
Deslondes, Charles, 126
Discontentment:
  manifestations of, 51–52, 104–7; statistics on, 107–8
Dissembling, slave:
  and behavior, 208; and personality, 112–14
Divorce, 80
Docility:
  fear and, 186–90; in concentration camps, 190, 222–23; personality and, 185–89; punishment and, 186–88, 193–200; sham, 188, 208
Domestic servant:
  aiding other slaves, 210; as "Sambo," 134, 200–201; loyalty to whites, 200; role in controlling slaves, 161; work of, 157–58
Dominance:
  in interpersonal relations and personality, 185–89; in slave family, 92
Douglass, Frederick, 23, 51, 71, 83, 94, 96, 105, 169, 193ff, 235
Drivers:
  role in controlling slaves, 161; role in protecting slaves, 210
Drunkenness:
  masters' abuse of slaves and, 162; of slaves, 209

Dubois, W. E. B., 32
Du Bose, John W., 24

Eakin, Sue, 234
Edwards, Paul, 234
Elkins, Stanley, 231, 237
Enslavement:
Middle Passage, 6–7; process of, 1–10, 14–17; reactions of Africans to, 5–9, 14–17
Equiano, Olaudah, 12–17, 38–39, 234
Escape of slaves:
mass attempts, 116–18; methods of, 109–10, 112–13; obstacles, 110–12; reasons for, 109
Etzioni, Amitai, 238
Ewe, 2, 26–27, 33

Falconer, James, 23
Family, African, 11–13
Family, slave:
children, 94–102; courtship, 85; marriage, 86–87; planters and, 79–82; role of men, 88–89, 92–94; role of women, 94; separation, 89–92; sex ratio, 77–78
Family, planter:
"mammy" and, 167; treatment of slaves and, 166–69
Faux, William, 50
Fears:
of slaves, 195–96; of whites, 139–42, 168–69
Feldstein, Stanley, 237
Felton, Rebecca, 235
Flint, Timothy, 236
Flogging:
internalization and, 194–99; resistand to, 211–13; slave behavior and, 196
Folklore:
African, 20–21, 25–27; aggression in, 56–59; slave, 49–50; socialization and, 56–59; tar-baby tale, 26–27; world view of slaves, 56–59
Fom, 2, 33
Food allotment, 158–59
Frederic, Francis, 233
Freedmen's Bureau, 90
Freeman, George W., 170

Frémont, John C., 106
Fulani, 2
Funeral rites:
African, 17–18; slave, 33–34

Genovese, Eugene, 237
Ghana, 26
Gibbs, Miflin, 234
Goffman, Erving, 188, 238
Grandy, Moses, 86
Gray, Thomas R., 127ff
Green, William, 93, 159, 168, 213
Grimes, William, 75, 96, 110, 165, 190ff
Gullah:
African languages and, 23–24; slave-white interaction and, 22–24

Haiti, 124
Hall, Basil, 236
Hall, Samuel, 22, 24, 198ff
Hallucinations:
fear of punishment and, 196; separations and, 197–98
Hausa, 2, 26
Heard, William H., 211
Hearn, Lafcadio, 28, 31
Henson, Josiah, 105, 159, 163, 165, 196ff
Herbemont, H., 177
Hewatt, Alexander, 29
Higginson, Thomas Wentworth, 67
Hildreth, Richard, 233
Holmes, Isaac, 31
Holmes, T. A., 171
Holsey, Lucius, 82, 98, 192ff
Housing, 159
Houston, Mathilda, 236
Hughes, Louis, 106, 159, 169, 192ff, 235
Humboldt, Alexander, 77
Hunger, 158–59
Hurston, Zora Neal, 59
Hutson, Charles, 235

Ibibio, 2
Ibo, 2, 12, 20, 26
Ichheiser, Gustav, 135
Identification with masters:
behavior and, 191; domestic serv-

ants and, 200–201; factors in, 190–93

Improvisation:
in African music, 19; in slave music, 54–55

Indians:
enslavement of blacks, 121; intermarriage with slaves, 121; maroons and, 121–24

Infantilism:
factors contributing to, 189–90; in concentration camps, 189–90, 222

Insurrection, see Rebellion

Internalization:
contributing factors, 185–86; factors preventing, 188–89; slaves and, 190–200

Jackson, Andrew (slave), 159, 168, 232

Jackson, Andrew (General), 122

Jacobins, 140, 142

Jamison, M. F., 48, 83

Jehovah's Witnesses, 224

Jefferson, Isaac, 165

Jefferson, Thomas, 165

Jesup, Thomas, 123, 124

Jones, Charles C., 68

Jones, Philip H., 164, 235

Jones, Thomas, 97, 195ff

Juba, 55

Keckley, Elizabeth, 95, 161, 211, 235

Kemble, Frances, 138

Kom, 2

Korn, Richard, 221

Lamar, John B., 176, 182

Lane, Lunsford, 63, 95, 97, 104, 208

Langston, John Mercer, 83, 192

Language:
African survivals in, 21–24; Gullah, 23–24; patois, 22–24

Lanier, Sidney, 55

Lanman, Charles, 236

Latin America:
African survivals, 39; rebellions, 124–25; slave trade, 39; sex ratio, 77

Latrobe, Benjamin, 30–32

Lee, Charles, 233

Lewis, George, 236

Lewis, J. Vance, 96, 97

Liberty County, Georgia, 81

Lindgren, Henry Clay, 237

Logsdon, Joseph, 234

Loguen, Jermain, 83, 98, 160, 197ff, 232

Long, John, 51

Louisiana:
Africanisms, 30–33; voodoo, 33

Lyell, Charles, 182, 236

McCall, George, 189

McCorkle, Lloyd, 221

McTyeire, H. N., 171

Mallard, Robert Q., 81, 235

Mandingo, 2

Manigault, Louis, 179

Mannix, Daniel, 8

Manumission, slave loyalty and, 192

Maroons:
attack plantations, 119; character of, 119; in Seminole wars, 121–24

Marriage, slave:
encouraged by masters, 80; legal status, 77–78; length of, 91–92; restrictions on, 86–87

Marrs, Elijah, 43, 98, 107, 165

Mars, James, 102, 195ff

Mason, Isaac, 74

Mauritius, 26

Medical attention for slaves, 164–65

Meredith, Samuel, 182

Merton, Robert K., 149

Middle Passage:
mortality, 7; Olaudah Equiano and, 14–15; reaction of Africans, 7–9

Militia, 125, 140

Miner, Valentine, 91

Ministers, White:
defense of slavery, 62–63; on duties of masters, 169–70; promote slave obedience, 62–63; religious instruction of slaves, 60–63; slave marriage and, 81

Ministers, slave
desire for freedom and, 63–64; sermons, 61–64; services, 61–67

Minor, William J., 80
Miscegenation:
  slave family and, 82–85; slave morality and, 82–85; slave traders and,
  83; white men and, 82–84; white
  women and, 84–85
Murder, of whites by slaves, 107–8
Music, African, 19
Music, slave:
  African survivals in, 19, 27–32;
  masters reaction to, 60–61; origins
  of, 27–32; role in slave life, 56–76;
  secular, 50–55; spirituals, 66–74
Mutinies:
  during mid-Passage, 7–9; on Mississippi River, 116

"Nat" stereotype:
  fears of whites, 140–41; relation to
  dominant slave personality, 141–
  42; "Sambo" stereotype and, 139–
  41; slave behavior and, 139–43
Neilson, Peter, 233
New Orleans:
  African music in, 30–33; voodoo in,
  33
Nichols, Charles, 237
Nichols, Thomas, 236
Nigeria, 12
Northrup, Solomon, 55–56, 83, 106,
  213, 234ff

Occupation of slaves:
  influence on self-esteem, 207; influence on treatment, 155–58
O'Ferrall, S. A., 236
Offley, G. W., 232
Olmsted, Frederick Law, 236
Osceola, 123
Overseer:
  and reaction of slaves, 176–77; and
  surveillance of slaves, 173–77; duties, 173–77

Paranoia of whites, 140–41
Parker, Allen, 211
Pascal, Roy, 228
Paulding, James K., 236
Pennington, James W. C., 232

Perception:
  in interpersonal relations, 135;
  stereotypes and, 135, 137–39
Personality:
  slave, 213–16; stereotypes and,
  135–36; theories of, 184–85
Peterson, Walter, 64, 235
Phillips, Ulrich B., 237
Plantation:
  churches on, 61; labor routine,
  155–58
Planter expectations:
  behavior of slave, 144; overseer
  and, 176; stereotypes and, 144
Planters:
  absenteeism, 172; characterized by
  slaves, 163; concern for slaves, 164–
  65; family life, 166–69; miscegenation, 82–84, 89; overseers and, 176;
  protecting slave health, 164–65;
  public opinion and, 169; restrictions on power, 166–72; rules for
  controlling slaves, 144–53; runaways and, 109; selective inattention toward slaves, 181–83; separation of slave families, 88–92; use
  of labor incentives, 145
Polygamy, 10–17
Poor whites:
  literary stereotypes, 138; relations
  with slaves, 202; slave contempt
  for, 177, 203
Pringle, Elizabeth, 235
Prison:
  as total institution, 220–21; behavior in, 189–90
Prostitution, 82–83, 84
Pulszky, Francis and Theresa, 235

Quarles, Ralph, 83

Randolph, Peter, 63, 110, 159
Rape of slave women, 83
Rebellion:
  Army and, 140; defined, 125;
  Louisiana, 126; militia and, 125;
  Nat Turner's, 126–30; New York
  City, 126; Stono, 117–18; topogra-
  phy and, 124; U.S. and Latin
  America, 124

Recalcitrant slaves, masters accommodation of, 179, 212–13

Recreation:
activities, 42–43; attitudes of masters, 43; frequency of, 42; role in slave life, 41–43

Religion:
defiance of masters, and, 75; docility and, 62–63; slave attitudes toward, 60–64; slave practice, 61–67; spirituals, 67–75; treatment of slaves and, 169–70; white missionaries, 60–61

Rewards:
as means of control, 145; slave labor and, 144–63; slave recreation, 42–43

Rhythm:
in African music, 19; in Juba, 55; in Slave music, 55–66

Ring shout, 65–66

Robinson, Lucy, 91

Robinson, W. H., 64, 88, 99, 105, 193ff

Roles:
overseers, 147–48; planters', 144–46; relation to personality, 148–50; slaves, 148

Role theory, 148–50

Roper, Moses, 60, 83, 84, 162, 169, 190ff

Ruitenbeek, Hendrick, 237

Rules of plantation management
slave behavior and, 148–53, 177; slave role and, 148; stereotypes and, 144

Runaways:
character of, 112–16; rebellious, 116; Sambo, 114–16; statistics on, 108

Russell, Marion J., 107

"Sambo" personality:
cruel treatment and, 195–99; predominant among house servants, 200–201

"Sambo" stereotype:
dominant slave personality and, 141–44; perception of outsiders, 135–36; projections of whites, 135; rebellious slaves, 139–44; relation to other slave streotypes, 141–44; roots of, 137–38; similarity to stereotypes of serf and Brazilian slave, 137–38

Selective inattention, 180–81

Self:
concept of, 184–85; factor in personality and childhood, 185

Self-esteem:
personality factors promoting, 185; slave, 204–8

Self-fulfilling prophecy, and rebellions, 142

Sellers, James B., 237

Seminoles:
maroons and, 121–24; war, 121–24

Senegal, 26

Separation of slave families:
extent of, 89–92; psychological impact, 197

Serer, 2

Sex ratios:
family life and, 77–78; U.S. and Latin American, 77–78

Schultz, Christian, 30

Significant others:
behavior and, 185–86; conjurers as, 45–49; parents as, 78–79, 99–100, 102–3; several on plantation, 201, 206; Sullivan and, 185

Simmons, J. L., 189

Slave behavior:
belief in inferiority, 199; contentment, 191–92; cruelty, 162–64; culture, 41–43; desire for freedom, 104–12; dissembling, 208–9; escapes, 104–18; fear of whites, 195–97; fighting masters, 211–13; group solidarity, 210; kindly treatment, 164–65; literacy, 207; loyalty, 191, 200; overseers, 176–77; rebellion, 117–30; religion, 63–66, 75; self-hatred, 199; significant other, 214; stereotypes and, 132–44; submissiveness, 195–200

Slave personality:
African origins and, 3; coercion, 151, 162–64; culture and, 41–42; parental models, 99–103; rebellions,

125–31; roles, 148–50; stereotypes, 132–44; variety in, 151–53, 186–216
Slave trade:
  African reactions, 7–9; character, 5–9; volume, 39
Slave traders:
  miscegenation and, 83; rebellious slaves sold to, 179, 210–13
Slave women:
  control of, 153; role in family, 85, 99–103
Slaves:
  African-born, 1–39; children, 94–103; clothing, 158; court decisions regarding, 107–8; culture, 41–75; family life, 77–103; holidays, 42–43; housing, 159; labor of, 155–58; marriages, 86–87; ministers, 61–64; number imported, 39; punishments, 162–164;
    branding, 163; *castration*, 164 religion, 60–75; separations, 89–92; stereotypes, 132–44; women, 85, 99–103
Smedes, Susan Dabney, 167, 182
Smith, Amanda, 96
Smith, Venture, 10
Socialization:
  of slaves, 94–103; of whites, 166–69
Southern writers:
  Brazilian writers and, 137–38; defense of slavery, 138; stereotypes of poor whites, 138; stereotypes of slaves, 137–39
Spaulding, H. G., 65
Spindler, Dearborn, 219
Spirituals:
  African origins, 27–28; imagery, 67–69, 73–74; means of communication, 68–69; references to freedom, 71–73; world view, 67–75
Stampp, Kenneth, 237
Starling, Marion W., 237
Stein, Stanley, 77
Stereotypes:
  comparative, 135–38; factors affecting, 135–38; literary, 132–44; relationship to personality, 135; roles, 144

Steward, Austin, 44, 88, 99, 102, 106, 107, 159, 161, 165, 196ff, 235
Stouffer, Samuel, 219
Stroyer, Jacob, 24, 69, 83, 102, 105, 168, 208ff, 235
Submissiveness:
  coercive power and, 186–87; personality and, 185–88; slave, 195–200
Suicides:
  among Africans, 1, 7; separations and, 197
Sullivan, Henry Stack, 184–85
Superstition:
  slave, 45; white, 48–49
Surinam, 124
Surveillance:
  in concentration camps, 221; in quarters, 206–7; internalization and, 185–86; masters and, 172; overseers and, 175–76; obedience and, 186
Sutcliff, Robert, 184–85
Swisshelm, Jane, 235
Sydnor, Charles, 237
Syncretism:
  in language, 21–24; in music, 19, 27–32; in religion, 17–18, 32–35
Szwed, John F., 27

Taylor, Orville, 114, 237
Taylor, Zachary, 124
Temne, 26
Thompson, John, 168
Thornwell, J. H., 170
Total institution:
  coercive power in, 189–90, 217–18, 225–26; compared, 217–26; defined, 189–90; plantation and, 189–90
Travis, Joseph, 129
Turner, Benjamin, 127
Turner, Lorenzo, 24
Turner, Nat:
  issue in Virginia legislature, 142–43; rebellion, 126–30

Vassa, Gustavus, 12–17, 38–39, 234
Vassouras, 77

Virey, Julien, 137
Voodoo, 33

Wall, Bennett, 237
Washington, Amanda, 164
Washington, Booker T., 94
Washington, George, 173
Watkins, James, 102, 159, 199ff
Watson, Henry, 84, 159, 161, 195
Webb, William, 43, 45, 61, 75, 99,
    105, 209
Wesley, John, 171
Whitehead, Margaret, 129

Whitmore, Charles, 180
Whittier, John Greenleaf, 232
Whydah, 33
Wigmore, John H., 228
Williams, James, 232
Woloff, 2, 26
Woods, Norman, 235
Work songs;
    among slaves, 52–54; in Africa, 19

Yoruba, 2, 3, 32

Znaniecki, Florian, 149

This impressive and original study views the institution of slavery from a new perspective—the perspective of the slaves themselves. Professor Blassingame challenges the timeworn stereotype of the slave as a passive and docile creature who lacked drive, purpose, and responsibility. He traces the development of the slave's personality traits, analyzes the patterns of resistance within the slave community, and proves conclusively that the slave had